Jersey Joe Walcott

Jersey Joe Walcott
A Boxing Biography

JAMES CURL

Foreword by Vincent Cream II

McFarland & Company, Inc., Publishers
Jefferson, North Carolina, and London

Unless otherwise noted, all photographs are from the author's collection.

"I'll Lick Joe Louis Again" article © SEPS licensed by Curtis Licensing, Indianapolis, Indiana. All rights reserved. Used with permission.

LIBRARY OF CONGRESS CATALOGUING-IN-PUBLICATION DATA

Curl, James, 1969–
  Jersey Joe Walcott : a boxing biography / James Curl ; foreword by Vincent Cream II.
      p.   cm.
  Includes bibliographical references and index.

  ISBN 978-0-7864-6822-5
  softcover : acid free paper ∞

  1. Walcott, Jersey Joe, 1914–1994. 2. Boxers (Sports) — United States — Biography. 3. African American boxers — Biography. I. Title.
  GV1132.W235C87   2012
  796.83092 — dc23
  [B]   2012009422

BRITISH LIBRARY CATALOGUING DATA ARE AVAILABLE

© 2012 James Curl. All rights reserved

No part of this book may be reproduced or transmitted in any form or by any means, electronic or mechanical, including photocopying or recording, or by any information storage and retrieval system, without permission in writing from the publisher.

Front cover image: World heavyweight boxing champion Jersey Joe Walcott (photograph courtesy Harry Shaffer, Antiquities of the Prize Ring); cover design by David K. Landis (Shake It Loose Graphics)

Manufactured in the United States of America

McFarland & Company, Inc., Publishers
  Box 611, Jefferson, North Carolina 28640
    www.mcfarlandpub.com

This book is for all the great fighters
who have not received their due

Acknowledgments

My thanks go to Mike Jones, Dante Fichera, Christopher La force, Henry Hasscup, Herb Goldman, Bob Collins, Maureen McLoone (President of the Merchantville Historical Society) Austin Killeen, Mike De Lisa, Mike Silver, John DiSanto, Don Cogswell, John Oaks, Tracy Callis, Jerry Fitch, Michael Foy (for his research services), Walter Sikorski, Jr. (for his information on Walcott's early years), Robert Yalen, Ken Poppen (for repairing my computer and keeping me up and running), Colleen Aycock, Phil Cohen, Harry Shaffer, Tony Triem, the New Jersey State Historical Society, and my wife Carol.

The following people deserve special thanks for their help with this project. Without their help this book would not have been completed: Vincent Cream (for the great information on his grandfather's early life and taking me on a tour of New Jersey and Philadelphia during my research trip), Dan Cuoco (who helped in so many ways I would need a paragraph to explain), Clay Moyle (for his great editing and suggestions), Ernie Aglugub (for his friendship, editing, suggestions and proofreading), Chuck Hasson (for all the great newspaper articles covering Walcott's early fights), and Mike Valentino (for his editing, corrections and suggestions).

I thank each and every one of you. If I have forgotten to mention anyone, I am sorry.

Table of Contents

Acknowledgments	vi
Foreword by Vincent Cream II	1
Preface	3
1. The Journey Begins	7
2. Roxie Allen, Jack Blackburn and Typhoid Fever	15
3. Sparring with the Brown Bomber	23
4. "Tiger" Jack Fox and Hard Times	29
5. Early Retirement	37
6. Bocchicchio	44
7. Stepping up the Competition	52
8. Win Some, Lose Some	58
9. Louis-Walcott I	69
10. Louis-Walcott II	86
11. The Cincinnati Cobra	97
12. Sweden, Omelio, and Johnny Shkor	108
13. Germany and Rex Layne	119
14. Winning the Title	132
15. Bringing the Title Home	147
16. Walcott-Marciano I: The Build-Up	159
17. Walcott-Marciano I: The Fight	165
18. Walcott-Marciano II: The Rematch	181

19. The 1950s and Hollywood	189
20. The 1960s and the Phantom Punch	194
21. The New Sheriff	199
22. The Passing of a Legend	204
Appendix: Jersey Joe Walcott's Fight Record	207
Chapter Notes	211
Bibliography	221
Index	225

Foreword
by Vincent Cream II

"Of all that I am, and all that I ever hope to be, I am, and always will be a chip off the great big rock that is my dad." My father Big Vince would always say that about Grandpop.

Approximately three years ago, I received a call from Jim Curl and after our initial conversation we were immediately bonded by our mutual belief that the story of Jersey Joe Walcott was a story that had to be written. I consider myself a fan and promoter of the life and times of the legendary Jersey Joe Walcott. As one of his grandchildren, I have been forever inspired by his incredible career as one of the true originals in the sport of boxing.

I was very young when Grandpop told me that his father was his first fan/promoter. Joseph Alexander Cream would tell anyone who was within earshot, "If this boy (8- to 10-year-old Arnold) gets the right manager and handler, he WILL be a champion!" The power of those words coming from his father inspired him to persevere through life's challenges to reach his ultimate goal and become a world champion.

Now, sixty years after his last fight, the story of triumph over poverty and adversity has finally been written. Jim has done a wonderful job of gathering the information necessary to make this a must-read for the friends and fans of Jersey Joe Walcott.

In the early seventies, towards the end of the summer before the first Ali vs. Frazier fight, Grandpop gathered up my brother Bill, my cousins Pete and Keith, and me. He told us he was going to take us to meet Ali. At that time, he refereed professional boxing and wrestling. Over the next two weeks, we went on an incredible odyssey as he refereed wrestling matches all the way from North Carolina to Miami. Imagine the famous Jersey Joe Walcott and his first four grandsons traveling in a low-key station wagon, hanging out and going to meet Muhammad Ali. Priceless! It was an unbelievable life experience.

He reminded us stay awake and observe things and places we had never seen. Grandpop inspired us to dream, and as you read his story, he will inspire you as well. Enjoy!

Preface

I first discovered Jersey Joe Walcott when I was about sixteen. I bought a videotape of the first heavyweight title fight between Jersey Joe and Rocky Marciano. Although the fight ended badly for Walcott, I was an instant fan. I loved the way he fought: he was so good ... he could box ... he could slug ... he was fast and slick. Even though I was just really beginning to understand boxing at that early stage in my obsession with the sweet science, I knew Walcott was a great fighter, but I didn't know how truly great he was.

I would spent the next twenty-plus years reading, watching and learning about the great fighters of the past before I came to a point in my life where I felt that I wanted to do something more than just be a student of boxing history. I wanted to contribute something to the fighters that I idolize and the sport that I love. My opportunity to do more came when I joined the International Boxing Research Organization in 2008. Since becoming a member of the IBRO, I had purchased several biographies from other members and was lucky enough to speak with the authors of these books. I began asking questions about writing a biography and what was involved in the process. My interest grew with each e-mail. Authors Clay Moyle (*Sam Langford: Boxing's Greatest Uncrowned Champion*) Bill Paxton (*The Fearless Harry Greb*) and Mike Silver (*The Arc of Boxing: The Rise and Decline of the Sweet Science*) were very helpful in answering my questions regarding the steps involved in putting a book together. After much talk, many e-mails and a lot of thought, I felt that a biography written about a fighter who truly deserved one would be a great way to give something back to my favorite sport. Writing a book was something I was confident I could accomplish (even though I am not a writer by profession) with a little help.

My next task was to choose a fighter that I felt deserved to be written about and had no biography. Jersey Joe Walcott was the first fighter that sprang to mind. There were two others that I gave some thought to, Ezzard Charles and Jerry Quarry, but Walcott just felt right. I was almost certain that there had not been a biography done on Jersey Joe, because if there had been I would have most likely read it. After some inquires to Dan Cuoco, the director of the IBRO, and a few other members I had met on-line, I confirmed that no biography had been done on Walcott. What a shame, I remember thinking, such a great fighter and nobody has written a book about old Jersey Joe Walcott.

I began the processes of research for the book and soon realized that Jersey Joe's life and boxing career is an incredible tale. The more I uncovered the more I realized how great Walcott really was and just how hard of a time he had before he made it. In fact Joe's life is a true rags-to-riches tale, perhaps more so than any other, and if you can bear to hear it again, a "Cinderella" story. I also realized through my investigation of Walcott's career that he had embarked on one of the greatest, yet least remembered, comebacks in boxing history.

After committing myself to writing about Jersey Joe, I decided to try to contact his family members. I was lucky enough to reach Vincent Cream, Walcott's oldest grandson. Vincent and I spoke on the phone for some time and Vincent told me several stories about his grandfather's childhood and post-boxing career. We then agreed to stay in touch and he would help me gather more information.

In October 2009, after researching for the better part of nine months, I realized that a trip to New Jersey would be necessary to further my research. While there I met Vincent Cream, his brothers Christopher and Bill, as well as his cousins Keith and Carlos. Vincent was nice enough to welcome me to his mother's house and share photographs of his grandfather and a scrapbook full of newspaper articles. Vincent also drove me all over Camden and the surrounding areas so I could take photographs and visit the Jersey Joe memorial, his grave site, and his old neighborhoods. The remainder of the trip was spent at the New Jersey State Archives and the Camden Historical Society pouring over hundreds of old newspaper articles, maps and directories. While the research yielded some great information, the trip was also a lot of fun.

The following June, in 2010, I made a trip to the annual Boxing Hall of Fame's induction weekend to further my research. I went there with the intentions of photographing Jersey Joe Walcott artifacts that the hall was sure to have. Unfortunately the IBHOF was sadly lacking when it came to

Jersey Joe paraphernalia. But I learned a lot about Walcott just by talking with the many knowledgeable boxing historians who attended the festivities. I was also fortunate enough to talk to the charismatic Bert Sugar. When I asked Bert what he thought about Jersey Joe Walcott, he said, "I think a lot about Jersey Joe Walcott." After talking for a while, he told me what I needed to do was "fill in the blanks" concerning Walcott's career and life. And that is precisely what I have tried to do. I hope with the writing of this book, and the two years of painstaking research, I have filled in some of the "blanks" concerning Jersey Joe's life. I also hope that I have done the man justice, and have written a fitting tribute, as well as a simply written book that is as enjoyable for you to read as it was for me to write.

—1—

The Journey Begins

The left hook landed with crushing force on Ezzard Charles' chin. The Cincinnati Cobra crashed to the canvas where the referee counted him out. Jersey Joe Walcott, after twenty-one years of boxing, five attempts at the title and at the ripe old age of thirty-seven, stood victorious as the new heavyweight champion of the world in 1951.

By knocking out Ezzard Charles, Jersey Joe Walcott completed one of the greatest journeys in the history of the sweet science, and finally realized his lifelong dream of becoming the heavyweight champion. The road Jersey Joe traveled to get to the title had been long and extremely difficult. To truly appreciate how hard Walcott's life had been prior to winning the title and how incredible his comeback was, you have to start the story from the beginning when Walcott was known as Arnold Cream before being called Jersey Joe.

Arnold Raymond Cream was born on January 31, 1914, at his grandparents' house at 115 Pine Street, just a few houses down the street from his own home.[1] Since Arnold did not have the luxury of being born in a hospital, an official birth certificate was not immediately filed. The lack of a birth certificate and the fact that Arnold started boxing at such a young age would lead many to question his actual age during the build up to his fight with Joe Louis in 1947. The issue of Arnold's age would continue to be a subject of debate long after he retired from boxing. Although every source (including Arnold himself in several interviews) indicates that Arnold was born in Merchantville, New Jersey, he was actually born just on the other side of the Merchantville border in an old section of Pennsauken called Homesteadville.

This was one of the oldest black communities in southern New Jersey and would eventually be known as Matchtown, because of a match-stick factory located in the area on Chapel Street. The area of Pennsauken that

Arnold was born in was a racially segregated neighborhood. Ethnic enclaves of Italians, Irish, Jews and Poles were common in Pennsauken, Merchantville, and Camden during Arnold's childhood and youth. The segregation of Arnold's youth didn't end in his neighborhood. It was ingrained in schools, in the workplace, in the armed forces, in entertainment and in daily life.

Arnold's parents may have been born thousands of miles apart, but as fate would have it they eventually met while living on the same street, Joseph at 107 Pine Street, Edna at home with her parents at 115. Joseph Alexander hailed from the tropical Caribbean island of St. Thomas, where he was born on January 30, 1872.[2] He was fluent in six languages and spoke with a heavy Islands accent. Joseph left home after his father passed away and eventually immigrated to the United States, settling in New Jersey circa 1889, when he was about seventeen years old.[3] When Joseph arrived in the United States, his original last name, Crime, would eventually change, because when Joseph pronounced the last name with his thick Caribbean accent the name Crime sounded like Cream. In an interview given in 1947 Arnold said he was thankful that the last name Crime had been changed to Cream, for obvious reasons. Edna Ella (Amos) was born in Jordantown, a small village within Pennsauken, in May 1888.[4] Edna's father, Charles, was a brickmaker, and her mother, Louisa, a housewife. Edna had three brothers, Walter, William and Howard, as well as four sisters, Marion, Ida, Bertha, and May.

Joseph and Edna, after courting for about two years, were married on June 4, 1909, by E.E. Parker with P.S. Parker as a witness. Joseph, who was sixteen years older than Edna, had been married once before to a woman named Mary. They had two daughters, Ella Eliza born in December 1892, and Thelma P. in June 1904. The records are unclear as to what happened to the marriage of Joseph and Mary. What is clear is that Joseph and Edna would spend the next twenty years together, and have twelve children, starting with Ruth in April 1907, Joseph in April 1908, Lester in August 1911, Arnold on January 31, 1914, followed by Edna, Norma, Naomi, George, Dorothy, Bertha, Robert and Barbara.

The Creams, like most families living in southern New Jersey during the early part of the twentieth century, were extremely poor. Arnold's father, a general laborer and mason, was a hard worker but with such a large family to feed, clothe and keep warm, he was hard pressed to provide for them on a laborer's pay. Arnold's mother, besides being a housewife and raising her large family, did side jobs such as washing and ironing to make a little extra money. A good day would bring in $1.50. Although both parents did their part to provide for their family, more often than not they barely had enough to eat. As a result of the lack of food and proper vitamins in their daily diet, Arnold, along with some of his siblings, suffered from rickets. This was a common disease during the early part of the twentieth century among poor folks (particularly children) that caused a softening of the bones due to a lack of vitamin D. Even though he and his brothers and sisters eventually overcame rickets, hunger was still a constant companion and the Creams would see more dinner times than dinners. Once when Arnold was twelve, he came in for supper and found his mother sitting at an empty table weeping. "Go back outside and play," she said, "we have no food." These hard times would only get worse after Arnold's father passed away from heart disease on May 21, 1929, at Cooper's Hospital in Camden. Joseph was laid to rest on May 26, 1929, in Jordantown Cemetery.

Arnold was just fifteen when his father passed away.[5] Joseph's early death forced the young boy to quit Homestead High School and begin working full-time to help take care of his family.[6] In the 1920s and '30s it was not unusual for a boy of fifteen (or younger) to quit school and go to work. Working was nothing new to Arnold; he had been doing it even before his father passed away. At the age of thirteen one of his first jobs was pushing a wheelbarrow filled with sand or gravel and unloading it into a cement mixer. "It lengthened my muscles, and I think, helped make me a sharper hitter," said Arnold.[7] Some of his other jobs were cutting lawns for the rich folks, running errands, working on an ice wagon, selling papers and working at the Campbell Soup factory. Always the nickels and dimes came home to Mom.

Although Arnold and his older siblings worked to help support the family, the Creams still struggled terribly, both financially and nutritionally. In an interview in 1947 Arnold had these words to say about not having enough to eat: "I'm sure postwar dietetic experts would change their theories about calorie requirements if they knew what the Creams got along on. The business of getting enough food was always problem number one. We could not go to relatives for help. More often there were relatives or friends in our house because they were worse off than we were, and had nowhere to go."[8] Recalling the days when there was no meat on the table, Arnold added, "For ten years in my house we thought we were feasting when dinner consisted of scrapple, beans and cabbage, without ham, of course. Sometimes we had potatoes instead of beans or bread; mostly we had less, much less. I won't try to detail our desperate poverty. The suffering that undernourishment can bring is not a story to be told play by play. But I ask the reader to remember that our family had hunger as a constant house guest most of the time. It is demoralizing. Poverty was a way of life. We didn't think about it then, because it was a part of us. But it is a wonderful thing to escape."9 Escape, Arnold eventually did, but it would take over thirty years of his life to do it.

Despite the fact that Arnold grew up underprivileged and could have easily turned to a life of crime and trouble, he didn't. In his own words he said, "I never did a wrong thing."10 A lot of credit certainly must be given to his mother Edna. She was no doubt a pillar of strength for her family and did her best to raise her children right. She was also a deeply religious woman, who insisted that her kids attend the Methodist church every Sunday. Her religious influence would follow Arnold for his entire life. As an adult he would regularly read the Bible and attend Methodist services.

Arnold spent his childhood and teenage years growing up in the neighborhoods of Merchantville, Camden, and Pennsauken. During these years the Creams lived at several different locations around the area. At some point in the 1920s they moved to 6201 Magnolia Avenue, where Arnold lived until his marriage to his girlfriend Lydia in 1933. His mother would live there until her death in 1943.

The neighborhoods that Arnold grew up in were established in the early to mid 1800s. The houses he and his family lived in were old and had none of the modern conveniences people today take for granted. There was no central heating, air conditioning, or insulation. The roofs leaked water and the cold air crept in through every available crack in the walls and around doors and windows. Many of the houses in his neighborhood didn't have electricity, indoor bathrooms, running water or glass in the windows. Heat was provided by a fireplace or burning coal in an iron furnace usually located in the basement. For light at night kerosene lamps were used. During much of Arnold's life there was not enough money to buy coal to heat the house. During the cold New Jersey winters the family was forced to huddle around the wood-burning stove in the kitchen to keep warm. Space was another problem and a luxury that the Creams did not have. The houses that Arnold grew up in had no more than three bedrooms, and most likely just two, for a family of at least twelve at one point living under the same roof. Often, the attic was turned into a room and several of the children would sleep there.

TV had not been invented when Arnold was growing up and the telephone was not yet a common household item, especially for a poor family. The one modern convenience that most families did have, even poor families, was the radio. During the late 1920s and all through the 1930s the radio was at the peak of its popularity. It was a major source of entertainment for kids and adults alike. Millions of people tuned in daily. Kids gathered around the radio and followed the exciting adventures of Superman and the Lone Ranger. Forty million listeners tuned in six nights a week to the *Amos 'n' Andy* show and daytime dramas like soap operas were becoming very popular. Jazz and Big Band was all the rage. Artists like Bing Crosby, Billy Holiday, Louis Armstrong, and Cab Calloway were a few of the popular hit-makers of the day. By the 1930s radio became the number one way to follow live-action sports and news. Friends and neighbors would gather around a radio and listen to the blow-by-blow broadcast of their favorite fighters or sit out on the front porch and listen to a baseball game. Radio brought sports into the living rooms of America.

Even though Arnold didn't have much while growing up there was still fun to be had. For entertainment during the summer months swimming in the Delaware River was a great way to cool off from the heat of a hot, humid afternoon. Fishing the river was another pastime enjoyed by many. If Arnold and his friends could scrounge up a few nickels they could see a movie at one of the neighborhood theaters or at the first ever drive-in movie theater, which opened in Pennsauken in 1933.[11] Of course every kid played sports. During the 1920s and 1930s the two most popular were baseball and boxing. Arnold and his friends played baseball in empty lots on homemade fields or held sparring matches around the neighborhood.

Kids growing up in Merchantville and Pennsauken during the '20s and '30s didn't want to be ballplayers, they wanted to be fighters and young Arnold was no different. One reason for this was George Cole's boxing gym; the other reason was that boxing was the most popular sport in the world. George Cole's was well known in the Merchantville area. Fighters like Sam Langford, Harry Wills, Joe Jeanette, Jack Blackburn and Jeff Clark, known as "The Joplin Ghost" and a cousin to Arnold, trained there. This group of fighters established a tradition unique to the Merchantville area, all the kids became fighters. As a youngster Arnold thought of Cole's gym "as a great high walled castle, always brightly lighted by the sun."[12] He would learn, after he spent some time training at Cole's, that his vision couldn't have been more mistaken. Years later when recounting his early career he would describe the gym as "a small, smoky, low-ceilinged place."[13]

Arnold's interest and talent for boxing became apparent at an early age. "In my neighborhood we boxed up and down the street from sun up to sun down. I fought as soon as I could walk. My father sparred open handed with me in the yard," said Arnold.[14] Around the age of nine or ten he began participating in neighborhood sparring matches. These matches were put on by the adults for entertainment. The grown-ups would hand out candy to any of the boys that were willing to fight a few rounds. Whenever one of these matches would get started Arnold's father would send for his son saying, "Go get Reds." "Reds" was a nickname Arnold had acquired because of a patch of red hair growing out of the left side of his head. At times Arnold would show up and pretend to be uninterested, saying that he didn't feel like boxing today. Of course this was just a ploy to get a pocket full of candy, and it usually worked. The eager adults would stuff the boy's pockets full of sweets. In return the young fighter would lace 'em up and box.

Even at a young age Arnold was naturally athletic and displayed a special talent for boxing. He was clever enough to outbox and out-fox the older, bigger neighborhood kids. Over the years he participated in countless neighborhood matches, becoming quite well known in Merchantville and Pennsauken for his boxing ability. These sparring matches would essentially make up Arnold's amateur career. From them he developed his own style of fighting and learned an assortment of moves and tricks. Years later as a pro fighter he would use these same tricks and moves when doing battle with greats like Joe Louis, Ezzard Charles, and Rocky Marciano.[15]

Joseph, realizing his son had athletic talent, gave Arnold his first pair of boxing gloves at the age of twelve. "It was a great event. Like some other kid getting his first fielder mitt," said Arnold.[16] Joseph was encouraging to his son, telling him some day he could be a world champion.

One evening as Arnold was putting out the trash and dinner was being prepared, out of nowhere Joseph exclaimed to Arnold's mother, "Let me tell you one ting, if this boy gets the right trainer and manager, he could become a champion." To this Edna replied, "Arnold just take the trash out; don't fill the boys head with such things Joseph." To that Joseph exclaimed in his thick West Indian accent, "Never you mind woman. I said if he gets the right manager and handler he will be a champion!"[17] Arnold was so inspired by the strong words of his father that he carried them throughout his boxing career and in his heart and mind for the rest of his life. And those same words would replay through his thoughts, like an echo from the past the night he won the title in 1951 from Ezzard Charles.

When Arnold got older the neighborhood sparring matches became more serious. In the 1920s and 1930s, due to the popularity of boxing, it was common for aspiring young fighters to stage boxing matches in makeshift boxing rings that were set up in basements, backyards or garages. On one such occasion an improvised boxing ring was set up in a basement by some of the older kids and young men from Arnold's neighborhood. A tough, local bully and known wife-beater was looking for a challenger. Arnold, who was only about fifteen or sixteen at the time, accepted the challenge and agreed to fight the man. The bully, who was a full-grown man and quite a few years older than Arnold, was considered to be a real tough guy. Arnold's friends, thinking it would not be a good idea for the teenaged boy to fight the older man, tried to talk Arnold out of the match. Arnold would have none of that. He climbed into the makeshift ring and to the shock of every one proceeded to outbox and defeat the older man.[18]

It was around this time that Arnold started hanging around some of the local boxing gyms in his neighborhood. Although officially he would start his boxing career at Battling Mack's, Arnold trained at a few different gyms around the Merchantville area. One of the local gyms he frequented during his early career was Sikorski's Boxing Gym. Before the Great Depression, Sikorski's was a bakery ran by Walter Sikorski and his wife. When the Great Depression hit, Walter was forced to close up shop. Mr. Sikorski, who just happened to be an ex-fighter (in fact, Sikorski had won the middleweight title of New Jersey), decided to turn the bakery into a boxing gym. With boxing being as popular as it was, it wasn't long before aspiring young pugilists from all over the neighborhood were training there. Eventually young Arnold found his way into the gym. He would spend several years training off and on at Sikorski's, where he and Walter formed a friendship that lasted for years. The young fighter would often stop by the Sikorski house after a workout. He and Walter would sit on the front porch, drink tea, and talk boxing for hours. Years later when Arnold was training to fight Joe Louis, Walter Sr. would bring his eight-year-old son Walter Jr. up to Grenloch Park to meet Jersey Joe and watch him train.[19]

It was at one of these boxing gyms during Arnold's early career that Jack Johnson, the former, and first, black heavyweight champion, stopped by. News of his impending arrival spread all over Merchantville and the surrounding neighborhoods. Outside of the gym, Arnold, standing in the rain along with a group of neighborhood kids and adults, excitedly awaited the legendary fighter's arrival, hoping to get an autograph or a chance to talk to the famous champ. Approximately three to four hours after his appointed arrival time, Johnson finally showed up in a big, fancy, black car. The former champion got out, dressed in an expensive black suit, wearing a top hat and sporting a cane. He also had two enormous Great Danes in tow that proceeded to run wild and terrorize the crowd. Johnson, being in a hurry, rushed past the group of fans with little more than a golden smile and a few nods and disappeared into the gym. Much to his fans' disappointment Johnson signed no autographs and had largely ignored them. It was at this point that Arnold vowed that if he ever became a famous boxer he would never ignore his fans or refuse to give out an autograph. It was a promise that he kept.

It was only a matter of time before Arnold eventually found his way into the boxing gym where he would get his start. Sometime around the age of fifteen or sixteen Arnold, along with some friends, stopped into Battling Mack's, at the intersection of 3rd and Walnut Streets in Camden, to watch some sparring. Mack's, like a lot of gyms during the era, was run by an ex-fighter. Battling Mack was a former lightweight from Camden turned gym owner and trainer. In an interview in 1947, Arnold described his experience: "In the ring were two lightweights, Joe Allen and a taller blond-haired chap named Johnny Lucas. I asked a man alongside me, how long's that big guy been boxing? 'About six months,' he replied pleasantly. Six months? Holy smoke! I said. I can fight better'n him. The stranger looked at me angrily. 'If you wannna watch these fellows, keep your mouth shut or stay out of here!' he snapped. 'You're a little too fresh! Y'understand?' I apologized so I could come again. I found out too late that that man was Lucas's manager, Eddie Prince."[20]

After his visit to Battling Mack's, Arnold's mind was made up. Two days later he went back with new sneakers and home-sewn trunks. He was going to be a prize fighter.

— 2 —

Roxie Allen, Jack Blackburn and Typhoid Fever

Having made up his mind to be a prize-fighter Arnold Cream enthusiastically showed up at Battling Mack's Gym in 1930. He was eager to train and dreamed of becoming a world champion. Arnold learned quickly that boxing is a tough sport. Eddie Prince, remembering Arnold's derogatory remarks about his fighter, thought he'd teach the young boy a painful lesson that would "send him home for good."

For five straight days Arnold was tossed in the ring with Roxie Allen, a top-notch welterweight from the Italian section of Camden. Allen, whose real name was Rocco Auletto, was born September 23, 1909, and his professional career started in August 1925 when he was just one month shy of his sixteenth birthday. Roxie was considered one of the best local fighters and had been fighting as a professional for over five years. Allen was instructed by Prince to give the young, inexperienced boy the "full treatment." It wasn't until sometime later that Arnold would find out about the plan Eddie and Roxie came up with to "send him home for good."

As Arnold later recounted: "Roxie tried all right, he knocked me down four or five times, cut my mouth, blackened my eye and gave me a bloody nose, all in two rounds. I took that kind of massaging for five straight days. At night I looked at my bashed face in the mirror, I tried to solve for myself the giveaways in the movements of my hands or feet that made it possible for Roxy [sic] to anticipate everything I tried to do. Furthermore, I quickly acquired a strong dislike for Allen, but time has changed my feelings. His influence followed me through my career and helped shape its present pattern."[1]

It was a rough start for Arnold but he toughed it out. Eventually, Roxie took pity on the young would-be fighter, and a friendship formed.

Roxie began mentoring Arnold, teaching him how to box properly. Encouraging the boy, Allen remarked, "Kid, you'll make a real fighter. You've got heart."[2] He even gave Arnold a used pair of ring shoes, his first. Over the next few months Arnold showed up at the gym and trained nearly every day. After a time Roxie realized that Arnold was serious about fighting, so he decided to help the young pugilist even more. He persuaded his half-brother Johnny Duaphin and Tommy Marsello, a junkyard owner, to become Arnold's manager and handler, respectively. They were the first of several in Arnold's long and rocky career.

Arnold trained at Battling Mack's for approximately eight months before his first professional fight. Like a lot of fighters during the era, Arnold's amateur career was virtually nonexistent. Instead he went directly into the punch-for-pay ranks. Training at Mack's, sparring with Roxie Allen, and boxing the kids in his neighborhood for candy was the extent of his amateur boxing background. In August, Arnold's manager came to him and told him to get in some steady road-work and boxing for a couple of weeks. "I have a fight for you over in Vineland," said Dauphin.[3] Arnold was so excited to have his first fight scheduled that he didn't even think to ask who his opponent was until the next day. For the next few weeks Arnold trained hard, working with Roxie at the gym and covering a lot of ground with his early morning road-work through the streets of Pennsauken, Merchantville and Camden.

Excited and perhaps a bit nervous, Arnold arrived at the Vineland Arena for his first professional fight on September 9, 1930. His match was the opening bout of the evening and scheduled for four rounds against a boxer from Philadelphia named Edward "Cowboy" Wallace. Not much is known about Arnold's first opponent. In 1933 a small-time gangster from Philadelphia named Edward "Cowboy" Wallace was shot and killed in connection with a robbery and the killing of police officer Charles Stockburger. Wallace's body was found in Bellmawr, near Camden, New Jersey, riddled with machine-gun bullet holes.[4] Chances are good that this was the same Cowboy Wallace that Arnold fought in his debut match, since Cowboy Wallace and Edward "Cowboy" Wallace were both listed as being from Philadelphia.

At the weigh-in, the sixteen-year-old Arnold Cream tipped the scales at 165 pounds. Still short of his full-grown height and weight, the teenager was already starting to mature into a powerfully built young man with broad shoulders and big hands. Wallace, who was about three years older than Arnold, weighed 155 pounds.

2 — Roxie Allen, Jack Blackburn and Typhoid Fever

Apprehensively, the young fighter made his way up the wooden steps into the ring, as the bright ring lights beat down their heat on his already warmed up and sweating body. The fighters were introduced and the referee gave his instructions. As the fighters returned to their corners, the bell rang to signal the start of round one. Wallace rushed from his corner to end the fight in a hurry. He swung one from the floor, but Cream danced away, as the "Cowboy" bored in and let loose a flurry of punches. Cream tied Wallace up, they broke, and Wallace hung a beauty under Arnold's right eye. Then came a series of fast exchanges when Cream, now thoroughly warmed up, saw an opening as his opponent shot a fast left. But Cream's right was faster and crossed the left with a short right with plenty of authority on it. Arnold hit the button, and down went Cowboy Wallace like a log.[5] The ten count was a mere formality.

Arnold was the winner with a KO in the first round. He collected his $15.00, paid his handlers and walked away with $7.50. The triumphant fighter rushed home to find his mother, still awake and worried, sitting up waiting for him. Arnold handed her the money and excitedly told her the results of his first fight. "Son," she said, looking her boy in the eyes proudly, "you will be champion of the world if they give you a chance."[6]

A month after his victory over Wallace, Arnold stepped into the ring for his second fight. He was originally scheduled to fight Indian Victor, but that fight fell through. Instead he was matched with Jimmy O'Toole, an Irishman from Brighton, New Jersey. O'Toole was on the comeback trail after a disqualification loss in his last fight. He was far more experienced than Arnold, having at least eleven fights to Arnold's one. The fight was staged at the Camden Convention Hall, just a few blocks from Arnold's house. The Camden Convention Hall was the premier place in Camden for sporting events from the time it opened, shortly after World War I, until it burned down in 1953. Arnold would become very familiar with the place, fighting there over a dozen times during his career.

The Cream-O'Toole bout was the second match of the evening and turned out to be an impressive showing for the teenaged fighter. Arnold came into the fight weighing 165 and a half pounds, with O'Toole at 165 even. From the opening bell Arnold outfoxed his more experienced foe. By the fourth round he was in command and dropped Jimmy to his knees with a well timed one-two combination. Bravely, the Irishman got up only to be hit by a hard, looping right hand from Arnold a few seconds later. The punch opened a deep ugly gash under O'Toole's left eye that instantly started to gush blood. Jimmy finished the round on his feet but was a beaten, bloody fighter. An examination of the cut at the end of the fourth round prompted referee Walters to stop the contest, since the cut was ruled too dangerous to let Jimmy continue.[7]

Happy with his win over the more experienced Jimmy O'Toole, Arnold jumped right back into the ring two weeks later against Frankie Mitchell (some sources report Frankie Matthews[8]) scoring a four-round technical knockout. The Mitchell fight was the last known fight that Arnold had in 1930. Arnold would fight only one recorded fight in 1931, against Carl Mays on April 20 at the Waltz Dream Arena in Atlantic City, New Jersey. A hard right to the head in round two sent Mays to the canvas for the count.

By 1932 Arnold had other things on his mind besides boxing. He was heavily involved with his girlfriend Lydia. The two had grown up in the same neighborhood and had been friends for years. As they matured into young adults, their relationship became more serious. Around November or December 1932, Lydia broke the news to Arnold that she was pregnant. In those days, marriage was the only option. On April 15, 1933, Arnold Raymond Cream married his childhood sweetheart, Lydia Eleanor Talton. At the time of the marriage Arnold was just nineteen, Lydia only sixteen. Lydia's parents objected, especially her father, Jessie, who was a Baptist minister. The wedding ceremony was performed at the United Methodist Church located at 5015 Chapel Avenue in Merchantville. Helen M. Hoxter and Richard Crocker served as witnesses. At the time of the marriage Arnold only had two dollars and five cents to his name. The marriage certificate cost two dollars; according to Arnold, he and Lydia had a nickel honeymoon.

Shortly after their marriage the young couple found a small house in Merchantville to rent. They settled in and prepared for the arrival of their first child. Arnold continued to work a daytime job and train to fight. Around this time the young fighter decided it was time to step up his boxing career. He headed over the Benjamin Franklin Bridge to Philadelphia, the City of Brotherly Love. Philly at this time was a hotbed of boxing activity. A lot of great champions had come from Philly. The city rivaled even New York for the privilege of being called the boxing capital. In no time Arnold found a suitable gym, the Arcadia at 123 North 13th Street.

The Arcadia gym was opened and run by fight manager, gangster, bootlegger Max "Boo Boo" Hoff. It was one of a number of popular boxing gyms that could be found in Philadelphia during the 1920s and 1930s. Visiting fighters from all over the world trained there when in town to fight.

If a young fighter were going to get somewhere with his boxing career, there was a good chance he would do it in Philly.

At this time Arnold decided the name "Arnold Cream" was not befitting a future champion. Like countless fighters before, he adopted the name of a past ring great. A fighter using the name of a great fighter from the past or altering his name was nothing new; fighters had been doing it for years. The practice was very popular with pre–World War II-era fighters. Using the name of a former great fighter was a sure way to get noticed. In Arnold's case he borrowed the name from the favorite fighter of his father and he, Joe Walcott, a.k.a., the Barbados Demon, the welterweight champion of the world from 1901 to 1904. As a kid, Arnold read everything he could get his hands on about the Barbados Demon. Arnold began using his adopted ring name in 1933. It wasn't until 1935 that he added "Jersey" as a way to distinguish himself from the original Joe Walcott and let everyone know where he came from.

It was at the Arcadia that Arnold caught the attention of one of the gym's trainers, Jack Blackburn. The lanky Blackburn had once been a great boxer, and had battled such legends as Sam Langford, Harry Greb, and Joe Gans. During a boxing career that spanned over twenty years and had perhaps as many as three hundred and eighty-five fights, Blackburn became a master boxer and gained a tremendous amount of knowledge. After retiring from the ring in 1923, Blackburn put his knowledge to use as a trainer. Jack guided Sammy Mandel to the lightweight title in 1926 and Bud Taylor to the bantamweight title in 1927. Blackburn was not just a great trainer. Today he is regarded by most boxing historians as a genius.

Walcott and Blackburn hit it off and became fast friends. The young fighter and his trainer shared two things in common, empty pockets and a love for boxing. After a time Jack began calling Walcott "Chappie." Under the old master boxer's tutelage Walcott began learning the finer points of pugilism. Blackburn taught Joe how to turn his right hand when he threw it, how to catch punches in the air and how to slip inside and outside of his opponent's punches.

Jersey Joe's confidence grew under Blackburn's teachings. The education he received from Jack was priceless. Unfortunately, Walcott had little opportunity to display the skill he was learning. Because the Great Depression had started to take a heavy toll on the business of boxing, Jersey Joe, like a lot of fighters, especially black fighters, had a hard time getting fights. Even when he could get a match, the money he made was not enough to live on. As a result Walcott had to continue to work a day job. While training at the Arcadia, he worked on an ice and coal truck for $12.00 a week. It was a physical job that kept him going from seven in the morning until midnight. Tossing around sacks of coal and heavy blocks of ice had one benefit, though, as it added muscle to his already muscular frame. Even though the job kept the Creams eating, it left Joe with little time to train and surely caused him to miss out on potential fights. Although he was not able to spend as much time training as he needed, he continued to fight when he could because he needed the extra money to feed his family and still dreamed of becoming a world champion.

On July 28, 1933, at the Pennsauken Arena, Walcott had a chance to display his skills against Henry Taylor, a tough, hard-punching young fighter from Philadelphia. The fight turned out to be an easy one for Walcott, a first-round technical knockout. It was the first time that Taylor had suffered such a loss.

A week after the Taylor fight, on August 4, Lydia gave birth to the couple's first child, Arnold Cream, Jr. Three months later on November 16, Walcott and Taylor fought a rematch at the New Broadway Athletic Club in Philadelphia. Joe had Taylor down three times in round one, but Taylor battled back to take command of the fight. This time it was Taylor who won, in a six-round decision that handed Jersey Joe his first defeat.

A few years after beating Walcott, Taylor became a much-avoided fighter. Finding opponents for Taylor became, according to one newspaper article, "like hunting polar bears in Africa." Taylor's manager, Sydney Landes, challenged top contender Nathan Mann in Mann's own back yard of New Haven, but the burly New England heavyweight champion flatly refused. Taylor, like a lot of good fighters, never won a title despite the fact that he never ducked an opponent and was willing to fight anyone, even bigger fighters.

In the spring of 1934 Blackburn showed up excitedly at the Arcadia one day waving a telegram and saying, "The Lord come to my rescue!"[9] The telegram came from old acquaintances Julian Black and John Roxbourgh. According to the telegram, Blackburn was offered a job in Chicago to train an amateur champion. The job paid $25 a week plus a percentage of the purses. Blackburn told Walcott that a money order was on the way and that the money was enough for both of them. "Pack your duds and come along. I'll make them handle you too, Chappie."[10] Walcott's response was not enthusiastic. His reply to Blackburn was that he would have to talk to his wife about perhaps following in a week or two.

The offer from Blackburn to go to Chicago was perhaps a golden opportunity, but unfortunately Joe missed out on that opportunity. Instead, fate stepped in. Later that evening when he got home, he had a headache and didn't feel well, so he threw himself into bed. The next day brought a high fever, vomiting, and stabbing pains in his back and abdomen. A trip to Cooper Hospital revealed that Joe had contracted typhoid fever. For three weeks his temperature was up and down and at times climbed as high as 105 degrees. Joe was bed-ridden for two months, his weight dropping from 190 pounds to 130. Confined to bed, Walcott was unable to get back to the Arcadia to talk with Blackburn before Jack left for Chicago. "Blackburn must have gone away thinking I did not care. But I did very much. If I hadn't gotten sick and been able to meet that man in Chicago, who knows, I could have been the champion before Joe Louis," Walcott would later say.[11]

While sick from typhoid in 1934, Joe was unable to work and had no alternative but to apply for assistance from the state. Walcott only accepted unemployment benefits when he had absolutely no other choice. He was, and always remained, a hard working man. Years later when he finally began to make some money, Jersey Joe paid back every cent he had received from the state.

Swallowing his pride, Joe went down to the state unemployment office and filed for welfare. The Cream family received $9.50 per week in the form of a relief check. The money was hardly enough to buy food and certainly not enough to pay the rent. As a result the Creams quickly fell behind financially. In no time the landlord showed up at Walcott's door with an ultimatum to pay or get out. Unable to come up with the money, the Creams were soon evicted. Over the course of the next several months, Jersey Joe and his family were forced to move from one rundown shack to another, always one step ahead of eviction.

Although he was extremely weak and could barely lift a rake, Jersey Joe was desperate. He was hired off of the relief rolls and took a CWA (Civil Works Administration) job as a gardener in the Camden parks for $15 a week. Combined with whatever work Lydia could get, the family managed to survive. Slowly over the course of the next several months, Joe began to gradually recover. He gained his strength and weight back and eventually got a job doing heavier labor on the roads. By the midpoint of 1935, Lydia was about three months pregnant with their second child. The Creams were going to need more money. Feeling fit enough to continue his boxing career, Walcott decided it was time to head back to the Arcadia.

It had taken a little over a year for Walcott to fully recover from typhoid fever. By the time he went back to the Arcadia to train and continue his boxing career, Blackburn was long gone, having accepted the job in Chicago to train a young amateur champion. That amateur boxer turned out to be none other than Joe Louis. Together, Blackburn and Louis would make history. As for Walcott, he would continue to struggle to survive for the next ten years before another golden opportunity came knocking on his door.

— 3 —

Sparring with the Brown Bomber

Once back at the Arcadia, Jersey Joe Walcott had a fight lined up in no time with Spanish fighter Lew Alva at the Pennsauken outdoor arena on August 27, 1935. It had been over a year since Walcott had climbed into a boxing ring. He was rusty and not in top shape. He decided that he better try to end the fight quickly. At the opening bell Joe started the fight fast. He jumped right on Alva and knocked out his overmatched opponent in the first round.

Following his one-round knockout of Alva, Walcott took on Brooklyn heavyweight Pat Roland at the Camden Convention Hall on October 10, 1935. The fight was scheduled for eight rounds, but Jersey Joe needed only four to knockout Roland.

Walcott's next fight was important; he was matched against fellow New Jersey fighter Al King for the light-heavyweight championship of Southern New Jersey, on October 29, 1935. The fight was at his usual hangout, the Camden Convention Hall. Joe stepped into the ring weighing 180 pounds, King at 174. At just over the two-minute mark of round one, Walcott caught King coming in with a perfectly timed hard right to the jaw. The punch sent Al to the canvas, his head banging against the hard ring floor. The combined impact of the punch and King's head hitting the canvas knocked Al out cold. His seconds rushed into the ring and attempted to revive him, but were unable. They moved their fighter to his dressing room and anxiously waited for him to recover. Jersey Joe was terror stricken, fearing he might have killed Al. As he waited for Al to regain consciousness, Joe prayed that his incapacitated opponent would recover. Finally, after two hours, Al awoke and was not seriously injured. For his victory, Walcott was awarded the title of light-heavyweight champion of Southern New Jersey.

Along with the title he was given a belt, which he proudly displayed to his friends and family members.

Having won a minor title, Jersey Joe became a boxing big shot around Camden, although this did nothing to help his financial situation and only a little for his boxing career. In fact, Walcott was in debt again and running out of credit. He and Lydia were being hounded by the grocery store, the milkman and the landlord for immediate payment. Needing money, Walcott agreed to face his old mentor Roxie Allen on November 26, 1935. Allen had been calling Joe out for some time and had openly challenged him, so a fight was arranged at the convention hall. Arriving for the fight, Joe was unexpectedly stopped at the entrance by a stranger who wanted to introduce Joe to a small dark man. "Here is the original," said the stranger.[1] "Meet Joe Walcott, the Barbados Demon himself."[2] Joe was absolutely thrilled and inspired by the incident. After all, Joe Walcott was Jersey Joe's idol. Although Joe didn't have a dime to his name to buy a ticket, he managed to get his hero a ringside seat.

The fight started off as a bit of a shock for Walcott. Roxie, in a burst of fury, floored Jersey Joe with a big left hook in round one for a count of seven. When Walcott got up, all of his old dislike for Roxie came flooding back. Once up, Walcott proceeded to batter Allen without mercy, finally knocking Roxie out in round eight with a left hook. The blow sent Roxie to the canvas, his head hitting the floor of the ring hard enough to make it bounce. Roxie's body stiffened and Jersey Joe again had the awful feeling that he might have killed an opponent. Roxie was taken to Cooper Hospital. That night Joe prayed for God to spare Roxie's life. The next afternoon Roxie regained consciousness, but remained hospitalized for ten days. After the fight the Barbados Demon paid Joe a visit in his dressing room, giving him a hug and saying, "Lots of fellers take the name Joe Walcott but you're the only boy I ever saw I was actually proud to have using it."[3]

For his victory over Allen, Joe walked away with $375. By the next evening, every cent of it was gone to pay the grocery store, landlord, milkman and a dozen other credits. By the next morning the Creams were living on markers once again. But somehow they managed to scrape by even with the increased demands of their second child, Elva, who had been born in November.

Since his return to the ring after his battle with typhoid, Walcott had racked up four victories, all by knockout. He had positioned himself to face his first top-ten-rated opponent. A week and a half before his twenty-second birthday on January 21, 1936, Walcott took on Al Ettore, a rugged and popular Philadelphia fighter. Born Albert Ettore on November 19, 1913, in Philadelphia, Al began his boxing career on March 14, 1930, at the tender age of 17, with a points win against Grover Hayes. At the time of his fight with Walcott, Ettore was ranked number nine with a record of 52-7-2 and 16 KO's. Al had been in the ring with the likes of Tommy Loughran, Jimmy Braddock and Willie Reddish. He would go on after his fight with Walcott to battle such notable fighters as Joe Louis, Maxie Rosenbloome, Arturo Godoy and "Two Ton" Tony Galento. Walcott came into the fight with an 11–1 record with a string of 11 knockouts.

The fight was supposed to be a coming-out party for Jersey Joe, and all of Camden was there to cheer him on. Regardless of the fact that most people were Depression poor, dozens of Walcott's hometown friends showed up along with a crowd of some 4,000 spectators. Since the Depression had started, attendance at the hall had been low. It was the largest crowd that the convention hall had seen in a long time.

The bout turned out to be a tough and exciting slugfest. When the bell rang for round one to begin, Walcott streaked from his corner. Since Jersey Joe had done only a little training for the fight, he wanted to try to get Ettore out early, and he nearly succeeded. With both fists swinging, Walcott quickly attacked his larger foe. Al ran into stiff head shots as Jersey Joe ripped across a hard right, then a left hook and drove sharp digs into Al's body. The fans loudly and excitedly roared their approval as Walcott nearly knocked Ettore off his feet during the opening round. Round one belonged to Walcott.

In the second round, however, Ettore appeared to find his bearings and started to take command after shaking off the effects of Walcott's vicious first-round assault. Al started to bomb Joe's ribs and kidneys with hard right-hand punches whenever the two fighters were at close quarters. During the infighting, Al had the advantage with his heavy blows to Walcott's body. His attack forced Jersey Joe to use movement and jabs to outbox and stay away from his bigger opponent.

Al forced the action in the third, fourth and fifth, winning the rounds and giving Walcott's ribs a merciless beating. In the sixth, a tiring Walcott made a stand. He shifted the tide of the fight back into his favor by buckling Ettore's knees with a hard right uppercut as the two were fighting against the ropes. Moments later as they battled in the center of the ring, Walcott landed a hard smashing overhand right that sent Al back to the ropes. Wham! Walcott landed another hard right that nearly floored Ettore; the punch opened a cut above Al's right eye that instantly started gushing blood. Al's handlers, in full cry earlier when their fighter was winning, were now clutching the ring's edge, dumb-struck. Their faces were chalk white and worried looking as Walcott rocked Ettore with staggering blows that turned Al into a crimson bloody mess. Lucky for Al the round ended a moment later.

The seventh round was a continuation of the sixth as Jersey Joe started right where he left off. Walcott crashed a left hook to the side of Al's face and crossed a right to Al's jaw that stopped him in his tracks. Al tried to retaliate with his effective body attack, but was unsuccessful. Walcott used movement to avoid Al's body punches while continuing to land bruising rights and lefts.

Although looking impressive, Walcott was tiring badly; his sixth-and-seventh-round rally was beginning to fade as the seventh round came to a close. Since Walcott was worn down from what seemed eternal hardship and not being in peak physical condition, he didn't have the stamina to put his opponent away. By the eighth round Ettore's brutal body attack had finally caught up with Jersey Joe. An exhausted Walcott collapsed at 1:08 of round eight from a hard right to the pit of the stomach, and he was unable to continue. Beaten by hardship and Ettore's brutal body attack, Joe suffered his second defeat and his first TKO loss. The Ettore fight was no doubt a huge disappointment for Walcott and his fans.

Four months after his fight with Ettore, Walcott was back in action. The evening of March 3, 1936, featured an "all heavyweight evening." Primo Carnera and Leroy Haynes headlined the main event at the Phillies ballpark. Jersey Joe Walcott and Willie Reddish were fighting the semi-windup. Instead of taking on a soft touch after his loss to Ettore (not that Walcott had any choice), Joe was matched against one of the most-avoided heavyweight fighters around, tough Willie Reddish. Willie was a former Philadelphia Golden Gloves amateur champion. He turned pro in 1932 and had been in the ring with some very good competition, such as Ettore and Haynes.

Newspaper columnist Lansing McCurley wrote his prediction a few days before the fight, saying that he did not think that the fight would go the distance and would end sometime around the halfway point. Matchmaker Peter Moran likewise predicted a knockout. In fact, Moran said, "If the fight doesn't end in a knockout I'll quit the fight game and never sign up another match."[4] Unfortunately, the fight did not turn out to be an exciting slugfest that ended in a knockout. It actually ended up being the opposite.

Walcott was awarded the decision after eight rounds of mostly body punching and a lot of clinching. It was a spectacle that annoyed one of Philadelphia's largest outdoor crowds from the first bell to the last. Apparently matchmaker Moran had made a mistake with this match, since both fighters had similar fighting styles that resulted in a boring fight.

In the spring of 1936 Jack Blackburn unexpectedly showed up at the Arcadia gym, looking for Jersey Joe Walcott. It had been two years since Walcott had spoken with Blackburn. Jack looked far more prosperous than he had the last time he and Walcott had spoken. Jack explained that he was looking to hire Walcott as a sparring partner for Joe Louis. Louis was in New Jersey training for his first fight with Max Schmelling. If Walcott was interested, the job paid $25 a round and guaranteed at least one round a day. "Whaddaya say?" asked Blackburn. Of course Walcott said yes. For a fellow who typically worked 50-plus hours a week and made $12 to $15 a week as a laborer, $25 a day for as little as three minutes of work was a fortune. It was the best news Walcott had heard in a long time, big money at last.

A few days later Walcott showed up at the Louis training camp at the Stanley Hotel in Lakewood, New Jersey. Louis' team had their quarters at the hotel. The Brown Bomber bunked at a house called the Albert Mansion. The hotel's owner, Harry Cohen, had pine trees cut and an area behind the hotel cleared. He then had an outdoor stadium built that could seat three thousand people as well as a workout area complete with a boxing ring. It was here in a shaded backyard area that Louis held his workouts. Cohen was hoping to make his hotel a regular place for Louis to train. He spared no expenses. Louis entered the ring to trumpet fanfare. A band played between each sparring session, with such songs as "I'm Sorry I Made You Cry "or "Let's Call It a Day." There was also a bandstand and nightly floor show.

There have been several different versions written about the sparring session between Jersey Joe Walcott and Joe Louis. In an interview in 1947, Walcott claimed to have decked Joe Louis during the first day of their sparring match and was subsequently fired by Blackburn after being paid $25:

> I crossed the right to Louis's head that made his eyes narrow. I stepped around and stab him with jabs. I kept in motion from side to side. The harder he tried the worse he looked. He dubbed his shots badly. As he lunged and missed with one big, angry left hook, I came back with a right to the face. It wasn't a hard punch and couldn't have hurt, but it was perfectly placed and enough to knock him off balance. He stumbled awk-

wardly across the ring. The rope saved him from falling face first, and he landed on both knees.

Technically it would have been a knockdown in a fight. Training camp observers, though, discount such mishaps to their star performer, and they possibly chalk that off as an error in foot work. But Joe's wife Marva and Blackburn laughed out loud. They were joined by Carl Nelson, Joe's detective bodyguard, and Julian Black. I think I could not suppress a smile. Louis became furious. Later that evening after dinner Blackburn took me aside. "I'm sorry, Chappie," he said, "but they decided that you ain't got the right style for Louis. You'll have to go." He counted out twenty five dollars into my hand.

I have to be a punching bag for the great Joe Louis too ... or no match, I said with some bitterness. Jack turned his head up at me with such a look of understanding, that I've never forgotten, he was a friend.[5]

Other versions of the sparring match have Louis knocking Walcott down and giving Jersey Joe such a whipping that Walcott quit outright. A third version, according to Walcott's grandson, as told to him by his grandfather, has Walcott knocking Louis down twice, in two separate sparring matches, and then being fired.

It has been accepted by some boxing historians that Walcott knocked Louis down. On the other hand there is little doubt that Louis knocked Walcott down, since there are photos from a newspaper that show in sequence Walcott falling to the canvas during his sparring match with Louis. Jersey Joe nevertheless had these words to say about the photos that were supposed to show Louis knocking him down: "Some newspapers even carried a series of movie photos purporting to show Louis flooring me. But that was as much baloney as Joe's statement that I never worked with him."[6]

However the sparring match went between Jersey Joe Walcott and Joe Louis, one thing is for sure: Walcott was fired and sent packing. Dejected, Jersey Joe hitched a ride on a grocery-store truck and headed back to Merchantville.

— 4 —

"Tiger" Jack Fox and Hard Times

"I once went an entire decade being hungry" — Jersey Joe Walcott

A week after the disappointing sparring session with Joe Louis, Walcott was back at the Camden Convention Hall facing Billy Ketchell, the "Millville Plowboy." Ketchell, whose real name was Basil Klucka, was a tough, strong, light-heavyweight who wasn't afraid to face many of the best fighters in his weight class. Walcott and Ketchell would fight a total of three times in 1936. Joe claimed that the fights were right up there with the most difficult of his career. The first fight on June 4, 1936, was a fast-paced ten-round draw. Twelve days after his fight with Ketchell, Walcott was back in the square circle. Because of some favorable press he had received after his sparring session with Louis, he was signed to fight in a Jack Dempsey–sponsored heavyweight tournament.

The event was held at the Coney Island Velodrome on June 16, 1936. Essentially, the tournament was designed to find the next "white hope," but fighters of all ethnicities were allowed to enter. Walcott was matched up against French Canadian heavyweight Louis LePage of Paterson, New Jersey. The former great heavyweight contender Joe Jeanette acted as Walcott's second. It must have been a great honor for Walcott to work with Jeanette, who was considered one of the greatest turn-of-the-century fighters.

Jeanette, who was born August 28, 1879, in North Bergen, New Jersey, began boxing on a dare at the age of twenty-five. Because the color line was in full force during Jeanette's time, black fighters didn't have a lot of options when it came to who they could fight. As a result colored fighters would repeatedly face each other. Jeanette battled Jack Johnson no less than ten times, Sam Langford fifteen times and "Battling" Jim Johnson seven times. Jeanette also fought Sam McVey five times, which included one of the longest marathon fights in boxing history. On April 17, 1909, McVey and Jeanette battle for three and a half hours over the course of 49 rounds. During the fight Jeanette was knocked down twenty-seven times and McVey nineteen times. In the end, exhausted with his eyes swollen shut, McVey was unable to rise from his stool, so Jeanette was declared the winner.

With such a fabled ring great in his corner to guide him, Jersey Joe was confident. Walcott went out and destroyed LePage, knocking him down once in the first, once in the second, and dropping him for good in the third. For his victory Joe received $125. But since he did not exactly meet the requirements for a "white hope," he was not asked to return.

On the evening of June 19, 1936, three days after the "white hope" tournament, Jersey Joe Walcott did what sixty million Americans did. He sat near a radio along with friends and family members and listened to the live, action-packed, round-by-round broadcast of the Joe Louis-Max Schmeling fight. Although this fight was nowhere near the political giant the second fight would be, it had nonetheless captured the attention of most of the world. There was trouble brewing in Europe, as Hitler and his Nazi's were preaching Aryan superiority and anti–Jewish ideology. As a result the fight turned out to be more than a simple boxing match. Schmeling, although not a Nazi, was viewed to some extent as representing the enemy. In fact some Jewish organization protested the fight, claiming that Schmeling represented Nazi Germany. In reality, Max was inadvertently mixed up with the trouble that was starting in Europe. Louis, on the other hand, was viewed as the hero of the free world. In the two short years that he had been boxing, Joe had become one of the most famous athletes on the planet as well as a hero and hope to blacks in America. The fight was America versus Germany and it wasn't just blacks that were rooting for a Louis victory; it was most of America, even some Southern whites.

As millions of Americans sat and listened to the fight, they were shocked at what unfolded. The contest turned out to be one of the greatest upsets in boxing history. Although Louis entered the ring as a 10-to-1 favorite, he was overconfident and not in top shape. Schmeling, on the other hand, had trained like a monk and had studied Louis' fighting style. Max claimed that he had found a weakness in Joe's style while watching films of the Louis fights. This discovered weakness led to his famous quote: "I see something."

The something that Schmeling saw was a chink in Louis' armor. When Louis threw a jab with his left hand, he dropped his left arm. This tendency to drop his left after throwing his jab resulted in Louis' face being wide open for a counter right-hand punch. Schmeling's plan was to counterpunch with his powerful right over Louis' left. The plan worked. Schmeling knocked out the previously unbeaten Brown Bomber in the twelfth round. The entire nation reeled under the shocking loss, especially blacks. When Jersey Joe Walcott looked out of his window after the fight at the streets of Camden, they were quiet. There were no celebrations after the Louis defeat.

Three days after Louis' unexpected loss at the hands of Schmeling, Walcott was in the ring with journeyman Phil Johnson. Little did he realize at the time of the Johnson fight that nearly fourteen years later he would fight Phil's then seven-year-old son, Harold. Phil and Harold would have the distinction of being the first father and son to fight and lose to the same fighter, both suffering third-round knockout losses to Walcott. Johnson was a stylish boxer possessing a sharp jab and a good punch. Unfortunately, Phil was not managed well and was over-matched during his early boxing career. As a result he became nothing more than a journeyman fighter, a stepping stone for future champions and top contenders.

The fight played out under the stars at the Phillies ballpark on June 22, 1936, on the eve of the Democratic National Convention. The main event featured two popular Philadelphia fighters, former Walcott opponent Al Ettore going up against Leroy Haynes. The famous "Cinderella Man" and heavyweight champion James J. Braddock was brought in as referee. The main event turned out to be lackluster, prompting newspaper writer Matt Ring to say, "All the fans got out of it was fifteen rounds of arduous cuffing, mauling and clinching, with nary a knock-down, not even a staggering blow to relieve the tedium. Good clean punching was so scarce that it evoked a roar from the crowd whenever some of it intruded on the proceedings."[1]

Thankfully the preliminary bouts provided some decent action for the thousands in attendance. The first bout of the evening proved to be exciting. Leo Duncan slammed Paul Pirrone all over the ring until he broke his left hand on Pirrone's skull in the fifth round and had to give up. Willie Reddish survived a thumping by Terry Mitchell in the last three rounds and gained a decision over the New Yorker in a six-round main preliminary. Jersey Joe Walcott scored a technical knockout in the third round when he broke Phil Johnson's nose with a right-hand punch that left his opponent bloodied and unable to continue. Paul Hoff suffered his first defeat as a professional at the hands of Gus Dorazio. Although the main event did not live up to the hype, the evening turned out to be a success with a sellout crowd of 15,000 spectators spending $40,000, the biggest gate in Philadelphia since Steve Hamas had defeated Max Schmeling at the convention hall two and half years earlier.

Twenty-two days after the Johnson fight, Walcott took on Billy Ketchell for the second time at the Pennsauken Arena. No doubt Walcott remembered how tough his previous fight with Ketchell was. The second fight turned out to be even tougher. In fact, the fight turned out to be one of the toughest of Walcott's career and would cause him to suffer through some of the most difficult times in his life.

In the first round Joe broke his hand on Ketchell's head and was unable to effectively punch with his right. Walcott had to use all of his craftiness and ring savvy to weather the murderous attack of Ketchell just to finish the fight on his feet. After ten hard-fought rounds the fight was ruled a draw. Following the fight, an aching Walcott was taken to Cooper Hospital to have his broken fist put into a cast.

With his hand in a cast, and the Great Depression well underway, jobs were hard to come by, especially for a black man. The Creams were soon back on relief checks and were barely scraping by. Desperate for money, Walcott removed his cast after only a few weeks and refractured his hand in a fight with Carmen Passarella. The fight, an eight-round decision victory, did little to help with Walcott's financial troubles or the healing of his broken hand. A trip to Cooper Hospital followed after the fight to recast Jersey Joe's broken knuckles. A month later, again out of desperation for food and rent money and no credit available to hold the Creams over until Joe's hand could heal completely, Walcott was forced to remove his cast early to fight Billy Ketchell again. The fight resulted in a ten-round decision loss for Jersey Joe as well as the refracturing of his hand for a second time. This time there would be no removing the cast early, warned his doctor; Walcott had to let his hand heal or face the possibility of permanent injury and a possible end to his boxing career.

Unable to fight because of his broken hand or find a steady job because of the Depression, Walcott was out of work for the better part of the next eight months. His wife, Lydia, worked as much as she could to help supplement their meager relief checks (when she could find work). Since she was pregnant with their third child, as her due date neared she had to stop working altogether. Joe and Lydia literally had to plead with the grocery store to get enough food to survive, as the Creams fell further and further behind.

Finally a little luck came Jersey Joe's way. He was rushed into a match against "Tiger" Jack Fox at the Rockland Palace in Harlem on May 22, 1937. Just a few weeks prior to the fight, on May 6, the German airship *Hindenburg* burst into flames as it was trying to dock at Lakehurst Naval Air Base in New Jersey. The giant zeppelin was completely destroyed in a matter of moments. Tragically, thirty-six people were killed. The world sat mesmerized as Herbert Morrison's impassioned broadcast of the disaster was replayed for days on every radio station available.

Tiger Fox was one of several popular Rockland Palace house fighters; Tiger was also one of the most dangerous light-heavyweights of the day. Born John Linwood Fox April 2, 1907, in Indianapolis (there is some debate over the subject of his age and place of birth), Fox began boxing at about the age of eighteen. Some sources claim Fox may have started boxing as early as the age of thirteen. Starting a professional career at such a young age was not unheard of during the early part of the twentieth century.

During a career that spanned twenty-two years, Fox had only one shot at a title, against Melio Bettina for the New York light-heavyweight championship, on February 3, 1939. Two months prior to the fight, Tiger got into a late-night argument with a woman named Edna Boyd. During the argument Edna stabbed Tiger with a ten-inch razor blade just below his heart. Initially doctors said Tiger would never fight again. He proved them wrong when he took on Melio for the championship. The fight turned out to be a disappointment for Fox; he suffered a technical knockout in round nine. No doubt the knife wound played a part in the outcome.

As far as fighting style was concerned, Fox was a counter-puncher who possessed a lethal knockout punch. Tiger's punch was good enough to score 94 knockouts in 151 recorded wins (Tiger claimed to have over 300 fights during his career), twenty-four of those in the first round. Fighting out of a slight crouch with his feet spread far apart and his hands down by his knees, Fox would regularly stick his chin out and make faces at his opponents, inviting them to hit him while bobbing and weaving to confuse an adversary. When an opponent did take the bait and attack, Fox would dodge and duck the blows and counter with thunderous haymakers, usually scoring a knockout.

When Jersey Joe Walcott took on Tiger Jack Fox, he was in no shape to be fighting one of the greatest light-heavyweights of all time, a fighter that Joe claimed was the single greatest fighter he ever faced.[2] Joe had not been in the ring in eight months and had done only minimal training. Furthermore he hadn't been eating properly and was underweight from lack of proper nutrition. Walcott came into the fight at 184 pounds, Tiger at 178.

Despite Walcott's condition, the first round began well for Joe. He connected with a solid right to Fox's chin that sent Tiger Jack through the ropes and out onto the apron of the ring where he laid still for seven seconds. Fox then jumped up suddenly and quickly rushed back into the ring. The crowd went absolutely wild. Nobody had ever knocked Tiger Jack out of the ring before. Once back in the ring, Fox proceeded to take command of the fight over the course of the next several rounds. By the eighth it was all Fox, as a tired, undernourished Jersey Joe Walcott took a frightful beating and was counted out. In Joe's own words, "I was counted out in the eighth round, counted out from sheer weakness."[3] Although defeated, Walcott put up a good enough showing for Al Douglas, the owner of the Rockland Palace, to want him back.

The next day Walcott's meager purse of $122 went to pay a dozen creditors. He cautiously took care of the most important ones first, but was still short on rent. His landlord gave him an ultimatum, "Pay or get out." Walcott, pointing to his wife who was due to have their third child any day, pleaded with the landlord and promised to pay him as soon as he could.

Jersey Joe's third child, Doris, was born on June 5, 1937. He kept his family fed by working down at the Philadelphia docks but was once again short on rent. The landlord's case was simply presented: "Get out by the end of the month."[4] Once again Walcott was forced to move his family from one ramshackle place to another.

On June 22, Walcott along with his cousin Willie "The Joplin Ghost" Amos and about a dozen friends and family members sat around a radio at Willie's house. They tuned into to the Louis-Braddock fight and listened excitedly as Louis knocked out the "Cinderella Man" in the eighth round. Walcott, although happy with Louis's victory, couldn't help but feel sad at how life had kicked him around. How he had missed out on the opportunity three years before to go to Chicago with Blackburn. Walcott's cousin Willie noticed Walcott's sadness, put his arms around Jersey Joe, and said, "You'll be next, Reds. Let them give you a break and you'll do it too."[5]

Jersey Joe's next fight was nearly four months later on September 3, 1937, a quick second-round knockout of Joe Lipps. He was then signed to fight another Rockland Palace regular, the dangerous slugger Elmer "Vio-

4 — "Tiger" Jack Fox and Hard Times

lent" Ray. At 6'2" and 195 pounds, Ray was a formidable opponent and was known as a thunderous puncher. This fight would mark the start of a three-fight series with Ray, beginning at the Rockland Palace on September 25, 1937.

Ray was born sometime around 1910 in Florida. As a young man he wrestled alligators for money but eventually found his way into boxing. He began his career by fighting in Battle Royals sometime around 1926 when he was known as "Bearcat Ray" and "Kid Violent Ray." These dangerous fights featured anywhere from three to ten colored fighters in the same ring, often times blindfolded. The fighters would beat each other senseless until only one remained. The last man standing was declared the winner.

Elmer "Violent" Ray, the much-feared heavyweight contender, during the mid–1940s. Walcott first fought Ray in 1937 at the Rockland Palace.

The fight actually turned out to be an easy one for Walcott. He took Ray apart quickly and ended matters with a hard right hand to the jaw and a left hook to the belly at the 43-second mark of the third round. The reason for Walcott's easy win may have had something to do with the fact that Ray, much like Jersey Joe, was barely scraping by and was undertrained and underfed. As Jersey Joe later said about his first fight with Elmer Ray, "I recognized Ray as a kindred soul as soon as I threw a right to the body. The spirit was willing but the stomach was empty."[6] For his victory over Ray, Walcott received $125 and an invitation by Al Douglas to come back in a few weeks to fight George Brothers. It was an invitation that the cash-strapped Walcott could not refuse.

On October 9 Jersey Joe was back at the Rockland Palace and in the ring to face Brothers. The fight started off easy for Walcott. He floored the former Golden Gloves light-heavyweight champion three times in round one. The three-knockdown rule was not in effect so Brothers was allowed to continue to get up and fight after the third knockdown. According to Irving Rudd, the Rockland Palace press agent who was covering the fight, some of the people in the crowd got up and started to make for the exits, since they figured the fight was going to be over quickly: "As one guy leaves he waves at Brothers and says, good-bye, boy. Don't get up or he gonna knock you down again! Brothers sits there looking at the fan, spits out a mouthful of blood and teeth, shakes his head, and just glares. Then he pulls himself up and carries the fight to Jersey Joe. Brothers lasts the eight rounds and comes off with a decision."[7] The fight was Walcott's last of 1937. While it had been a hard year for Jersey Joe, the hard times were far from over.

—5—

Early Retirement

Walcott started off the first half of 1938 with half a dozen fights, about one a month. These fights along with his daytime job kept his family afloat financially, albeit just barely. In January, Walcott fought twice. First up was Freddie Feducia, a tough Italian from Newark, New Jersey, who had only lost only one fight in his last fifteen starts. The fight was the semi-windup to the Al Ettore-Gus Dorazio main event held at the Philadelphia Arena on January 1, 1938. Jersey Joe easily outboxed Freddie for the first six rounds. In the seventh Freddie burst forth in a wild rally and knocked Joe down for a count of two. Feducia continued his rally into the eighth and final round, but it was too little too late. Since Walcott had already swept the first six rounds, he was awarded the eight-round decision.

Walcott, at this point, was part of Pete Morans stable of fighters fighting out of Philadelphia. Moran was matchmaker for the Adelphia Athletic Club and was one of the great boxing hustlers from Philly during the 1930s and 1940s. Pete's stable of fighters included Leroy Haynes, Mickie Keach and Frank Donofrio. Walcott's manager at this time was Bill Brooks. Brooks decided to keep Jersey Joe on a busy schedule and quickly had Joe signed for a fight.

Walcott continued his winning ways by earning a decision over Jim Whitest, on January 10, at the Olympia Athletic Club in Philly, breaking his opponent's jaw in the process. A month and a half after the Whitest victory, Jersey Joe was signed to fight journeyman Art Sykes. Walcott scored a fourth-round knockout over Sykes with a right to the jaw.

Less than three weeks after the Sykes fight, Jersey Joe faced Lorenzo Pack at the Camden Convention Hall. Pack, who had been in the ring with the likes of Tiger Jack Fox, "Two Ton" Tony Galento and Leroy Haynes, was a tough guy and was not afraid of Jersey Joe. Prior to the fight Lorenzo was boasting, according to Walcott, that he would "Splash me all over the Camden landscape."[1] Pack fought as if he intended to make good his boast. In Walcott's own words: "Nobody ever hit me so hard and often. In the fourth round I drew him to me with a right that was deliberately short. I shifted to a left hook that burst on the point of his chin. Like Al King and Roxy Allen, Lorenzo crashed backwards, slammed his head against the floor and went completely unconscious."[2] Jersey Joe was once again filled with the terror that he might have killed an opponent. Fortunately, Pack's head cleared the next afternoon.

Since the start of 1938, Walcott had racked up four wins. This was good enough to get him a rematch with the dangerous Tiger Jack Fox. After a close ten-round brawl at the Camden Convention Hall on May 10, Tiger Jack was awarded the decision. A few weeks later, Walcott dropped another close decision to a former Joe Louis opponent, Roy Lazer, at the Fairview Arena in Camden. Having lost two in a row, there was suddenly little demand for Walcott's services.

The second half of 1938 was extremely bleak for Jersey Joe and his family. As the holidays approached, the Creams were penniless and Joe had not fought in nearly six months. The jobs he had managed to get were sporadic and didn't pay very well. To add to his worries, Joe was reminded daily that Christmas was approaching. His oldest son Buddy and daughter Elva were anxiously awaiting the arrival of Santa Claus and what he might bring.

Jersey Joe was rushed into a match against Bob Tow on December 23, just two days before Christmas, as "the Lord rescued us from disappointing the little ones."[3] Starring in the main event of the boxing and wrestling show at the Camden Armory before a crowd of 5,500 Walcott easily outpointed Tow. He lost only one round of the fight, the fifth, when Tow used an effective body attack to win the round. When the bout was over, Jersey Joe was awarded the decision and $75, allowing Santa Claus to come on schedule.

Although the Tow fight was a victory, Walcott had decided that he needed to make an effort to get out of the uncertainties of boxing. He applied for a job on the Pennsauken Township police force, but the expected opening never came. Jersey Joe spent the next two years taking any job that came his way and fighting occasionally.

In June 1939 Walcott's fourth child, Ruth, was born. Two months later, Jersey Joe took on Hungarian fighter Al Boris at the Meadowbrook Bowl in Newark, New Jersey. Boris possessed a slam-bang style that helped him little against the slick Walcott. Joe won an eight-round decision and received $90. The following November, Walcott was back at the Rockland Palace. This time he was taking on a fighter named Curtis "The Hatchet Man" Sheppard.

Although raw and inexperienced, Sheppard already had a reputation as a powerful puncher. He began his professional career in 1938 with a one-round knockout of Larry White. Before his pro career he had a successful amateur career. Sheppard made it to the finals of the New York Golden Gloves tournament in the light-heavyweight division but lost on a decision to Gus Alexander. In the same year, on March 21, Sheppard won the intercity Golden Gloves championship at heavyweight by a decision versus Dan Meritt. His fight with Jersey Joe would be the first of two for the pair. Walcott earned an eight-round decision over the inexperienced "Hatchet Man," who at the time only had nine professional fights under his belt. For the win Walcott was paid $100.

Jersey Joe began 1940 with a six-round decision win over journeyman "Tiger" Red Lewis. He had won four in a row and was on a roll. It was once again time for Walcott to step it up and face a top-ten opponent. That opponent turned out to be a giant of a man, number-four-ranked contender Abe Simon, nicknamed "Sky Scrapper Abe."

At 6'5" and weighing anywhere from 250 to 260 pounds, "Big Abe" was the largest fighter that Jersey Joe ever fought. He was born Abraham Simon on January 1, 1913, in Long Island, New York. As a teenager of sixteen, Abe was larger than most full-grown men. Standing well over six feet tall and weighing in excess of 200 pounds, Abe's freakish size was found to be caused by an overactive pituitary gland, which caused rapid growth in the teenaged Simon. One story tells how when Abe, at sixteen, showed up for class the first day and said to the teacher in his deep bass voice, "My name is Abe Simon, where do I sit?" The teacher replied, "Anywhere you want."

As a full-grown man Abe was massively built and strong. He had huge feet (one report has his feet size at eighteen) and massive hands; in fact, Abe owned some of the largest hands ever recorded on a heavyweight fighter.[4] He also had huge shoulders and his chest measured 48 inches unexpanded, 52 inches expanded. But for all his fearsome appearance, Abe was a gentle giant, not only big and strong but also very intelligent. In high school Abe excelled in academics as well as athletics and was offered a scholarship to Yale, but turned it down so he could pursue his boxing career. One little known fact about Abe is that he collected and ran Lionel trains.

Abe's professional boxing career started in 1935 with a second-round knockout over Jim Dowling. From there Abe racked up twelve more wins, ten by knockout before suffering his first defeat, a decision loss at the hands of Lou Nova, who would go on to battle Joe Louis and defeat Max Baer twice. Abe would continue on after the Nova loss, winning most of his fights and eventually challenging Joe Louis two times for the world's heavyweight title, going thirteen rounds in the first fight before being knocked out. On the strength of his performance in the first match with Louis, Abe was given a second chance. Louis, always better in rematches, was all business and dispatched Abe in the sixth round. After the Louis rematch Abe retired from boxing, having compiled a 36–10–1 record with 25 knockouts. Simon went on to work as a referee, bouncer, and actor. He appeared in several TV shows and movies, most notably two all-time classics, *On the Waterfront* starring Marlon Brando and *Requiem for a Heavyweight* starring Anthony Quinn.

Abe's biggest win would come against Jersey Joe Walcott. The fight took place on February 12, 1940, at Laurel Gardens in Newark, New Jersey. "Skyscraper" Abe entered the ring at 256 pounds to Walcott's reported 192. Walcott claimed he only weighed about 180 pounds for the Simon fight. Coming into the fight, Joe was out of shape and hungry, having only eaten a few potatoes along with some tea the day before. This was hardly the nutrition needed to fight a man the size and strength of Abe Simon. In fact, Walcott said he had never entered a fight before feeling like he had less energy. Although in poor condition and with a stomach literally growling from hunger, Walcott performed well, for a while. Jersey Joe won the first few rounds easily by out-jabbing and out-maneuvering the bigger, slower Simon. Walcott landed a number of hard right hands and left hooks, shaking up the bigger fighter on several occasions. Eventually though, after wrestling with and being mauled by the massively strong Abe for six rounds, Walcott's lack of conditioning and improper diet finally caught up with him. In the sixth round Big Abe landed a powerful right hand to Walcott's jaw, sending him to the canvas. Too exhausted to rise and continue, Jersey Joe was counted out. He was beaten more by fatigue and hunger than by Abe's fighting ability. Walcott later said about the Simon fight: "Although I had been winning all the way, my arms grew terribly heavy. By the sixth they would no longer obey me and my whole frame gave way. When I stumbled into Simon's glove, there was nothing left."[5] Years after the fight with Walcott, Abe conceded that Jersey Joe had punched harder than any other fighter he fought, including Joe Louis.

5 — Early Retirement

Following the loss to Simon, Walcott was fed up and discouraged. The defeat was another setback in a career filled with setbacks. After fighting for the better part of ten years, his career was going nowhere. After years of fighting for small purses, bluffing his way through fights because he was out of shape, being ripped off by shady managers, and not making enough money to support his family, Jersey Joe finally decided he had enough.

No longer did Jersey Joe have the dream of winning the heavyweight title. Gone was his boyhood enthusiasm he shared with his late father as they spoke of past ring legends. Boxing was now nothing more than a dangerous job to fall back on when there was no other way to make money to feed his family. It was with a heavy heart that he decided to give up his dream of winning the heavyweight title, but what choice did he have? How could he continue when there was never enough money to train or eat properly? After all, he was the responsible head of a growing family with a wife who was only a few months away from giving birth to their fifth child. What Jersey Joe needed was a steady job with a steady income, something his sporadic boxing career could not provide. In February 1940, the

When Jersey Joe retired from boxing in 1953 after his loss to Rocky Marciano, having a street named after him in Camden, New Jersey, was as much a dream as being heavyweight champion.

26-year-old Walcott made the difficult decision to retire from boxing. It wasn't the first time Joe had quit the ring. He had done it several times before, but this time he was serious.

Just about the time Jersey Joe was hanging up his gloves, a young middleweight from Cincinnati was making his professional debut. His name was Ezzard Charles. Unknown to either at the time, their destinies would eventually collide in several battles.

A few days after the decision to end his boxing career, Walcott picked up a job working on a coal delivery truck but the job only lasted a few months. When winter ended, so did the job. In July, Lydia gave birth to Vincent, their fifth child. With another hungry baby to feed, Walcott took whatever job he could find. For the next year and a half he worked at quite a few different occupations, including such filthy jobs as garbage collector and septic-tank cleaner. Although employed most of the time, these jobs, like all the others, barely paid enough to support the Cream family and keep the bill collectors at bay. Consequently, Joe was constantly living on credit and was never able to get ahead.

Shortly after Walcott decided to stop boxing, former heavyweight champion Jack Johnson came to Merchantville looking for Jersey Joe Walcott. The ex-champion stopped at the house of Joe's former teacher, Miss Lena Skelly, and sent word for Walcott to come over, which he did. After Walcott arrived, Johnson explained that he was interested in managing and training him. His response to Johnson was that he would have to think it over. But after the loss to Simon, Walcott's mind was made up and even an offer from the famous former heavyweight champion did not tempt Walcott back into the ring. For the next year and a half, Jersey Joe worked at whatever manual labor jobs he could find to feed his family.

On December 7, 1941, the Japanese attacked the United States at Pearl Harbor, drawing the U.S. into World War II. As a result of the war, jobs were created and workers were needed to maintain ships for the military at the New York shipyards near Camden. It was here that Walcott landed a decent wartime job. He started off as an unskilled laborer and worked his way up to caulker and chipper. On a good week he could make as much as $85. But his take-home pay was usually around $58. Although the shipyard was a decent job, Jersey Joe continued to have financial difficulties, as he was constantly in debt to creditors and living paycheck to paycheck.

Walcott worked at the shipyard from 1942 to 1944. In June 1944, out of necessity to earn some extra money, he fought two easy fights against nondescript opponents. He won both fights easily, even though he had not fought in four years and four months. The first fight was an eighth-round decision win over New York heavyweight Felix Del Paoli. The second was a third-round knockout over Elis Singleton. The extra money from the two fights went quickly, since Joe was in debt to several people such as the grocery store owner and landlord. On December 14, Lydia gave birth to their sixth child, Carol, and the Creams were scraping the bottom of the barrel again. In Walcott's own words, "I couldn't have gone any farther down the drain if I had pulled the stopper out myself."[6]

Although Jersey Joe had the two fights in June, his attitude towards boxing had not changed. In fact, he even reverted to using his birth name, as a comeback was the farthest thing from his mind as he worried about how he was going to support his family and a new baby. But destiny in the form of a neat looking, little, Italian man was about to step into Arnold's life and change it forever.

— 6 —

Bocchicchio

Destiny came disguised as a neat looking Italian man

It all began as a shopping trip to Ptomkin's poultry store in Camden in late 1944, four days after Arnold's daughter Carol was born. While shopping, Arnold was introduced to Felix Bocchicchio, by Mr. Ptomkin, the store's owner. Felix, dressed in a grey pin-striped suit and tie, was a neat looking, little Italian man with a slight build. He gave the impression of being every bit the 1940s gangster, with jet-black hair that was slicked straight back, an ever-present Lucky Strike cigarette hanging from his bottom lip, and a limp from an old bullet wound when he walked. Felix was also the local fight promoter and president of the newly opened Camden Athletic Club. Together with his long-time friends Vic Marsillo and Bart Guarino, Felix had just recently opened the Camden Athletic Club and was staging the club's boxing shows at the Camden Convention Hall. Felix and Vic had known each other for years and used to put on fight cards at the old Camden Armory. Formally, Vic was acting matchmaker and a fight manager. Bart Guarino had the official title of matchmaker.

Felix Bocchicchio was a well-known figure around New Jersey and Philadelphia. He was also a well-known underworld criminal, gambler, and gangster. In fact Felix was described by writer Bill Kelly as "being so crooked that he had to screw his socks on."[1] Felix's nickname was "Man O War," after the famous race horse. He was born August 31, 1907, in Philadelphia shortly after his parents immigrated to the U.S. from Italy. Felix's father, Andrew, was a barber. He plied his trade in a shop he owned and operated in Philadelphia. His mother, Claudine, was a housewife. Felix grew up on the tough streets of Philly along with his two brothers, Nicky and Ronald. As a young man Felix worked at a pharmacy but soon became involved in a sordid life of crime.

Felix Bocchicchio (right) became Jersey Joe's manager in 1944, resurrecting Walcott's boxing career and putting him on the road to winning the heavyweight title.

His first arrest was reported in 1925. His rap sheet grew from there to include such acts as larceny, holdups, assault and battery, state liquor violation, white slave trafficking, and prison breaking. His list of known accomplices included such gangsters as Angelo Bruno, Peter Casella, Pasquale Massi, Dominick Pollino, Louis Campbell, and the legendary mobster Charles "Lucky" Luciano, the father of modern organized crime.

By 1930 Felix was incarcerated in the Northumberland County Jail in Pennsylvania. Upon his release he made his way to New Jersey where he continued his criminal activities. By 1934 Felix was a suspect in the murder of Camden police detective William Feitz; he was also a suspect in several break-ins around the Camden area. In 1935 Felix was tried and acquitted for a tavern robbery. In 1936 Bocchicchio was picked up for involvement with pinball machines, which were considered illegal gaming devices at the time.

By the summer of 1936 Bocchicchio had moved to Mount Ephraim, New Jersey. It was here that he met Vic Marsello. Felix and Vic started promoting fights around this time, as Felix more or less became a somewhat respectable businessman. After his career as a fight promoter and manager was over, Felix and his brother Anthony owned and operated the Bo-Bet Motel and KO Car Wash in Mount Ephraim, New Jersey. Felix would live there until his death on June 18, 1975.

Having been introduced to Arnold, Felix explained that he was a fight promoter for the newly opened Camden Athletic Club and was looking for a good local heavyweight fighter to promote, someone who could draw some attention and help boost ticket sales, which had been low as of late. In fact, after having talked with Roxie Allen a few days before, Felix had been looking for Jersey Joe Walcott. "This is funny," said Felix. "I ran into Roxie Allen the other day, and told him what I needed to boost the boxing business in Camden was another pair attraction like him and you. Roxie said, 'I'm through with boxing, but go after Walcott. He's around and he's no more than thirty.' I was thinking of digging you up."[2]

At the time Felix had offered no proposition, instead he told Arnold: "Say if I can help you in any way, don't be afraid to ask. My office is at the Camden Athletic Corporation on Market Street."[3] Arnold's next step was dictated by the demands of an empty pocketbook, a family with six children and Christmas a week away. He went to Bucchicchio's office the next day. Felix was unavailable so Arnold left word that he had stopped by, along with his address on Magnolia Street.

The next evening, much to Arnold's surprise, Bocchicchio stopped by his house. It's a good bet that Felix had not visited many homes that were in the condition that Arnold's house was in. It was a ramshackle two-bedroom two-story shack, one of a row of such houses in the Matchtown neighborhood. The house had wind and light seeping in through the countless cracks in the woodwork, no glass in the windows and a hole in the front door big enough to put a football through. The hole was covered with an old dingy piece of brown burlap tarp. The windows were covered with cardboard, and the paint which once covered the house had by now mostly flaked away. A stove in the kitchen where the family would huddle around to keep warm provided the only heat—when there was enough coal to fire it up. Years later in an interview Bocchicchio described entering Arnold's house: "The children were huddled around the kitchen stove and there were just two bedrooms for eight people. Even if Arnold would have turned down my offer to fight I would have still done something for his family, they really needed it."[4]

Once in the Creams' house, Bocchicchio seemed more concerned with getting some coal for Arnold and his family than he was about getting him to fight again. Felix's only reference to fighting came as he was leaving. "If you want to fight again, I'll get you a manager and get you started. I'll make one promise. Whatever you earn you'll get. All you need is a little confidence."[5] What Arnold really needed was some coal. Felix took care of Arnold's request. The next day, two days before Christmas, Bocchicchio had a ton of coal delivered to the Creams' basement. "I think we never had a happier Christmas," said Arnold.[6] From then on he would often refer to Felix as "his good angel."[7] Seeing that Bocchicchio was a man of his word, Arnold made up his mind to go and talk with Felix. It was one of the best decisions he ever made, a decision that would affect on the rest of his life.

On Tuesday, the day after Christmas 1944, Arnold walked the few blocks from his house over to the Camden Athletic Club, which was located at 221 Market Street. He happened to meet up with Felix on the corner of Market Street and 3rd Street, right outside of Bucchicchio's office.[8] Together the two spoke and Felix gave Arnold his sales pitch, "So do you want to fight again?" was Bocchicchio's question to Arnold.[9] "I'm not sure," replied Arnold.[10] "Mr. Felix, my family is getting along and I don't know if I want to take a chance on fighting again. Boxing never got me nothin' before, and all I want is a steady job so my wife and kids can eat regular and I can put coal in the cellar. I'm over thirty and just plain tired of it all."[11] Looking to close the sale, Felix replied, "Look, I'll give you money up front, and I'll make sure you have enough money each week to take

The corner of Market and Third streets, the location where Felix Bocchicchio, Jersey Joe's manager, had his office at the Camden Athletic Club (upper floor window with air conditioner). On this same corner, Bocchicchio talked Jersey Joe into returning to the boxing ring.

care of your family."[12] "I don't know," replied Arnold.[13] "I guess one more shot wouldn't kill me," Arnold conceded.[14]

With coal in the basement and a cash advance on future earnings from Felix, the burden of finances and food was finally off of Arnold's mind. He was now set to return to the ring. At thirty years old, an age when most fighters have already won titles and are well into their championship reigns, Jersey Joe Walcott was just getting set to return and start his incredible climb to the heavyweight title. He was about to show the world what he could do with proper training, management, and food.

Felix, as promised, brought in Joe Webster, a wealthy café owner to manage Walcott. He then went to the commissioner, John Hall, and had Walcott's boxing license reinstated. Next Bocchicchio set Joe up with a new trainer, a middle-aged Italian guy named Nick Florio.

Nick Florio was born in 1904, the year his family emigrated from Italy to the United States. The Florio family settled in the Bronx, New York. It was in the Bronx that Nick and his brother Dan grew up and became involved in the fight game. As a young man, Nick was a bantamweight fighter. After his boxing career, he and Dan began training and managing fighters. Together the two brothers had been in the boxing business since the 1920s and had done a little of everything. The Florio brothers had trained a who's who of fighters that included Roland Lastarza, Nick Barone, featherweight champion Battling Battalino, lightweight champion Tony Canzoneri, and NBA world featherweight champion Petey Scalzo. After Walcott retired, Nick would continue to train fighters, eventually working as a cut man with Floyd Patterson and a young Cassius Clay.

The first thing Florio did was get Walcott into a regular training and eating routine. For the first time ever, Jersey Joe began working out and eating the way he should have been doing during the early part of his career — three square meals a day with plenty of meat and vegetables and a lot of road work. Nick turned out to be a great trainer for Jersey Joe. Together over the next few years they would develop such moves as the famous "Walcott shuffle," a forerunner of the Ali shuffle, and the "Walkaway." Together they would also perfect Walcott's feinting and hand movements.

It was the first time in Walcott's boxing career that he had world-class training (besides the year he spent with Blackburn) and could actually concentrate on getting into fighting shape. Although he had to continue to work at the shipyard during the early part of his comeback, he did not have to work the grueling 50+-hour weeks. He was able to spend a lot more time in the gym (without being worn out) than he had been able to do at any previous time during his early career. Webster and Bocchicchio planned to keep Walcott on a busy fighting schedule, by having him fight about once a month. The two wasted no time getting Walcott his first fight.

Jersey Joe Walcott made his return to the ring on January 11, 1945, against journeyman Jackie Saunders, at the Camden Convention Hall. He knocked out the left-handed Saunders in the second round. Two weeks later Jersey Joe faced Johnny Allen on the 25th of January. The fight, held at the Camden Convention Hall, was a disappointment for Walcott and almost ended his comeback. Still rusty, Walcott lost a disputed eight-round decision to Allen. After the fight, Walcott was very upset and disappointed. He told his handlers that he was definitely going to hang up his gloves. Bocchicchio and Marsillo wouldn't hear of it, and after much talking, they convinced Jersey Joe to continue.

To get Walcott's confidence back after his loss to Johnny Allen, Bocchicchio and Webster matched Jersey Joe against Austin Johnson, an inexperienced fighter with only eight professional fights. Walcott easily outpointed Johnson at the Camden Convention Hall, and was awarded a six-round decision. With a win under his belt, Walcott fought a rematch with Johnny Allen. Jersey Joe squared matters with Allen by winning a solid decision over the Philadelphia fighter.

Next up was big Joe Baksi, a former coal miner from Kulpmont, Pennsylvania. Baksi was ranked number four in the world and considered a good prospect. He had defeated some good competition such as Lou Nova, Lee Savold, Tami Mauriello and Gus Dorazio. Baksi represented Walcott's first real test on his comeback. A win here would go a long way.

Business at the shipyards had slowed and thanks to advances from Bocchicchio and the assurance that his family was taken care of, Walcott was able to take a few weeks off from work and dedicate himself to serious training. Jersey Joe trained at Ted Gleason's camp at Greenwood Lake, New Jersey. He got up early every morning for long runs through the green countryside and ate three big meals a day. Experienced heavyweight contender Lee Savold joined Walcott during his training camp. Lee just happened to be training at Gleason's at the same time. The two fighters became friends and spent the next few weeks working out together.

Working with Lee was a blessing since Savold had inside information on Baksi, having faced the big Pennsylvanian three times. As Jersey Joe later recalled: "Lee Savold one of the smartest fighters I know worked with me. We practiced little things together and drilled as very few boxers do. The experience sent me against Baksi with absolute confidence. I felt like a colt even though it was my most important fight in five years and I had passed my 31st birthday."[15]

Before a crowd of 3,500 fans on August 3, 1945, at the Camden Convention Hall, Jersey Joe entered the ring a solid and lean 188 pounds. Baksi came in at a fit 212 pounds. From the opening bell, Walcott used a strategic retreat, superior boxing skills and speed to outbox his larger opponent. Walcott upset Baksi's timing and rhythm throughout the fight and used a trick on Baksi that would later become a famous Walcott move, the "Walkaway," in which Walcott would half turn and walk a few steps back to draw an opponent in and then turn and strike with a quick punch. Jersey Joe had this to say about the tactic: "I faked a movement in one direction and went in another. I let Baksi maneuver me into striking range and half turning walked casually away. When he thought he had me solved I teased him with jabs and shook him with rights."[16] After tiring out his opponent, Walcott uncorked a sizzling attack in the tenth and final round that left his opponent groggy and bloody at the bell. The only official, referee Paul Cavalier, scored the fight 6-3-1, giving Jersey Joe a ten-round decision.

The Baksi fight was a huge upset win for Walcott. The victory propelled Jersey Joe into the top ten of heavyweight boxers for the first time in his career. News of the fight's results were sent all over the country: "Jersey Joe Walcott is new heavyweight hope."[17]

Excited with Walcott's upset victory over Baksi, Felix and his team started thinking big. But first Felix and Webster decided to match Walcott against a couple of journeymen. Jersey Joe first faced Johnny Denson at the Camden Convention Hall on September 20, 1945, scoring a quick second-round knockout. Walcott then disposed of Steve Dudas a month later on October 23 by a fifth-round technical knockout. Team Walcott was now ready for bigger challenges as the postwar boxing climate unfolded, with heavyweight champion Joe Louis returning to civilian life after three years in the military service.

—7—

Stepping Up the Competition

Starting in November 1945 Bocchicchio and Webster decided it was time to step up the level of competition that Jersey Joe Walcott faced. The boxing landscape in 1945 was littered with a lot of good fighters. There were seasoned journeymen contenders as well as truly great boxers. If team Walcott was going to make some real money and get a shot at taking Joe Louis' title, Jersey Joe would have to face the best in the heavyweight division.

Bocchicchio's plan was straightforward. He matched Walcott against the toughest and most-avoided fighters around. First up was the number-five-rated contender, Lee Q. Murray. Lee was a real spoiler, and a big hitter. Nobody on the way up wanted to fight him. In fact famed fight trainer Ray Arcel called Lee the biggest hitter in the division next to Joe Louis. Lee was also a seasoned professional and had been in the ring with the likes of Henry Taylor, Willie Reddish, Curtis Sheppard (four times), and wartime interim champion Jimmy Bivins (three times). The fact that Lee was riding an eleven-fight winning streak in Baltimore rings was used to build up the fight.

The two fighters met on November 11, 1945, at the Baltimore Coliseum. However, the fight turned out to be a real stinker. Walcott hurt the normally rugged Murray early in the fight and crowded him so closely that Lee was unable to do anything to Walcott. Murray's vaunted punch was never a factor. The 6'3" 207 pound Murray was disqualified in the ninth round for not trying. Joe was awarded the decision since he was the aggressor all the way and had won every round. For his victory over Lee, Walcott received a check in the amount of $2,000. It was the first time in his career that he had earned a four-figure paycheck, and it had taken him fifteen years to do it. Walcott's heavyweight ranking went from number nine to three after his big win over Lee.

Curtis "Hatchet Man" Sheppard was the gatekeeper. To get to the top of the heavyweight mountain, Walcott had to get past him. Jersey Joe had done it before, as he had beaten Curtis in 1939. But this time Sheppard was a much more seasoned fighter than when he and Walcott had fought six years earlier at the Rockland Palace. Sheppard was now a top-rated contender, and like Murray was avoided by most fighters on the way up. Curtis had also added to his experience since his first meeting with Walcott by fighting a number of tough contenders like Jimmy Bivins, Gus Dorazio, Joey Maxim, and Murray. Sheppard was another dangerous puncher. Archie Moore, the "Old Mongoose," said the "Hatchet Man" was the hardest puncher he had ever came up against in over two hundred fights, and Sheppard hit harder than Rocky Marciano. Sheppard had once hit a fighter so hard he broke the man's collarbone; he was also the only fighter to ever knock out the iron-chinned Joey Maxim.

On December 10, 1945, Walcott met "Hatchet Man" Sheppard at the Century Athletic Club in Baltimore. Jersey Joe entered the ring weighing a fit 192½ pounds, and was in great shape. Curtis came in at 191½ pounds. For the first three rounds Jersey Joe completely baffled Sheppard. Walcott used stinging jabs, right crosses, and fancy footwork including the "Walcott shuffle" and the "Walkaway." Jersey Joe used these signature moves to effectively draw Curtis into more than one sucker punch.

In the fourth round the always dangerous Sheppard unleashed one of his powerful rights. The punch nailed Walcott on the jaw and dropped him for a few seconds. Most fighters would have been finished, but Jersey Joe was in top shape. He took the blow and recovered quickly. Motivated by the knockdown and perhaps thinking Walcott was hurt after such a punch, Sheppard went on the attack in the fifth and sixth and did enough to win both rounds. In the seventh Walcott reestablished his dominance and from then on it was all Jersey Joe. By the tenth and final round Walcott was in complete control. He landed several smashing punches on Sheppard's chin and the "Hatchet Man" hit the canvas, being counted out at the 2:15 mark. It was a very good win for Jersey Joe Walcott. He received $2,400 for his victory, as he steadily worked his way up the heavyweight ladder toward number one.

Walcott and journeyman Johnny Allen fought a rubber match on January 30, 1946, just one day before Walcott turned thirty-two years old. It was an easy win for Walcott. He rocked Allen early in the fight and ended matters in the third round, courtesy of a walloping right hand. Following the Allen fight, Bocchicchio and Webster felt it was time for Walcott to face the best fighter he had not yet faced on his comeback, Jimmy Bivins.

Jimmy was born December 6, 1919, in Dry Branch, Georgia. At some point during his childhood the Bivins family moved to Cleveland, Ohio, where Jimmy began boxing. As a teenager he was picked on in school. Deciding that he had better learn how to defend himself against bullies, Jimmy soon found his way into one of the local boxing gyms. After a time, the young boy discovered that he had a talent for fighting. As for the bullies, they soon discovered that Jimmy had a talent for fighting as well.

As an amateur, Jimmy went on to win several championships in the welterweight division. He eventually turned professional at the age of twenty and soon gained the nickname "Cleveland Spider Man," because of his unusually long arms. In his fifteenth pro fight, Bivins defeated a much more experienced Charley Burly, one of the great black "Murderer's Row" fighters of the 1940s. Jimmy won four more fights before losing a decision to future light-heavyweight champion Anton Christoforidis. He went from there and campaigned through the light-heavyweight division. Eventually Jimmy grew into a heavyweight and by the mid–1940s was one of the best in the division.

During World War II, when Joe Louis had been drafted and the heavyweight title put on ice, Bivins emerged as the dominant heavyweight. From January 1942, just a month after Pearl Harbor, to February 25, 1945, Jimmy lost only one fight, a decision loss to Bob Pastor. During World War II, Jimmy won the light-heavyweight "duration" title in 1943 when he defeated Ezzard Charles. The following March 12 Jimmy outpointed Tami Mauriello to win the heavyweight "duration" title. After World War II ended, Louis predicted that Bivins would be the next heavyweight champion. Unfortunately for Jimmy, his fight with Walcott would ruin his chance at a title fight with the Brown Bomber.

By the time he faced Jersey Joe Walcott, Bivins was on a twenty-seven fight win streak (one of the fights was a draw). He had defeated such boxers as Ezzard Charles, Archie Moore, Joey Maxim, Melino Bettina, Anton Christoforidis, Tami Mauriello, Lee Savold, Gus Lesnevich, Joey Maxim, Lee Q. Murray and Curtis Sheppard. Bivins had proven himself to be a truly great fighter.

In early February 1946 matchmaker and fight promoter for the Cleveland Arena, Larry Atkins, reported that a bout between Bivins and Walcott had been signed. The fight was scheduled for the 25th of February. News-

7 — Stepping Up the Competition

Jersey Joe receives some expert lessons from his trainer, Dan Florio (right). (AP Photograph)

paper reports of the upcoming tilt acknowledged that since his return to the boxing ring a year and a half earlier in an endeavor to feed his family, Walcott had scored fourteen knockouts in nineteen fights.[1] This achievement caused some newspaper reporters to compare Walcott's recent rise from poverty to that of Jimmy Braddock, the famous "Cinderella Man." They called Jersey Joe the new "Cinderella Man" of boxing. Other writers called him "The Brown Cinderella Man." Reports on the fight also said that the winner of this fight would be the next in line to get a shot at Joe Louis for the title, if Louis beat Conn in their upcoming rematch. A fight with Louis is exactly what Walcott wanted; ever since his 1936 sparring match with Louis, he felt that he could beat the Brown Bomber.

Team Walcott packed their bags and headed to Cleveland, Ohio. This was it. This was the make-or-break fight for Jersey Joe Walcott. A defeat here would place Walcott permanently in the journeyman category. A victory over the highly regarded Bivins would prove that Jersey Joe Walcott was for real.

At the old Cleveland Arena before a crowd of 12,166 fans, the largest of the season, Walcott and Bivins went at it. While Jimmy entered the ring a slight favorite at 3-to-1, this made no difference. Jersey Joe used his superior boxing ability, speed, and movement to dance around the slower Bivins. Walcott jolted Bivins early on with rights and lefts to the head and body. In the fifth, Bivins caught Walcott with his "Sunday punch," a right to the head, and shook up Walcott briefly. Jersey Joe took the shot with a grin and moved right back in. During a heated exchange, Jersey Joe put Bivins on the canvas in the seventh, for a count of eight, with a perfectly timed right to the jaw. It was the first time in seven years that Bivins had visited the canvas. When Jimmy got up, Walcott battered him around the ring for the remainder of the session. In the eighth, Walcott continued to outmaneuver Bivins by landing hard rights and lefts. Jimmy did manage to tag Jersey Joe with several solid rights during the round, but by this time Bivins was beginning to tire and had lost some of the steam on his punches. The ninth and tenth rounds followed the same pattern as the rest of the fight, with Walcott grinning, punching, shuffling, feinting and dancing as Jimmy came forward trying to land roundhouse punches.

The scoring for this fight was a little strange. The first scorecard read 6–4 for Bivins, the second 9–1 for Walcott, and the last had it 5–4–1 for Bivins, but the official with the last scorecard gave the fight to Walcott because of the knockdown. One newspaper described the bout as a "sizzling fight" and went on to say that the Cleveland title aspirant Bivins went into the ring as a favorite but left it badly beaten and disillusioned. It was an impressive and important victory for Jersey Joe Walcott.

Walcott later talked about the importance of the Bivins fight: "In February 1946 when Louis was already signed to fight for his second fight with Billy Conn, he predicted that the next heavyweight champion would be Jimmy Bivins, a long armed heavyweight who hadn't been defeated in twenty seven fights. Not many people knew about me, *nobody* mentioned me. But that same month I whaled the *sawdust out of* Bivins in Cleveland, his home town. I floored him with a right and left to the chin for the count of eight in the seventh round. He managed to stick it through, and I will say this for Louis's judgment. On the night I met Bivins he was the best fighter I ever faced."[2]

Bivins never received a shot at the title. Following his loss to Walcott, Jimmy also lost his next two bouts, to Ezzard Charles and Lee Q. Murray. He would go on to continue his boxing career for another nine years and have a somewhat average record. After retiring in 1955, Jimmy worked as a boxing trainer and a driver for a bakery in Cleveland.

7 — *Stepping Up the Competition*

After the Bivins fight, Team Walcott celebrated with a party back at their hotel. Joe, normally not a drinker, shared a bottle of champagne with his handlers. The fight catapulted Walcott to the number-one contender spot and earned him more money than he had ever made; his confidence was at an all-time high. Team Walcott began calling out Joe Louis for a shot at his title. One report had Walcott brashly saying, "Now I want to box Louis. I know I'll knock him out because I trained with him at Pompton Lakes when he was preparing for Schmeling. In two days I floored him three times with 16 ounce gloves. With light gloves I'd tear his head off. He's too easy to hit."[3]

Unfortunately for Walcott, he would have to wait twenty-two months, and have eight more fights, before he would get a shot at Louis' heavyweight title.

— 8 —

Win Some, Lose Some

Walcott was happy to enjoy some time off with his family after his victory over Bivins in Cleveland. But it didn't last long. He was back in training after only a few days off and in the ring with journeyman Al Blake at his old stomping grounds, the Camden Convention Hall, on March 20, 1946. During the past year Walcott's popularity had increased immensely. Four thousand spectators showed up at the Convention Hall, most of them fans of Jersey Joe. They had come to cheer on their local hero and rising star.

The Blake fight was an easy win for Walcott. He scored a technical knockout at the 2:17 of the fourth round. However, the win over Blake didn't do a lot for Joe except keep him busy and in fighting shape. A better opportunity came up the following month. Joe Baksi withdrew from a scheduled match with top-contender Tami Mauriello a week before the fight due to an injury. Bocchicchio rushed to New York to try to secure a match with Tami. He knew that a win over the well-known Mauriello would go a long way for Walcott. Felix met up with Mike Jacobs, the fight's promoter. Jacobs, also known as "Uncle Mike," was the founder of the 20th Century Sporting Club and the world's top boxing promoter. He was also the promoter for Madison Square Garden as well as Joe Louis. Jacobs refused Felix's offer for a match with Mauriello. He explained that he had already promised Mauriello a match with Louis in September if Tami beat Baksi. But since Baksi had pulled out, there was no way that Jacobs and Mauriello were going to jeopardize a big payday by fighting Walcott. Instead, Jacobs matched Mauriello against the less-risky John Thomas. The hard-punching Mauriello knocked out Thomas in the third round to earn his title shot against Louis.

Following the failed attempt to secure a fight with Mauriello, Walcott's management team spent the next two months looking for a match for their fighter. After Walcott's recent success in the ring, suddenly nobody wanted to fight him. After much effort, and weeks of negotiation, Team Walcott finally put together a match with ranked-contender Lee Oma. A date at Madison Square Garden had opened up due to the cancelled Sugar Ray Robinson-Marty Tippy championship fight. To get the fight, Bocchicchio and Webster had to put up a guarantee of $35,000 for Oma to agree to fight Walcott. This meant that Walcott and his handlers would hardly make any money on the match. It was a gamble. If Walcott lost, it would mean a huge setback with very little profit. If he won, it would guarantee Team Walcott a number of bigger fights and paydays. Mike Jacobs made the announcement that the fight was set for May 24. It was an exciting time for Jersey Joe. His fight with Oma would mark the first time he would be fighting at the famous Madison Square Garden. It was every fighter's dream to fight at the Garden; Jersey Joe had hit the big time!

Lee Oma was a bit of a clown. His approach to boxing and training could be compared to that of former heavyweight champion Max Baer. Lee would often enter the ring in less than top physical shape, as indicated by a flabby midsection, and at times goof off more than fight. During his fight with Bill Weinberg, both fighters were actually disqualified in the seventh round for clowning around. Oma was often viewed as a fighter that could have been very good if he had only taken his career more seriously. At his best, he could compete with the top men in the heavyweight division. At his clowning worst, he would lose to third-rate fighters.

The afternoon before the fight there were rumors going around that Lee was not in top shape and might not "do his best." After hearing these rumors, Chairman Eddie Eagan of the New York Boxing Commission went to Lee's dressing room and warned the fighter that no funny business would be tolerated. The rumors caused the odds on the fight to fluctuate wildly. By fight time, Walcott was a 13-to-5 favorite.

In the main event, Jersey Joe Walcott, "The Brown Cinderella Man," took on "Loose-Leaf" Lee Oma before a crowd of more than 11,000 roaring fans at Madison Square Garden. If people were unable to get to the Garden to see the fight live, they could listen to the exciting blow-by-blow broadcast on the radio. The fight was available on WOLS, 1230 on the radio dial, broadcast as part of the *Gillette Cavalcade of Sports*.

The Oma fight turned out to be a dull affair. Walcott easily outpointed the out-of-shape Oma, who was described as "flabby." In the first round (some sources say second) Walcott floored Oma with a hard right. From then on Lee was on the run. Jersey Joe pursued the side-stepping, backpedaling Oma for ten rounds. He gave his overmatched opponent's rib cage a fierce beating throughout the bout. In the final round Walcott opened up and gave Lee such a battering that the dark-haired Oma was groggy and bleeding from his mouth and nose as well as a gash on his cheekbone. Jersey Joe won with such ridiculous ease that two of the officials gave Oma but one round each, and that due to a foul. The third official was kinder, awarding Oma three rounds.

Although the crowd at the Garden was a nice turnout, it was short of the expected 18,000 because the railroads were tied up by a strike. As a result the fight did not make as much money as anticipated. Felix had to dip into reserve money to cover the payment to Oma, as Jersey Joe walked away with only $1,000 after a night's work.

On July 29, Mike Jacobs announced that a match was made between Jersey Joe Walcott and Tommy Gomez. Gomez, a World War II hero and Purple Heart recipient, was one tough customer. While in the service Gomez fought at the Battle of the Bulge. He was wounded during the battle just after the 310th infantry crossed the Rohr River on February 6, 1945. Tommy, along with a group of nine volunteers, was sent on a mission to take out a German roadblock. During the assignment the group ran into heavy German fire. While fighting in the battle, Tommy was hit by 16 pieces of shrapnel as well as a machinegun bullet through his chest. The bullet missed Tommy's heart by just two inches. During his recuperation, the doctors that patched up Tommy said that he would never fight again. Tommy proved them wrong by making a successful comeback after his discharge. Since his

World War II hero Tommy Gomez, according to Walcott, was one of the hardest punchers he ever fought.

return to the ring after his time in the military, Tommy had scored six wins by knockout, three of those in the first round. Having fought and lived through the Battle of the Bulge, Gomez said he was not afraid of any man wearing a pair of gloves.

On August 16, 1946, at Madison Square Garden, Walcott climbed into the ring with the power-punching Gomez. The winner of the bout had a good chance of getting a title shot at Joe Louis. Slightly shorter than Walcott, but very muscular, Tommy packed 190 pounds of solid muscle onto his 5'10" frame. The brawny Gomez was yet another feared puncher among Walcott's list of opponents. In 56 pro fights he had scored 43 knockouts.

The Gomez fight was short but exciting. Gomez, possessing no boxing skills to speak of, took the fight to Jersey Joe in round one. He came out with his fists swinging, looking for a knockout. But Walcott used his superior boxing skills to outbox and stay away from the swarming slugger. In the second, Gomez once again came straight in swinging. When he managed to land a massive blow to the base of Jersey Joe's neck, Walcott knew he was in a fight and needed to get Gomez out of there as quickly as possible. Jersey Joe had this to say about the punch: "The single hardest punch I ever stopped came from Tommy Gomez, the Tampa heavyweight. He landed a right half on my neck half on the base of my skull behind my ear in the second. I clinched; it stunned me and then hurt for a week afterwards. I decided to finish him as quickly as I could."[1]

As hard as Tommy could hit, and as tough as he was, he was no match for a boxer with the skills and ring generalship that Jersey Joe possessed. The cagey Walcott caught Tommy in the second and floored him. The count reached five as the round ended. Sensing that his opponent was ready to go, Jersey Joe burst from his corner in the third. He started the round quickly and floored Tommy with a hard right to the jaw, for a nine count, midway through the session. Gomez got up but was dropped again by a smashing right hand. Again Tommy bravely rose, only to take more punishment on the ropes as Walcott mercilessly pounded his foe's midsection with bruising shots. The 11,600 fans were on their feet screaming loudly as referee Frank Fullman stepped between the fighters and put an end to the bout at 1:21 of the third round. Walcott's take from the fight was $12,000. Jersey Joe was finally making big money and he was mentioned regularly in the newspapers.

It was around this time that Jersey Joe finally made enough money to be able to move his family out of poverty. After more than thirty years of hardship, he was able to purchase a ten-bedroom house in a very nice area of New Jersey as well as a couple of Cadillacs. One could imagine how exciting it must have been for the Cream family, especially the children. After living in a small house and having to share a room with several siblings, it must have been thrilling for each child to have his or her own room. Never again would the Creams be hungry, cold, or cramped.

After his victory over Gomez, Team Walcott found themselves perched precariously, and perhaps a bit apprehensively, on the brink of a title fight with Joe Louis. Louis, on the other hand, already had a date in September with Tami Mauriello, so Jersey Joe would have to continue to wait. In the meantime a fight between Elmer "Violent" Ray and Walcott was mentioned as a possibility, but that was about as far as the negotiations went. Ray's manager Tommy O'Loughlin claimed that he tried to get a match with Walcott, but that Walcott's managers turned him down. Perhaps Bocchicchio didn't want to risk a shot at Louis by matching Walcott with the thunderous punching "Violent" Ray.

Instead of a fight with Elmer Ray, Walcott was matched with the slick,

Joey Maxim (left) fought Jersey Joe three times between August 1946 and June 1947.

but less powerful punching, Joey Maxim. Maxim, a good-looking dark-haired Italian from Chicago by way of Cleveland, was a very good fighter. As an amateur he had won the national AAU championship at middleweight as well as two Golden Gloves titles. As a professional (at the time he faced Walcott) Joey had been in the ring with several top-notch boxers including Ezzard Charles, Curtis Sheppard, Jimmy Bivins and Lee Oma. After his fights with Walcott, Maxim would go on to win the light-heavyweight championship in 1950 and became the only fighter to ever stop the great Sugar Ray Robinson.

In a fight that saw the temperature in the ring reach more than 100 degrees, Ray Robinson, weighing all of 157 pounds, challenged Joey Maxim (weighing 173) for the light-heavyweight title. Ray, using his superior boxing ability, built up an early point lead but the heat and Joey's heavy punches were starting to take their toll. In the tenth, due to the effects of the severe heat, referee Ruby Goldstein had to be replaced by back-up referee Ray Miller. In the second half of the fight, Joey started to come on. By the thirteenth round Ray was exhausted and suffering from the effects of heat prostration. On his way back to his corner Ray collapsed. He was unable to answer the bell for the fourteenth, even though all he had to do was remain on his feet to win a decision. Maxim was awarded the fight on a technical knockout. It was the only time Sugar Ray Robinson was stopped in a career that saw over 200 fights. At the fight's end the judging scorecards all had Ray comfortably ahead, 10–3, 9-3-1, and 7-3-3.

The Walcott-Maxim fight was scheduled for August 28, the same night that Elmer "Violent" Ray was doing battle with Lee Savold at Ebbet's Field in New York. Before a crowd of 7,700 people, the largest ever at the Camden ballpark, Jersey Joe lost a close disputed ten-round decision to Maxim. The major reason for his loss was the fact that in the second round Jersey Joe broke a bone in his right hand and dislocated a knuckle in his left hand. He was unable to fight effectively from then on. In spite of the pain of two broken hands, Walcott toughed it out for the full ten rounds. When the fight was over, referee Paul Cavalier, the only official, had it 5-3-2 for Maxim. The Camden crowd loudly booed the decision. The Associated Press had the fight 6-3-1 for Walcott. Maxim's manager, the famous Jack "Doc" Kearns, the same manager that had guided Jack Dempsey to the heavyweight title, agreed to a rematch "anytime" to prove that the fight was no fluke. Following the fight, Jersey Joe admitted that Maxim was one of the cleverest boxers he had ever faced.

The loss to Maxim did little to tarnish Walcott's reputation, though.

He was still viewed as one of the top challengers for the Brown Bomber's title and deserving of a title shot. After all, it wasn't his fault that his hands didn't hold up and that he was the recipient of what most considered to be a bad judging decision.

On September 18, 1946, Walcott saw a fight with Louis almost ruined by a massive right hand from Tami Mauriello. In the first few moments of the first round Tami landed a bomb of a right hand on Louis's chin that turned the Bomber's legs to rubber and drove him across the ring into the ropes. Louis was hurt badly and only a punch or two away from being knocked out. But being too slow to capitalize on the stunned Louis, Tami let the moment pass. A moment was all Joe needed. Once his head cleared, the angry Brown Bomber destroyed Mauriello, knocking him out in two minutes and nine seconds of round one. Jersey Joe must have breathed a sigh of relief. As for Tami, perhaps somebody should have told him to be careful what you wish for.

Even though Walcott had repeatedly won fights and had been mentioned as a possible opponent for Louis, Mike Jacobs started another campaign to find the next opponent for Joe Louis. He proposed an elimination match between Walcott and Elmer "Violent" Ray. By September 28 negotiations were underway for a match at Madison Square Garden. The winner would be virtually guaranteed a shot at Joe Louis. Jacobs paid Walcott a visit a few weeks before the fight at Felix's Camden office. The promoter told Walcott, "Joe, if you get over Ray you'll fight Louis."[2]

By early October the fight was signed. The two fighters would meet November 15. Walcott was confident he could whip Elmer since he had beaten him in 1937. But there was one big difference this time. Elmer was a lot more experienced than when he and Walcott last met. The last time the two faced off, Elmer had a record of 2-5-2 and was inexperienced. Ray was now a seasoned professional with a record of 75-11-4 with 62 knockouts. He was a huge puncher, considered by most observers to be right up there with Joe Louis and Curtis "Hatchet Man" Sheppard. Going into the fight, Elmer was riding a 48-fight win streak; 42 of his opponents had been flattened. Twenty-nine of them were knocked out in three rounds or fewer. It was an extremely dangerous fight for Jersey Joe.

Walcott came into the fight a 2-to-1 favorite. He weighed a solid 191½ pounds, with Ray at 191¼. Walcott's trainer Florio, now joined by an assistant trainer and longtime friend of Walcott, Joey Allen, wanted Jersey Joe to box and use movement to stay away from the power-punching Ray. They trained at Greenwood Lake, New Jersey. Together the team formulated a plan that called for plenty of movement, feints and footwork from the cagey Walcott.

The Ray fight turned out to be a total bust for Walcott. Elmer refused to be out-maneuvered by Jersey Joe. The big slugger stayed as close as he could to Walcott and flailed away. This strategy threw Walcott off his game plan and forced him to fight Elmer's fight. According to Jersey Joe, here is what happened during the fight: "I bowled Ray across the ring with a left in the opening round and should have finished him then, but my legs strangely wouldn't respond. To this day I don't know why. My right hand was broken in the fifth and I stuck to left hooks the rest of the fight. The decision was split and I lost by a point. I cried in the dressing room. I felt that I had let Felix down even though our piece of the gate was $18,000. When he came in I said, Felix, I'm through. I can't fight anymore."[3] The loss set back Walcott at least a few months.

A few days later, after having an opportunity to think things over, Walcott reconsidered his words to Felix. He realized that his loss to Ray wasn't as damaging as he originally thought. He had almost held even one of the most-feared, hardest-punching heavyweights in the world with only the use of his left hand for half the fight. Walcott had taken Ray's famous "killer" punches without being hurt. Maybe he hadn't done as badly as he thought.

After climbing so far up the heavyweight rankings, Jersey Joe slipped a little as a result of the two losses. But it wasn't in his character to give up. Putting the losses behind him, he pressed on toward his goal of obtaining a shot at Joe Louis and the heavyweight championship of the world. Team Walcott decided to move forward as quickly as they could. Their plan was to erase Walcott's two losses by getting him back into the ring with Maxim and Ray. Victories over the two boxers would go a long way toward restoring Walcott as the number-one heavyweight contender.

In December, Felix and Webster met with "Doc" Kearns and Mike Jacobs. Together the managers and promoter negotiated a rematch with Maxim. The fight would take place at the Convention Hall in Philadelphia on January 6, 1947.

Over 9,000 fans showed up to see if the first fight between Walcott and Maxim was really a fluke. Most fans thought that Walcott would knock out Maxim this time. As it turned out, the closest that Walcott came to flooring anyone was referee Charley Dagger, whom he accidentally hit over the eye in the second round.

With the great Mickey Walker, ex-middleweight champion, yelling out instructions from Maxim's corner, Joey began the fight with piston-like left jabs. Several of these found their mark on Walcott's face, jolting his head back with their impact. But Jersey Joe took these punches with a smile and unleashed his own attack that concentrated on Maxim's soft-looking midsection. In the fourth round both fighters were guilty of low blows. In the fifth Walcott caught Joey with a solid right and staggered him badly. Maxim spent the sixth round recovering from the wallop he took in the previous session and didn't do much. In the seventh round Walcott stopped smiling and a more serious look came over his face as he tried to knock out Maxim. The last three rounds saw both fighters slugging it out toe-to-toe as the fans came to their feet and roared their approval. Maxim came out on the losing end of the slugfest with Walcott but he did manage to shake Jersey Joe with a hard blow just below the heart as Walcott was coming in. When the brawl was over Walcott earned a hard fought ten-round decision. Two of the judges voted in favor of Walcott, while the referee had it even. Maxim's manager Kearns felt that Maxim had won and called for a third fight. But Team Walcott wasn't interested in an immediate rematch with Maxim just yet, as they had a score to settle with Elmer Ray first.

In early February 1947 the rematch with Ray was signed. The fight was scheduled to take place at the Orange Bowl in Miami. Walcott arrived a few weeks early to acclimate himself and continue his training. Seats at the Orange Bowl were divided 50/50 between whites and blacks. They were sold for $3 to $12 apiece, with ringside seats being a little more expensive. It was the first boxing match ever held at the Orange Bowl featuring two black fighters. Ray was a slight 6-to-5 favorite.

Iron-chinned Joey Maxim lost his third fight with Jersey Joe in Hollywood, California, in June 1947, setting the stage for Walcott's first shot at a heavyweight title fight with Joe Louis.

On the night of March 4, Walcott ended Ray's streak of fifty-one wins before a crowd of more than 10,000 fight fans. Walcott's experience and boxing ability were the keys to the victory. Jersey Joe changed his stance often and used his famous "Walkaway" move to throw Elmer off his game and disrupt his timing. Walcott used his slick moves to draw Elmer into lefts and rights. These punches, along with crowding Ray at times, put Ray down in the first, third and fourth rounds for no-count knockdowns. In the sixth round Ray took the offensive play away from Walcott but the hard-punching Ray was never able to figure out Walcott's tricky style. Although he did manage to rock Walcott with some powerful shots at various times during the fight, Ray was unable to follow up. At the end, Jersey Joe was awarded a close split decision. Two of the officials had it for Walcott; a third scored the fight even.

After successfully avenging Joe's losses to Maxim and Ray, Team Walcott was now ready for their shot at Louis. It was announced on March 21 by Abe Green, president of the National Boxing Association, that Walcott's manager Joe Webster had issued a formal challenge to Louis. Green said he would accept Walcott as a proper challenger because he was among the top contenders for the title. The challenge was filed citing a rule that the champion has to defend his title at least every six months, and Louis was past his due date. Webster also announced that he would put up a guaranteed $250,000 for a fight with Louis. Even though Louis was past his stipulated defense date, Walcott was forced to wait by the boxing powers that be. Louis and Jacobs were looking for a fight that would draw a bigger crowd than a fight with Walcott was expected to draw. The problem for Louis was there simply wasn't anyone else left to fight, and would soon discover that there was no way to avoid a fight with Walcott.

For the time being, Team Jersey Joe wanted to stay busy and cash in. There was some talk about a rematch with Joe Baksi, but Jersey Joe instead opted for a rubber match with Maxim. Before the third fight with Maxim, though, Walcott and his family took a well-deserved vacation to Havana, Cuba. After a few weeks of relaxation, the Creams returned to New Jersey. Jersey Joe departed shortly thereafter for the land of sun and movie stars, Hollywood, California.

The Walcott-Maxim rubber match was promoted by none other than Ol' Blue Eyes himself, legendary Hollywood actor and singer Frank Sinatra. The fight was at Gilmore Field, the home of minor league baseball team Hollywood Stars, on June 23, 1947. Movie stars such as George Raft (accompanied by his bodyguard "Killer" Gray), Lana Turner, Marilyn

Maxwell and Tyrone Power were on hand to witness the event. As an added bonus, heavyweight champion Joe Louis fought a four-round exhibition match with Francisco De La Cruz. Despite the appearance of Louis and several Hollywood movie stars, the turnout for the fight was only 9,600, far short of expectations. Most of the blame for the lack of ticket sales and interest in the fight was placed on the fact that many newspaper writers either ignored, or belittled, the fight during the buildup.

Sinatra's debut as a boxing promoter turned out to be a disappointment. The fight, billed as "fight of the year," was anything but. It actually turned out to be unexciting and at times left the crowd booing loudly. In the eighth round Walcott launched a right to Maxim's kidney that landed well below the belt. The punch put Maxim down. The crowd booed the low blow and showered the ring with fight programs. Maxim got up, protesting the blow to referee Reggie Gilmore. For the remainder of the fight, Maxim limped and held his side, occasionally grimacing in pain. When it was over, Joe walked away with a split decision. The day after the fight Maxim's manager, "Doc" Kearns, said he would file a complaint about the low blow that Walcott landed and seek to have the decision reversed. But it was to no avail.

Walcott had done it. He had avenged his two defeats and regained his status as the top contender to challenge Joe Louis for the heavyweight title. The following month, after his fight with Maxim, Walcott was offered a fight with Swedish heavyweight Olle Tandberg. Felix declined the offer. Instead, Team Walcott decided to sit tight, not risk a loss, and hope that a fight could be arranged with Louis. They didn't have to wait long. Negotiations for a fight with Louis began in July; by July 31 a fight was announced. Walcott was finally going to get his title shot! Of course, very few knew who Jersey Joe Walcott was, or gave him much of a chance to dethrone the champion. While he was not a "household name," that would all soon change. On December 6, 1947, the day after his battle with Louis, most of the civilized world would know who Jersey Joe Walcott was.

—9—

Louis-Walcott I

Joseph Louis Barrow was born four months after Jersey Joe Walcott on May 13, 1914, in Lafayette, Alabama. Like Walcott, Louis was born into poverty and faced many of the same struggles while growing up. Unlike Walcott, when Louis started boxing he had the support and financial backing of Julian Black and John Roxborough, two wealthy black businessmen, to help guide and manage him. And of course Louis had Jack Blackburn to teach him how to fight. Although initially Blackburn was reluctant to take on a colored fighter because the color line was still in effect in the 1930s, making it difficult for a black fighter to make it, he accepted the job.

While Walcott struggled in obscurity for years, Louis was nurtured. After a successful amateur career that saw Joe win several Golden Gloves championships, he turned professional in 1934. Under Blackburn's teachings, Louis ran his record up to 24-0 with 20 knockouts before losing his first fight to German heavyweight Max Schmeling. Louis quickly rebounded and won his next seven in a row. He then faced the "Cinderella Man," Jimmy Braddock, for the heavyweight title. Eight rounds later, Louis was the new heavyweight king. From 1937 to 1942 (until his enlistment into the U.S. Army), Louis defended his title twenty times including avenging his loss to Schmeling. During this time, Louis had become a true American hero and was the most popular boxing champion since Jack Dempsey. While in the military, Louis defended his title once against Abe Simon and fought nearly 100 exhibition fights. Louis entertained millions of troops and was given the Legion of Merit award for his "incalculable contribution to the general moral."

After his discharge from the Army on October 1, 1945, Joe Louis was anxious to get back into the boxing ring. He was in debt to his promoter, "Uncle" Mike Jacobs, for $100,000 and owed the IRS another $81,000 in back taxes. Louis needed to fight. His postwar return bout was a rematch against Billy Conn in 1946. Louis and Conn had met previously in 1941 in a thrilling battle. The fight went thirteen rounds with the 174-pound former light-heavyweight champion using his lightning speed to outbox the heavyweight champion for the first twelve rounds. Going into the thirteenth, Conn led on two of the scorecards and was even on the third. Instead of playing it safe and boxing for the last two rounds, Conn got cocky when he wobbled Louis with a big left hook. He decided to try to knock out the champion, which was a big mistake. Standing toe-to-toe with Louis, the lighter Conn was no match. The Brown Bomber began to land devastating lefts, rights, and uppercuts. Tough as nails, Conn took some massive blows but was eventually knocked out.

Due to the excitement of the first fight, the second fight drew a huge crowd of 45,266 and brought in nearly $2,000,000 but failed to live up to the excitement of the first fight. Louis scored an easy eighth-round knockout over the now slower and heavier Conn and made half a million dollars from the fight. Next up was Tami Mauriello, whom Louis took care of in one round and made several hundred thousand dollars. After dividing the money and paying his debts, there wasn't much left. Louis needed another fight. He asked Mike Jacobs to get him another opponent. There was only one problem: Louis had cleared out the heavyweight division. By 1946 he had beaten everyone, at least everyone that would draw a good gate and a decent payday. There was some talk of a tilt with Joe Baksi but the talks fizzled out after Baksi was beaten by Swedish fighter Olle Tandberg, who in turn turned down an offer as well to face Louis.

Eventually Sol Strauss came up with a plan for an exhibition fight. Sol at this time was running the day-to-day operations of the 20th Century Sporting Club. In December 1946, Mike Jacobs suffered a stroke. His lawyer and cousin Sol took over operations while Jacobs was recuperating. Sol's plan was to match the comparatively unknown number-one contender, Jersey Joe Walcott, against Louis. Walcott was so lightly regarded that originally the fight was scheduled as a ten-round, non-title exhibition at Madison Square Garden on November 14. However there was a rule stipulating that since the fight was ten rounds the belt would be at stake if Walcott knocked Louis out. If the fight went the distance Louis would retain his title, even if Walcott won every round. This arrangement didn't go over well. Eddie Eagan, chairman of the New York State Athletic Commission, said, "Walcott would be regarded as champion if he banged out a knockout against Louis."[1] Abe Green, president of the National Boxing

Association, said, "If Walcott won by a knockout no commission would deny Walcott's title claim."[2]

Ultimately this exhibition fight arrangement stirred up so much controversy that it had to be changed. There was the fear of possible "post-bout disputes and repercussions" if Walcott won by a knockout.[3] Sol and Chairman Eagan eventually decided to promote the bout as a full-blown, fifteen-round title fight. Both fighters agreed to the change. Louis' only request was that the fight be rescheduled for a later date so that he could have more time to train. The new date was set for December 5, 1947, at Madison Square Garden.

From the beginning and all through the buildup of the fight, the press criticized Walcott. In no time at all, his age became a huge subject of debate. Just about every sportswriter claimed that Jersey Joe was at least 38 years old. Others said he was 40, or older. "Anything under 50 could be correct," said Jack "Doc" Kearns. Sportswriters dubbed him "Pappy," a nickname given him because they thought he was old. Words like "elderly," "ancient," and "aging" were commonly used to describe Walcott. Jersey Joe himself maintained that he was 33 years old. But since he was born at home and not in a hospital, he could not prove his age with a birth certificate that was filed when he was born. "We could not prove we were born," Walcott would say in an interview years later.[4] "Only the IRS believed us."[5] A copy of a birth certificate that was filed in 1936 was acquired from the Camden Bureau of Vital Statistics by Francis Albertani, the press liaison officer in Walcott's training camp. This certificate showed Jersey Joe's birth date to be January 31, 1914. However most people continued to believe he was older than he claimed to be, since the birth certificate was not officially filed at the time of his birth.

Not being very well known, most people did not realize that Walcott had started boxing at about the tender age of 15 and had his first professional fight at 16. A lot of sportswriters and fans may have assumed that Jersey Joe was older than 16 when he began boxing. Therefore they assumed he was older when he fought Louis. Some residents of Camden who claimed to know Walcott were interviewed before the fight. They also claimed that Walcott was older than he said he was. Jersey Joe's answer to this was that people may have been confusing him for his older brother Joseph, who was five years older than him. During Walcott's early years, Joseph was known to hang out at the boxing gym and do some fighting as well. Of course, having adopted the ring-name "Jersey Joe Walcott" did not help matters, as some people may have assumed that Joe Cream, Walcott's older brother, and "Jersey" Joe Walcott were one and the same. It is easy to see how some people might have mixed up the two. To further add to the confusion, there is at least one source that says Walcott may have fought under the name Joseph Arnold Cream (his older brother's full name) in an early fight. But this was most likely Joseph doing the fighting. However you slice it, the simple fact is Walcott was only 33 years old at the time of his fight with Louis. This meant he was only four months older than Joe Louis.

It wasn't just Walcott's age that sportswriters criticized, it was his fighting ability as well. They said he wasn't a real contender. It was reported that although Walcott was the top contender he was a second-rate fighter and was not deserving of a shot at Louis' title. As one columnist wrote, "Walcott has no right whatsoever to be in the same ring with Louis. He is probably 40 years old, has six children, and can't fight a lick."[6] It didn't end there. Former heavyweight champion Jack Dempsey got in on the act by saying that "Walcott is not a real contender" and that "there are no real contenders left. The field is wide open."

Just about every boxing fan and newspaper columnist greatly underestimated Walcott's boxing ability. They gave him no chance at all to beat Louis. The question wasn't whether Louis would win. The question was in what round would Louis knock out Walcott? The general consensus was that Louis would beat Jersey Joe in five rounds or earlier. One reason the press and fans thought Walcott would lose so easily was because he had lost to some average, and even below average, fighters. In fact, he had lost to two of Louis' knockout victims, Al Ettore and Abe Simon. Of course most, if not all, of the members of the press covering the fight had no idea why Jersey Joe had lost to second-rate fighters. They didn't realize the terrible hardship he had endured during his early career and how he fought at times on short notice with little or no training, or even enough food. They just assumed he was not very good.

Walcott was also criticized because of his record, which was 44-11-2 at the time. What the public didn't realize was that his record was very misleading. First of all, under different circumstances it would have been much better. Secondly, Walcott had a lot more fights than were recorded on his record and may have had several more wins. Some newspaper articles claimed that Jersey Joe said he had about 130 fights. A conservative estimation is about twelve to fifteen more than were on his record. Nobody will ever know for sure how many of his early fights went unreported, or how many times Walcott climbed into the ring in some tank town in order to feed his hungry family.

One thing was for sure, by the time Jersey Joe climbed into the ring to fight Louis he was a master boxer who knew how to handle himself. The cagy veteran had been swapping punches for seventeen years. During his career he had learned every trick in the book and even invented a few along the way. He had been exposed to every type of fighting style and knew how to deal with every situation. The newspapers did get one thing right: Jersey Joe was "a ring veteran."

It was during the fight's build-up that the 1936 sparring session between Walcott and Louis came back to haunt both fighters. The story of Walcott knocking Louis down during the sparring match caused quite a stir and helped to hype the fight a little. At the time, Louis' response to the story was that he did not even remember who Jersey Joe Walcott was. However, in his autobiography *My Life*, Louis wrote that he did remember Walcott and that he knew Jersey Joe was "a damn good fighter."[7]

The fighters retired to their respective training camps to prepare for the title battle. Louis set up camp at Pompton Lakes, New Jersey. The reports from the Louis camp confirmed that Louis was in great shape. Some said he was in better shape than when he had fought Billy Conn in 1946. Louis himself said he was taking Walcott seriously and therefore training hard. He stated in one interview that he considered Jersey Joe a serious threat and a hard puncher. When Louis broke camp, he had boxed over 85 rounds and had run over 300 miles. One account said that Louis looked "wonderful" and at 33 he was as good as ever. These reports were a little misleading. No doubt Louis was in good shape, but at 33 he was starting to slow down and had lost some of his incred-

Walcott, at the Grenloch Park training camp, takes some time off from training for the 1947 Louis fight.

ible hand speed. The four years he was away from boxing by serving in the military had done him no good. The simple truth was, Louis was not quite the fighter he was before the war, and he had lost a step. But he was still a force to be reckoned with, as the best heavyweight in the world.

For his training Walcott went into seclusion at Grenloch Amusement Park in New Jersey, which was at the time closed down. Walcott rented the park and had a boxing ring and workout area set up in a large white building next to a lake. During his training Joe's advisors kept him away from the press and allowed no interviews, although his workouts were open to the public. This was done on the grounds that they wanted Jersey Joe to fight Louis with the plan that Team Walcott had devised. They did not want him receiving any well-intentioned, but confusing advice that sometimes comes with interviews. Walcott and his trainers, Florio and Joey Allen, worked hard on formulating a plan to fight Louis. Florio figured Louis would try to pressure Walcott, always coming forward. The last thing Dan wanted was for Walcott to get into a slugging match with the Brown Bomber. The fight plan was to have Jersey Joe use every trick in his impressive repertoire. It called for a lot of movements, including shoulder and hand feints, counter-punching, and his signature "Walkaway" move. The line of attack was to confuse Louis with quick shifts and cute tactics.

Jersey Joe would need to be in tremendous shape to fight fifteen rounds with all this movement. To accomplish this he was up every morning at the crack of dawn, running between five and eight miles. While jogging Walcott wore heavy-sole laborer boots and often slogged through mud. Once back at the gym he would do two rounds of shadow boxing, two rounds on the speed bag, ten minutes skipping rope, and two rounds on the heavy bag. He then followed up by doing hundreds of sit-ups and pushups. For sparring, Bocchicchio hired some good sparring partners, including the veteran Leroy Haynes, tough Austin Johnson and Philadelphia fighter Eddie Wilson. Together Walcott and his trio of sparring partners worked between five to ten rounds a day. After the daily training, Walcott's personal chef fixed everybody dinner, usually steak. At times Walcott would don the chef's hat and cook Saturday evening dinner for his siblings, trainers, and sparring partners. After dinner, Joe would frequently visit with his sisters and brothers who often came to the camp. Together they would play cards and listen to the radio.

Walcott and his team trained hard for eight weeks. The reports coming out of his camp were that Jersey Joe was hitting hard and beating up his sparring mates. Head trainer Dan Florio said a few days before the fight:

9 — Louis-Walcott I

Jersey Joe plays with Austin Johnson, Jr., the son of his sparring partner, during the training for his first fight with Joe Louis, in 1947.

"He's in wonderful shape. He's better now than when he whipped Bivins in Cleveland a couple of years ago, and nobody gave him a chance then either."[8] By fight night, Jersey Joe was a finely tuned fighter, hell bent on winning the heavyweight championship.

On the evening of December 5, 1947, Jersey Joe Walcott stood ready in his corner to face Joe Louis, the man considered by nearly everyone to be the greatest heavyweight champion of all time. The odds against Walcott lifting the crown from the champion were an incredible 20-to-1. Back home in New Jersey at the Cream residence, Walcott's family excitedly awaited the start of the fight as they gathered around the television along with about thirty friends and family members. It must have been thrilling for his kids to see their father on television, only moments away from fighting for the heavyweight title.

At Madison Square Garden the two fighters and their handlers stood in their respective corners. Walcott and his team were going over last-minute instructions as announcer Harry Balogh read the introduction at ring center. His voice came out of the speakers loud and clear, drowning out the noise of the crowd. "This is the final and stellar presentation. Fifteen rounds for the heavyweight championship of the world. Presenting the capable challenger from Camden, New Jersey, his weight 194½ pounds, he's wearing black trunks with black stripes, Jersey Joe Walcott!" A loud roar went up from the crowd. "From Detroit Michigan, the internationally famous, Detroit's Brown Bomber and the heavyweight champion of the world, weighing 211 pounds and wearing purple trunks, Joe Louis!"[9] An even louder roar went up from the crowd. The fighters approached ring center and received their instructions from referee Ruby Goldstein. A few seconds later, the bell sounded to signal the beginning of round one.

From the start of round one Walcott began pumping the jab, snapping Louis' head back and circling to Joe's right. Louis, on the other hand, having said that he intended to try to get the fight over quickly, jabbed twice and threw a right hand with everything he had. The punch just missed Jersey Joe's jaw. It was obvious that the punch was thrown with bad intentions. The two fighters then exchanged a series of hard blows as Louis came forward and Walcott danced, feinted, and circled. Two jabs and a hard right from the champion drove Walcott into a corner, a spot he didn't want to be. Louis swarmed Jersey Joe, following up with a barrage of fast lefts and rights. Trapped in a corner, Jersey Joe had no choice but to battle his way out. He fought back ferociously by throwing a right, left, right combination; the last punch had the full weight of his powerful shoulders behind it and caught Louis flush on the side of his face, dropping him backwards onto the seat of his trunks. The crowd rose with a roar at the unexpected knockdown. Cameras began flashing by the dozens. Louis, more surprised than hurt, was up at the count of two. Once on his feet, he headed straight for Jersey Joe and threw a right-hand bomb that grazed Walcott's jaw. Jersey Joe instantly retaliated with a hard right of his own and then continued to dance and move around Louis. Both fighters were throwing hard dangerous punches with a lot of force; in fact Louis almost

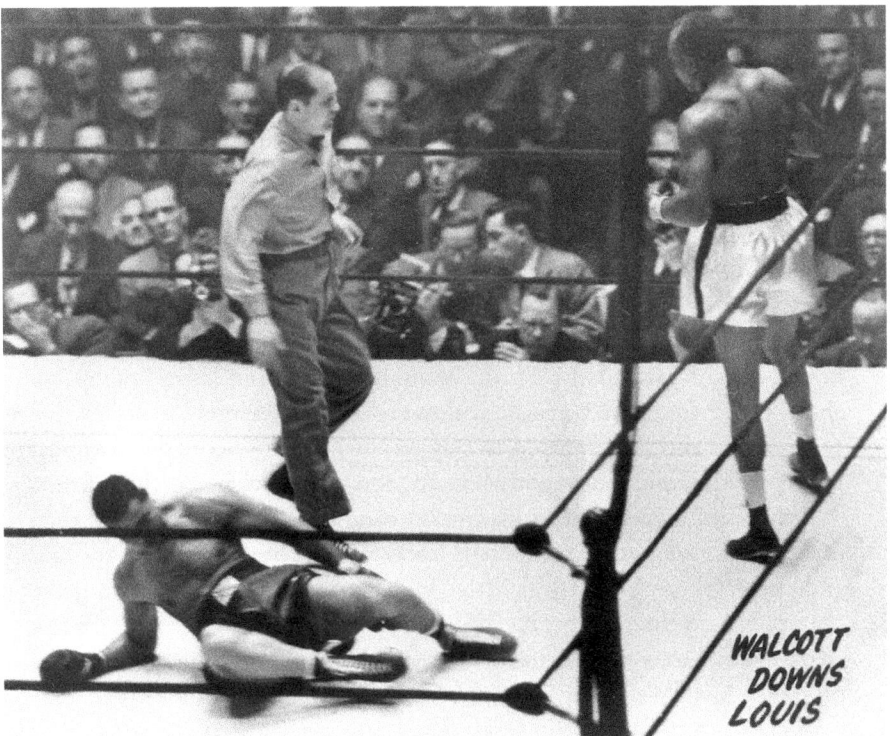

In his first heavyweight title fight, at Madison Square Garden in December 1947, Walcott floors the great Joe Louis.

slipped and fell after missing a powerful right-hand blow. Walcott took advantage of the slip and attacked with a right hand and had Louis momentarily up against the ropes. Joe quickly removed himself and the two continued to slug it out until the bell sounded.

Round two started with Louis stalking Walcott. He tried to catch Jersey Joe with a right but Walcott dodged the blow and moved out of range. Joe bore in and forced Walcott up against the ropes but Walcott tied Louis up, pushed him off and again moved out of range. Jersey Joe then flicked out a quick jab and two hard right hands; the last right caught Louis on the chin and momentarily buckled the champion's knees. Louis continued to come forward but appeared a little less anxious to charge in and mix it up. His face was already turning red where Walcott had landed the two rights. Jersey Joe was outboxing the champion with his tricky moves and beating him to the punch. By the end of the second round, Louis had a frustrated look on his face.

Walcott continued to outbox Louis at long range in round three by backpedaling and side-stepping. Louis did manage to catch Jersey Joe with a few long sneaky jabs. But Walcott fired back with a left hook to Louis's chin that shook the champion. Jersey Joe then danced around for much of the round in a manner that seemed to annoy and frustrate Louis but delighted the crowd. The two fighters exchanged several stiff jabs throughout the round while looking for openings. Near the end of the round Jersey Joe got in a heavy right that hurt Louis. He threw another hard right that just missed its mark as the bell rang to signal the end of the third round.

Louis waved to a friend as he got off his stool to start round four. He came out with two hard jabs, the second one catching Jersey Joe on the chin. He then jabbed again, following the challenger as Jersey Joe backpedaled and side-stepped to stay out of range. Walcott shot two fast jabs at the champion, dropped his hands and walked away. He then turned back and fired a quick jab. Louis continued to come forward. Walcott then turned and took another two steps back. Again Louis continued to stalk and come forward. But Walcott's "Walkaway" move was upsetting the champion's rhythm. Each time Walcott dropped his hands and took a few steps back, Louis would have to reset before continuing his forward progress. The "Walkaway" was also allowing Walcott to time the champion's advances. Once again Jersey Joe dropped his hands and took a few steps backwards. This time, though, when Louis reset and came forward Jersey Joe was waiting. He threw a perfectly timed right hand as the champion came in. The punch smashed into Louis' face. All of Walcott's power and weight was behind it. The blow knocked Louis backwards and drove him to the canvas, putting the champion down hard. The Brown Bomber was hurt; he had run right into the punch. The crowed was on its feet as Louis wisely took a count of eight. As soon as the champion was up, Walcott charged right in and threw a hard right hand that Louis barely avoided. The champion tried to keep Walcott off by jabbing and holding, but Jersey Joe threw another right that caught Louis on the right side of his head. Louis tied up the charging challenger again. Walcott pushed him off and fired a fast left-right combination that landed on the champion's face. Louis wobbled and again held onto Walcott. But Jersey Joe was aiming for a knockout. He pushed Louis off and threw another hard right hand that Louis somehow ducked. Walcott kept the pressure on the champion for the remainder of the fourth round by throwing hard lefts and rights. The bell sounded. It was a good round for Jersey Joe.

To everyone's surprise Louis began backing up a bit in round five.

The crowd shouted in awe at this phenomenon. Maybe Louis was growing tired of chasing the elusive Walcott and this was his way of trying to draw in the challenger. Maybe he needed some extra time to recover from the knockdown in the previous round. Whatever Louis was attempting to do, Jersey Joe was having none of it. Walcott kept dancing and moving, refusing to be drawn in. The champion soon went back to chasing the challenger. At this point, Jersey Joe tried to draw Louis into another devastating right hand by using his "Walkaway." But the champion wasn't taking the bait. Instead he landed two jabs to Walcott's face. Jersey Joe retaliated with a left hook to Louis' chin and then for a portion of the round switched his stance and fought left-handed. The two fighters exchanged stinging jabs. Louis then landed a hard left hook to the head. Walcott came back with a fast right to the champion's body. Louis subsequently landed his own hard right hook to Walcott's rib cage and sent over a left to the other side of Jersey Joe's body. Walcott backed up and connected with two fast jabs. Louis jabbed back as the bell sounded.

Round six started the same way that the fifth session had. The champion again started backing up, trying to draw Walcott in. Jersey Joe spat contemptuously. He then fired a jab aimed at the champion's swelling left eye; Louis fired one in return. Walcott shot over a hard right that Louis blocked with his open glove. Walcott then connected with a left to the body. The champion landed two solid jabs, snapping Walcott's head back. Louis stopped backing up and began to stalk Walcott again. Joe threw and missed a hard left and right to Jersey Joe's head. Louis quickly followed up the missed punches with jabs to the head and stomach and a hard left hook to Walcott's body. Walcott shot over a right uppercut that caught the champion on his shoulder and a left hook that hit Louis in the face. Walcott then landed a left and right hook to the champion's body. Louis fired right back with a powerful jab that caught the challenger flush on the chin. Walcott missed a couple of hard rights. The two fighters exchanged lefts and rights in mid-ring. Walcott landed a hard right and took one to the chin in return from the champion. The two fighters roughed each other up in what was an even sixth round.

Walcott started round seven by dancing and moving from side to side. Louis was finding it difficult to get a stationary target. The champion did manage to reach Walcott a few times with long sneaky lefts that jolted the challenger's head back. After eating a few jabs, Walcott drove home a left to Louis' face. The champion shot out a jab and missed with two more. Walcott nailed Louis with two rights to the jaw and Louis came back with a left jab to the chin as Walcott landed a right hand and took a left and right in return. Louis then drove a hard right to Walcott's face before the two then traded left hooks. Walcott then landed two lefts and a hard right to the champion's jaw. The two fighters then exchanged a barrage of savage blows with Walcott getting the better of the exchange as the seventh round ended.

Walcott started round eight by straightening up Louis with a hard right and then landed two more that reddened the champion's face. Walcott jabbed well, concentrating on Louis' nearly swollen-shut left eye. The champion pecked away with jabs trying to find an opening. He continued to stalk the elusive challenger, finally forcing him up against the ropes where he unleashed several solid shots to Jersey Joe's body and a hard right to his chin. Walcott fired back with a right of his own to Louis' body. The champion sent over a stiff, hard jab to Walcott's face but Jersey Joe took the punch and fired back. Confident, Walcott stopped his backpedaling and stood his ground. Jersey Joe seemed full of pep. He exchanged several hard blows with Louis at the end of the eighth round.

After slipping from a Louis jab, Walcott stung Joe with a right cross to begin the ninth. Moments later blood was flowing down the left side of Jersey Joe's face from a powerful Louis left hook. Walcott was cut. The blood prompted Louis to go on the offensive. The champion forced the action and hit Walcott with a long overhand right that hurt the challenger and drove him into the ropes. With Walcott pinned up against the ropes, Louis came on strong by landing several crushing body blows. But Walcott fought back savagely, hurting Louis with a right. Although hurt, Louis showed a lot of heart and continued to hammer away at Jersey Joe. He caught the challenger with a hard right that wobbled Jersey Joe. Shaken up by the champion's two-fisted assault, it looked for a moment that Jersey Joe was on the way out. But the crafty veteran escaped off the ropes and landed a hard right hand wallop to Louis' face. The champion was momentarily hurt by the punch. Walcott then tried to box Louis, but the two were soon swapping hard punches in an even exchange as the ninth round ended. The ninth round was really the turning point of the fight, as Jersey Joe recalled in a 1948 article in the *Saturday Evening Post*:

> The round that won the fight for me and the one that was most misunderstood by ringsiders was the ninth. For two minutes stepping up the speed of my feinting I found it possible to punish Louis with long rights to the face. He landed two head punches that backed me against the ropes on the south side of the Garden ring. This time instead of going for my body he decided to level straight for my head. But I fell into a rhythm

with his lefts and rights. I rolled with every punch. Because I rolled with punches it may have looked as if my head were rocking under the drive of his gloves. Meanwhile, though I fired every time I straightened up and caught Louis moving into my punches. I could have ducked out or side stepped if I wanted to. But my fists were doing the real damage. The defending champion acknowledged that by backing away. The movies verify what I say. Louis knew that he wasn't going to nail me that night.[10]

Perhaps sensing that he was a little behind, Louis was anxious to begin the tenth round. He was up off his stool even before the bell sounded. He came out wearily following the challenger, looking for an opening. But Walcott's defense continued to baffle the Brown Bomber as it had done all night. Walcott finally opened up with a long left hook that caught Louis on the chin and made his legs a bit shaky for a second. The two fighters traded quick rights before Louis was finally able to drive Walcott back into a corner. The champion landed a couple of hard body shots. But Jersey Joe quickly fought his way out of the corner with Louis in hot pursuit firing jabs as Walcott retreated. Walcott continued to backpedal and sidestep for most of the round. His tactics seemed to confuse the champion. At times Jersey Joe would stop his retreat and fire a wild punch that would often land. The two fighters would then exchange quick flurries of punches and Walcott would get back on his toes and box the champion. Louis continued to be the aggressor and kept after Walcott. He forced the action for most of the tenth round.

Louis continued to force the action in round eleven. He started the round with two solid lefts to Walcott's body. He then fired two stiff jabs that landed on Walcott's face. Walcott retaliated by stabbing Louis with a fast left jab to his face. Both fighters then connected with left hooks. They exchanged hooks again and Walcott followed up with a hard right to Louis' chin. Louis fired right back with a right of his own to Jersey Joe's jaw. A hard right from Walcott caught Louis coming in. At close quarters both fighters began to exchange devastating body blows. Louis then drove Walcott back with a left hook and hit him with a fast stiff jab. He followed the jab with an overhand right that caught the challenger square on the chin. The punch was hard. It stopped Jersey Joe in his tracks and stunned him for a second. From Walcott's corner, Florio screamed at the top of his lungs, "Head down!" Walcott fired back at Louis with an overhand right to his jaw as the eleventh round ended.

By the twelfth round, both fighters bore the marks of a tough, hard fight. Jersey Joe was cut and bleeding. Louis's left eye was swollen nearly shut. The skin on his face was red and raw from Walcott's jabs, and his lips were smashed and puffed up. The round opened with Louis stalking Walcott. He landed a left to the challenger's body. Jersey Joe clipped Louis with a left and took a left to the face in return. Walcott began peppering away with jabs, targeting the champion's swollen left eye, and then shot over a hard right to Louis's head. Walcott continued to land jabs as he backed away and side-stepped Louis' punches. Louis scored with a hard left and right to Walcott's head. Jersey Joe came back with a left to Louis' chin. For a time the action slowed as the champion followed Walcott around the ring. Jersey Joe suddenly came to life and landed two lefts and a right to Joe's face, but took a hard left to his face as he connected with a left-right combination. He outboxed the Brown Bomber for most of the twelfth round. The two fighters swapped jabs and hooks at the bell.

By the thirteenth round, Walcott was seemingly ahead. Jersey Joe started the round with a right that grazed the champion's jaw and caused blood to flow from Joe's nose. Louis kept moving in, following the crafty challenger who was dancing on his toes and firing jabs and an occasional right hand. Louis tagged Walcott with two jabs to the head as Walcott backed away. The challenger then attacked by landing a right and two lefts to the champion's face. They exchanged right hooks and Louis slammed a left into Jersey Joe's jaw. Walcott swung one from the bleachers, but missed and fell. Quickly, Walcott sprang to his feet. The two fighters exchanged a series of smashing blows in the center of the ring. Walcott hit Louis with a left and right hook to the head. Louis landed two jabs to Walcott's face. As the end of the thirteen round neared, the two fighters went at it toe-to-toe, throwing bombs as the bell rang.

During the break between the thirteenth and fourteenth rounds Florio instructed Jersey Joe to box and "stay away" from Louis. Since Dan felt that Walcott was ahead, he didn't want him to take any unnecessary chances, like Billy Conn did in his 1941 match with Louis. Florio knew that Louis was a deadly finisher. Even though Louis was behind, he was a dangerous fighter right up to the last second. The Brown Bomber could take out an opponent at any moment, with a single murderous punch. Jersey Joe had to be careful. Walcott followed his trainer's instructions. He got moving as Louis came out jabbing. Jersey Joe backed-up and side-stepped, but the Brown Bomber was still able to force Walcott to the ropes and land some ripping body punches. Walcott quickly escaped and continued to box beautifully. He was on his toes dancing, side-stepping, and backpedaling. He flicked out occasional jabs and quick flurries of punches. At times he would stop and the two fighters would exchange a few hard punches, but then Walcott would get back on his toes and dance away. An exhausted Louis could do nothing but follow the elusive Walcott to try to catch him.

During the break before the final round, Dan reminded Walcott to "stay away" and that's what Jersey Joe did during the fifteenth round. He danced around like a dervish, with the champion in hot pursuit. Louis got jolted with a jab that bloodied his nose and had difficulty catching up with the challenger. The crowd began to boo Walcott's retreating tactics. Louis continued to follow Walcott and miss punches. Jersey Joe made little effort to fight during the final round. Instead, he side-stepped, backpedaled, and danced. There were only a few brief exchanges of punches throughout before the bell sounded, signaling that the fight was over.

The exhausted fighters went to their corners. Bocchicchio, Webster, and Florio immediately swarmed Walcott and embraced him. Each thinking as most did, that Jersey Joe had just pulled off a huge upset and won the heavyweight title. Louis, on the other hand, disgusted with his performance and probably thinking that he had just lost his title, wasted no time in attempting to leave the ring even before the official decision was announced. His handlers stopped him before he could get away. They explained that if he left he could be disqualified. Louis then donned his robe and awaited the official verdict. Announcer Harry Balogh read the decision: "Judge Frank Forbes scores six rounds for Walcott, one round even, eight rounds for Louis. Referee Ruby Goldstein scores seven rounds for Walcott, two rounds even, six rounds for Louis. Judge Martin Monroe scores nine rounds for Louis, six rounds for Walcott. The winner by majority vote and still the heavyweight champion of the world, Joe Louis!"[11]

The response from the crowd at the Garden was instantaneous. The 18,000 fans voiced their disagreement with loud, thunderous booing. Trainer Dan Florio could be seen holding his head in his hands in disbelief. Jersey Joe and his handlers were shocked at the outcome. A moment after the decision was announced, Louis walked over to Walcott's corner and approached Jersey Joe. "I'm sorry, Joe," was all that Louis said.[12] Walcott took this as an admission of defeat on Louis's part. Louis later said that he only said that because he had fought so poorly. The battered champion then proceeded to exit the ring and head for his locker room. Walcott and his handlers stayed in the ring as the crowd continued to boo then cheer when Walcott's hand was raised by Florio.

Immediately following the shocking decision Felix and Webster approached Commissioner Eagan and demanded justice. Eagan said that they could take up the argument at his office on Monday morning.

After the crowd had died down, Walcott and his handlers followed a cordon of policemen through a narrow tunnel under Madison Square Garden and made their way back to Jersey Joe's dressing room. Once there, the disappointed Walcott sat on a rubbing table. Nearly in tears, he answered questions from the press. "I don't believe it, I thought I won big," said Walcott.[13] So did Walcott's trainer Florio who said, "He won the fight. If he didn't I don't know anything about fighting."[14] Jersey Joe added, "I was never hurt at any time, although he punched hard especially in the ninth when he had me against the ropes.... I knew all the time what I was doing. After the first round I knew I could beat him."[15] When asked if he would like to meet Louis again, Walcott's face lit up for the first time with a real grin, not one that he had forced for the benefit of photographers. "I sure would as soon as I could get him, I would fight him tomorrow," Walcott said enthusiastically.[16]

Across the hall from Walcott's dressing room, the battered champion was being examined by doctors and questioned by the press. Louis was a mess; his left eye was completely swollen shut and had a cut below it. His lips were smashed and swollen as was his jaw. His right hand was also bruised and puffed up. The examining physicians were sure the hand was broken. "Do you think Walcott was a second rate fighter tonight?" asked one of the members of the press. "No, I was," replied Louis.[17] When asked about a rematch, Louis said, "He deserves one."[18] As to why he tried to leave the ring before the decision, Louis said, "I was disgusted with myself."[19] After getting cleaned up and answering questions, Louis was taken to the hospital for further examinations.

Despite the disappointing loss to Louis, the fight was still a victory for Jersey Joe. He had taken the great Joe Louis to the edge of defeat and was only the third fighter to go the full 15-round distance with the champion. Jersey Joe had given Louis his worst beating since his loss to Max Schmeling, ten years before. As a result of the fight, Walcott became an international celebrity overnight. His performance earned him the best sports comeback of 1947. His comeback overshadowed the fine comebacks by the New York Yankees, Joe DiMaggio, George McQuinn and the California football team. Finally after seventeen years of anonymity, Jersey Joe Walcott was famous.

Years later in an interview, Walcott revealed his feelings about the Louis fight and its outcome: "Like thousands of people who saw it, I thought I won the fight. I thought I won big. But out of my respect and admiration for Louis, I never felt bad about not getting the decision. He was such an idol to the world. I think that anyone that dethroned him would be the most hated guy in the world."[20]

A rematch with Joe Louis was a natural. But first there was the backlash of the unpopular decision to deal with and a meeting to appeal the judges' decision.

—10—

Louis-Walcott II

The day after the 1947 fight against Joe Louis, Jersey Joe Walcott and his handlers arrived to a hero's welcome at Central Airport in New Jersey. A few thousand fans and a fifteen-car caravan headed by Camden mayor George E. Brunner waited to lead Walcott, the "uncrowned champion," and his team on a triumphant "welcome home parade" through downtown Camden. The mayor, who had telegraphed his protest to the New York State Athletic Commission said, "The Camden commissioners, chamber of commerce, business and sport figures have joined to make Jersey Joe's homecoming the most outstanding demonstration ever held for a Camden athlete."[1]

Jersey Joe had very little time to enjoy all the attention coming his way. His weekend was busy. On Saturday he was taking care of one of his children who had become ill and answering phone calls from friends and family members who wanted to congratulate him and talk about the fight. On Sunday he met with Webster and Felix at the Camden Athletic Club to plan their appeal.

During the weekend, hundreds of calls and telegrams from angry fans flooded the New York State Athletic Commission office claiming that Jersey Joe was "robbed" and that something needed to be done. Sportswriters as well were writing about how Walcott was the recipient of a bad decision and how he had made Louis look like a bum. The decision was so bad that one of Louis' biggest supporters, columnist Jimmy Cannon, remarked that if the winner had been anybody else there would have been a full-scale investigation into the officiating. A poll was taken of all of the sportswriters at ringside. Of the forty-two, twenty-six had it for Walcott, while sixteen gave the champion the nod. Although the majority of the fans and press thought that Walcott deserved the decision, there were those that argued that Walcott's strategy of playing it safe and "running" for the last two rounds because he was ahead on points had lost him the fight. You can't win going backwards was Louis' response. If a fighter was going to win the heavyweight title, especially against a champion as popular as Louis, he would have to take the title from the champ. As Jersey Joe had found out, winning a decision was nearly impossible.

Commissioner Eagan couldn't, however, ignore the overwhelming public response. After speaking with Webster and Walcott on the phone Sunday, Eddie set up a meeting for Monday. Team Walcott arrived Monday afternoon and pleaded their case before the Athletic Commission in an attempt to have the decision overturned. Later in an interview, Jersey Joe summarized his appeal:

> We made it clear that we did not question the integrity of the officials but we added: We contend that Mr. Forbes, the judge, scored the contest for Walcott, but failed to properly record the conclusion he was constrained to make under the boxing rules of the commission. We challenged Mr. Forbes particularly because he scored twelve points for me to nine for Louis, and yet voted for Louis on the grounds that Louis had taken eight of the rounds. Forbes' decision, together with that of Judge Marty Monroe overbalanced Referee Ruby Goldstein, who voted for me. We cited a rule which states that the winner of a lesser number of rounds may be awarded the decision where in the judgment of the ring officials, said contestant has inflicted the greater amount of damage and has proven his superiority over his opponent during the contest and finished in better physical condition. A sentence added to that same rule as recently as 1945 served as a basis for our case. The total points of such a winner over a fewer number of rounds shall be more than those of his opponent. Our unpublished statement contended that the latter sentence placed a control over the degree of discretion permitted an official and that therefore it was binding on the official as evidence that I had proven my superiority. As for inflicting the greater damage, everyone who saw the bout knows who did that. A look at the two of us after the fight left only one answer to the question who finished in better condition. As to who proved his superiority, we cited another much ignored rule which sums up my whole feeling about boxing. Credit should be awarded where ring generalship is conspicuous. This comprises such points as the ability to grasp and take advantage of every opportunity offered, the capacity to cope with all situations which may arise, to foresee and neutralize an opponent's method of attack to force an opponent to adopt to a style of boxing he is not particularly skillful. Our final argument was that the commission should make a legal ruling on what should have been the correct interpretation of Forbes' point score in the control it exercised on the question of superiority.[2]

Despite the convincing argument that Walcott and Webster presented, there was no way that the decision was going to be changed. The two men sat silently at the long meeting table as Eagan informed them that the decision would stand. In short Eagan said, "This commission has no desire to interfere with the exercise of the discretion and judgment of competent appointed officials." The commission did, however, congratulate Walcott on his splendid performance. Eagan then added that since Joe Louis has always been a true sportsman, the New York Commission assumes that Louis will give Walcott another chance. Neither Walcott nor Webster had any comment on the Commission's ruling. If Jersey Joe wanted the title, he would have to face Louis again.

As early as two days after the fight, Joe Louis was agreeing to a rematch with Walcott. He didn't like the outcome of the first fight, saying that he was disgusted with the way he had fought. He blamed his poor performance on the fact that he had been overly concerned with his weight. Against the advice of his trainer Manny Seamon, Louis ate and drank very little food or water for two days prior to the fight. He had "dried out" in an attempt to come in at a respectable weight. Louis said that doing so had left him feeling weak during the fight and that next time he would be in better shape. Joe was also not accustomed to the negative reaction from the press and his normally adoring fans. Ultimately, Louis wanted to retire after the first fight with Walcott, but knew that he couldn't do it on such a sour note. He would have to face Walcott again. However, this time he said he would retire, win or lose. "On my word of honor I will retire. Win, lose or draw. I've had enough," said Louis.[3] He added, "I've been around a long time."[4] Plans for a June 1948 rematch were quickly underway.

On January 31, 1948, Walcott took a break from negotiations to celebrate his 34th birthday. A party was put on at Merchantville High School, where several hundred friends and family members showed up to mingle with the "champ" as he was known, and to wish him well in his rematch with Louis. Despite being another year older, Walcott said he "never felt better in my life."

By mid–February, the Walcott-Louis match was all but set. There were reports that a rematch could possibly net a $2,000,000 gate. There had only been two of those in the history of boxing: Dempsey-Tunney II in 1927 and Louis-Conn II in 1946. There was just one problem: Walcott and his team were not happy with the terms of the contract being offered. The contract stipulated that Walcott would receive 20 percent of the proceeds from the net gate and television (Webster and Walcott were hoping for 30 percent) and 22.5 percent of profits from radio and movies. Louis would receive 40 percent of all proceeds. Team Walcott decided to hold

Walcott and trainer Dan Florio (left) relax between Jersey Joe's two fights with Joe Louis.

out, hoping to fatten the deal but eventually were given a two-week deadline by Louis, who threatened to instead sign to fight light-heavyweight champion Gus Lesnevich. Louis said, "You'd think Walcott was the champion the way he wants to call the shots."[5]

In the end Walcott reluctantly accepted the one-sided contract. He made his acceptance public on February 26, 1948, at a ceremony put on by Harold H. Roswell, publisher of the *Police Gazette* magazine, and Camden mayor Brunner. The ceremony was held at the Camden Convention Hall, with the purpose to present Walcott with the *Police Gazette*'s "World Championship" belt. The *Police Gazette* said it believed Walcott had beaten

Louis in December 1947 and recognized him as champion. Walcott, dressed in his black and white fight trunks and robe, was presented with the diamond studded "honorary" belt before 7,500 fans. He gave a speech and confirmed that he would fight Louis again, even though he was not particularly pleased with the contract, and postulated that Joe Louis, the 20th Century Boxing Club, and the New York Boxing Commission were "trying to be dictators of boxing in this country."[6] The next day, Team Walcott left for New York. On February 27, 1948, at the 20th Century headquarters in New York, Walcott signed the preliminary contract at 2:00 P.M. and posted the required $5,000 guarantee that he would show up. The official signing took place on April 14. The rematch was scheduled for June 23, 1948, at Yankee Stadium, an outdoor venue, rather than the indoor Madison Square Garden site of the first fight.

Jersey Joe was a very busy man over the months of December through March. He spent time with his family, went to church, negotiated the rematch, made guest appearances, fought exhibition matches, and refereed fights. On December 22, Walcott was at the Boston Garden refereeing a tilt between Bob Montgomery and Joey Angelo. In February, Jersey Joe refereed the amateur semi-final and main event matches for a charity event put on by the March of Dimes, in Beckley, West Virginia. Then it was on to Charleston, South Carolina, where he refereed an amateur match put on by the black-branch YMCA building fund. He was a guest speaker at the event as well, telling children who were interested in boxing about his much disputed match with Louis. On March 10, Walcott made his first appearance in a boxing ring, in Chicago when he fought a four-round exhibition fight with his sparring partner Austin Johnson. Jersey Joe enjoyed his time off but as April approached it was time to set up training camp.

Team Walcott set up camp at Grenloch Park on April 15, complete with signs that read "Training Camp of the Champ." Walcott spent the first two weeks primarily doing road work and calisthenics. This included ten-mile hikes up lush green tree-covered mountains and rolling terrain wearing heavy boots in the warm, humid weather. After two weeks of intense road work, his camp was opened to the public and he began sparring sessions on May 2. Walcott and his handlers anticipated larger crowds and more press coverage than last time. In preparation there was an outdoor workout area erected, with plenty of seats where large gatherings of fans and the press could watch Jersey Joe skip rope, pound the heavy bag, spar or conduct interviews.

For sparring, Walcott once again called on Austin Johnson. He also hired ex-opponent Curtis "Hatchet Man" Sheppard as well as newcomers Billy Norris, Charley Robinson, and Cliff Dyes. For this fight, Walcott worked on improving his defense, footwork, speed and left hook. At times during sparring he would wear heavy boots as well as heavy tights around his waist and legs, to use the extra weight to make him faster.

To further improve his footwork and speed, Walcott went through footwork drills with the fastest man in the camp, Florida middleweight Cliff Dyes. The training that Jersey Joe put himself through was intense. To attest to this, Walcott's foot became infected because of blisters caused by all the running and sparring. A doctor advised Jersey Joe to stay off his feet for a few days. Luckily, the infection was not severe and he resumed his training after a couple of days of rest. After a full nine weeks of training, Jersey Joe had done over 350 miles of road work and had sparred over 100 rounds. He was in fine physical shape. So impressive was his condition that Curtis Sheppard, Walcott's chief sparring partner, said: "Walcott is fast as lightning, which makes him ten times faster than Louis. Walcott is smarter, craftier, and a better thinker than Louis and Walcott punches hard enough to flatten Louis any time that he connects solidly. The guy is terrific. He'll knock Louis out in seven or eight rounds."[7]

As anticipated, the press showed up to cover Walcott's workouts in greater numbers and asked a lot of questions. One question asked was how a fighter like Jersey Joe could come from nothing and almost win the most coveted prize in sports. Florio answered the question this way: "He always had the ability," said Dan.[8] "He was just never given the opportunity before. Now that he has the confidence he has shown what he can do."[9] Walcott was asked what he was going to do with all the money he was going to make fighting Louis. To this Walcott responded that he wanted to have a house built for each of his six sisters and three brothers and put enough aside to send his kids to college. The press also wanted to know what kind of style Walcott would use against Louis this time. The first time Walcott used a lot of movement, counter-punching and his "Walkaway" move to throw Louis off. Walcott responded: "I don't know what my plan of battle is yet; I'm going to fight as I'm told. Boxing is like a football team, there's a captain and a coach. One guy calls the signals; I'm the guy who carries the ball."[10] Regardless of what Walcott had told the press, the plan was to stick with what worked in the first fight. Florio wanted Walcott to again use a lot of movements and feints. He did not want Jersey Joe to stand flat-footed and mix it up with the Brown Bomber.

Louis began his preliminary training at Bear Lake, Michigan. He spent about a month there doing road work, calisthenics, and chopping logs. To make sure he was in top condition for the fight, Manny increased Joe's usual road work from six miles a day to eight miles. Manny wanted Joe in top shape for this fight. When asked about Joe's weight, Manny said, "He can weigh 210, 212, 215 or he can weigh a ton. One thing I do care about, however, and that is having Joe at the peak of form."[11]

On May 20, after several weeks of training at Bear Lake, Louis and his team arrived in New York to begin the second phase of Joe's training, which included sparring. Manny hired some new sparring partners to help Louis prepare for Walcott's speed and tricky style. He figured that the cagey Walcott would again be on the move throughout most of the fight. To prepare Louis for this, Manny wanted fast sparring partners, preferably ones that could run the 100-yard dash in at least ten seconds. He found one, Richard Hagen, a twenty-year-old Chicago Golden Gloves champion of 1947. "He can run as fast as Walcott," said Seamon. "Louis will catch Walcott this time no matter how fast he runs." Manny also hired "Tiger" Roy Taylor, who was extremely fast and had a style of fighting that was similar to Walcott's. With the help of his new sparring partners, Louis got himself into great shape.

As the fight neared, both fighters expressed their confidence. Louis predicted a knockout. Moreover, he said, "No drying out this time. I'll be good and strong for this one. I'm going in there trying to put over the knockout punch just as fast as I can. I'll catch him this time unless he jumps over the ropes and runs back home. I'm 50 to 75 percent better than last fight."[12] Upon hearing that Louis was in great shape, Walcott replied, "I'm glad to hear that Joe is in good shape because I want him with all of his strength so he'll be able to go a few rounds before I take care of him."[13]

Several ex-fighters gave their predictions of the fight's outcome. Former heavyweight champions Jack Sharkey and Jack Dempsey chose Walcott by a knockout. However, as the fight neared, Dempsey changed his pick to Louis by a knockout. Light-heavyweight champion Gus Lesnevich had it for Walcott and so did Max Bear and fight manager Dumb Dan Morgan. Of the 282 members of the Associated Press that were polled, 230 picked Louis while 52 thought Walcott would win. Although not as badly underestimated as he was during the first fight, Jersey Joe was still a 13-to-5 underdog. And most people felt that Louis would win because he had always proven himself better in rematches.

On June 22 Walcott woke up early and went for a five-mile run. Afterwards he rested and finished packing his things. He and his team then motored to New York City that afternoon and checked into their midtown hotel. The next day both fighters showed up at around noon for the official weigh-in. Walcott tipped the scales at 194¾ pounds, Louis at 213¼.

Not long after the weigh-in, the news broke that the fight was postponed due to severe rain and was rescheduled for the 24th. To keep himself occupied during the setback, Walcott took in some movies at a nearby theatre. He paid 85 cents to see a double feature. On June 24 it was still raining. The fight was again canceled and rescheduled, this time for Friday the 25th. Finally after two days of rain, the weather cleared and the fight was given the go-ahead. By this time both fighters were anxious to get in the ring. The fans were anxious as well to see the highly anticipated rematch. Despite the two-day delay 42,667 fans showed up and paid over $900,000. Although not the crowd that was anticipated, it was still a decent turnout considering the two cancellations.

In what one newspaper called a "golden Floperoo" the fight turned out to be nothing like the first. Louis, determined not to chase Walcott in this fight, decided to box the challenger. He patiently stalked the elusive Walcott, waiting for him to tire. He would then go for the knockout. Walcott, on the other hand, not wanting to get into exchanges, kept his distance and was on the move, dancing throughout most of the fight. He tried to frustrate Louis by bobbing and weaving and using his trademark "Walk-away" move. At times Jersey Joe tapped his gloves together before initiating bursts of punches and looked to land counter right hands. These strategies made for an unentertaining fight. The crowd booed throughout most of the fight, except on the rare occasion when there was an exciting exchange. In the third round, Walcott gave the crowd something to cheer about when he caught Louis with a smashing right to the jaw that dropped the champion on to his haunches for a count of one. In round eight Louis caught the backpedaling side-stepping Walcott with a solid left hook and a couple of stiff jabs that shook up the challenger. But the intermittent exchanges were not enough to keep the crowd satisfied. Referee Frank Fullam, aware of the crowd's displeasure, began telling Walcott to pick it up and start fighting. By the eleventh round Fullam urged both men, saying, "Hey, one of you guy get the lead out of your ass, and let's have a fight."[14]

About the time the referee urged the fighters to fight, Walcott started dancing and giving Louis a lot of movement. He was dodging Joe's jabs and firing right-hand punches. Walcott was boxing beautifully but being perhaps a little careless when all of a sudden Louis landed a hard right that

Joe Louis (left) and Jersey Joe go at it in action from their second fight, in June 1948.

caught Jersey Joe flush on the side of his face. The punch momentarily turned Walcott's legs to rubber. Louis, sensing the kill, pressed forward, firing a right-left combination followed by a right to the body. The force of the blows drove Walcott into the ropes. Louis landed another right to the body and a right to the head, followed by a left hook that Walcott ducked. Louis then landed another right to the body, a right to the head and an upper cut preceded by a left hook just as Walcott threw his own left. Jersey Joe shot a right and a left, followed by a right, as the two warriors exchanged hard, furious punches.

In the heat of battle, Jersey Joe was making the same mistake that Billy Conn had. Instead of dancing away from the ropes and away from Louis, Walcott thought for a moment that he could trade punches with the Brown Bomber. It was a mistake that would cost him. Louis landed a right that caught Walcott hard, causing his head to turn from the impact. Louis then followed up with a fast barrage of blistering lefts and rights. The punches landed flush on Jersey Joe's face. After taking five or six solid shots from arguably the most accurate, hardest punching heavyweight in history, Jersey Joe dropped to the canvas. He landed on his back, drooling blood from his mouth. The crowd was on its feet as the referee waved Louis to a neutral corner and began his count. A stunned Walcott rolled over onto his hands and knees and shook his head to try to clear the cobwebs. He rose slightly but fell back down. Bravely, he forced himself to his feet, but it was too late, as the referee had reached the count of ten just a moment before. Jersey Joe was counted out at 2:56 of the eleventh round.

When the fight was over, Louis was given a standing ovation by fans who thought that they had just witnessed his last fight. Walcott, disappointed and battered, made his way back to his dressing room. Once there he sat for a while as Florio and Allen attended to him. They applied an ice pack to his swollen face and cleaned up the cut under his left eye. After a time the press was allowed in and began asking questions. When asked what happened, Walcott explained it this way: "I thought I had him then the referee kept telling me to come on and fight. He didn't tell Louis, just me. His constant hounding got me confused. I changed my style of fighting and this happened. I was fighting the referee instead of Louis."[15] Somebody asked if Walcott was ever hurt during the fight. "He never hurt me until the eleventh round. I thought I had him licked until I made a mistake," Walcott said sadly.[16] "I don't know what it was but he caught me with a powerful punch. I only remember that first punch, they say he hit me some more, I don't remember."[17] When asked if he would keep on fighting at the age of 34 or retire, Walcott said that despite his age he would continue his career and his goal of winning the championship: "It's always been my ambition. I think I can still win it."[18]

A few doors down, Louis was being interviewed as well. From his dressing room, Joe announced his retirement, saying: "This was for you, Mom. This was my last fight."[19]

The second defeat to Louis was a bitter blow to Walcott. He was sure he was going to defeat Louis to win the heavyweight title. Disappointed, Walcott and his team headed back to New Jersey. Little did Jersey Joe realize at the time that his greatest boxing triumphs were still yet to come.

—11—

The Cincinnati Cobra

Joe Louis's unofficial retirement after his fight with Walcott in 1948 left the heavyweight division in turmoil. His announcement prompted a bitter war that took place behind the scenes among three promotional entities: the 20th Century Sporting Club, the "Seven Angels" (so-called because of the seven millionaires that ran the company), and Jack Solomon, a London promoter. The scramble was on to find the next heavyweight champion, and each promoter was determined to gain control of him. All three of the promotional companies had their own idea of staging elimination tournaments that would eventually produce the two top contenders to fight for Louis' vacated title. There were several contenders mentioned to participate in these tournaments: Jersey Joe Walcott, Ezzard Charles, Gus Lesnevich, Joey Maxim, Lee Savold, Joe Baksi, Freddie Mills, Bruce Woodcock, and Elmer "Violent" Ray; there was even talk of a comeback by Billy Conn.

Jack Solomon proposed a heavyweight competition and invited American heavyweights to participate. Sol Strauss and the 20th Century Sporting Club were trying to get a Walcott-Lesnevich or Walcott-Charles fight that would start a series of elimination bouts, as were the "Seven Angels." Sol and Mike Jacobs were also thinking of matching Charles with light-heavyweight champion Lesnevich. A fight between these two boxers would have determined two titles at once, the light-heavyweight and heavyweight title. But Lesnevich's manager, Joe Vella, refused, saying, Charles would knock out Gus, and at this stage of the proceedings he wasn't going to get him hurt. Gus, on the other hand, felt that he and Walcott should bypass the tournaments and fight for the championship. Since he had beaten Melino Bettina and Tami Mauriello, the number one and two contenders, Gus felt that he deserved to fight for the vacant title. And since Walcott was one of the top-rated contenders, it was only logical that the two should meet.

As it turned out, Gus got his wish. In August, the "Seven Angels" Promotion Company managed to put together a match between Walcott and Gus before Sol and 20th Century could. The announcement of the fight came out right around the time that Jersey Joe announced that he and his long-time manager, Joe Webster, would not be renewing their contract. "I'll handle my own business arrangements from now on," Walcott told a reporter.[1] Joe added, "Webster and I remain the best of friends. There has been no dispute between us, but he's too tied up in his restaurant business."[2]

The fight with Lesnevich was scheduled for September 21, 1948. The two fighters were co-featured along with middleweights Tony Zale and Marcel Cerdan in an elimination tournament called the "Tournament of Champions." The idea was that the winner would fight the winner of the Ezzard Charles-Jimmy Bivins fight, presumably for Louis' vacated title. In fact, Walcott had already been offered $60,000 to face either Charles or Bivins by Capital promoter Florence Turner. The "Seven Angels" along with the rest of the promotional companies were eager to gain control of the next heavyweight champion. Whoever gained control of the next champion was hoping to break the monopoly that Mike Jacobs and the powerful 20th Century Sporting Club had on boxing and Madison Square Garden.

Unfortunately for the "Seven Angels," their plan did not work out. On September 17 it was announced that the Walcott-Lesnevich fight was cancelled. Gus had slipped down the steps of the post office in his hometown of Cliffside, New Jersey, and suffered a broken toe (some reports say ankle). It would be a month before he could fight again. Since a suitable opponent could not be found on such short notice, Walcott was dropped from the card. The cancellation left Walcott and his team looking for another opponent. In late November, Felix Bocchicchio met with promoter Larry Atkins to try to arrange a fight with the winner of the Bivins-Maxim fight on December 7, but negotiations fell through; instead Maxim and Charles were matched for a February 1949 tilt. Until a fight could be arranged, Walcott kept himself in shape with light training and an exhibition match with Earl Griffin at the Camden Armory on December 14, 1948.

After 1948 quietly came to a close, the new year began with Walcott and his team still having a hard time securing a fight. In fact, Walcott was having such a hard time that there was some talk of his traveling to the Netherlands West Indies to fight a six-round exhibition with Baba Adams on January 29. Reports said that Jersey Joe was guaranteed $5,000 plus traveling expenses. The records do not say if the bout ever took place. The new year began to look up when Joe Louis contacted Jersey Joe in February. Louis wanted to know if Walcott would be interested in a fight with Ezzard Charles for the vacant world heavyweight title. Of course, Walcott and his team jumped at the opportunity.

On March 1, 1949, Joe Louis called a press conference and officially announced his retirement from boxing. He would now be turning his attention to promoting fights. Shortly after his last fight with Walcott, Louis along with Arthur M. Wirtz and James D. Norris, two wealthy businessmen from Chicago, formed a promotion company called the I.B.C or International Boxing Club. Once the partnership was formed, Louis asked for and was granted permission by the National Boxing Association to promote a title fight for his vacated title. Like James J. Jefferies did after he retired as undefeated champion in 1905, Louis chose the two fighters he felt deserved to fight for his title. Louis decided on Jersey Joe Walcott and Ezzard Charles, the two most outstanding contenders. The fight was scheduled for June 22 at Comiskey Park in Chicago.

Officially, the Walcott-Charles fight was for the National Boxing Association version of the heavyweight title. This meant that every state except New York would recognize the winner as champion. The New York State Athletic Commission refused to recognize the winner as champion, even after Joe Louis had asked Commissioner Eddie Eagan to recognize the winner as champion, because according to Eagan, they wanted to stage more elimination tournaments to determine the two top contenders to fight for the title. It also meant that the top European and British promoters would not recognize the winner as "world" champion either. They too had their top contenders and their own ideas of elimination bouts that would hopefully produce the next world champion. All of this mattered little to Walcott and Charles, who both saw the fight as a golden opportunity. It would be Walcott's third crack at the heavyweight title. He felt sure he would win the championship this time, even though he was going up against a truly great fighter in Charles.

To say Ezzard Charles was a great fighter is an understatement. He was an outstanding fighter, but one who never really received the credit he deserved. This was mostly due to the fact that he, like Walcott, fought in the shadow of the great Joe Louis. Most boxing fans did not see Charles as a standout during his time because there were a lot of great fighters then. Sadly, Ezzard has been nearly forgotten today by the mainstream boxing public. Despite his greatness, he is one of the most underrated and least-remembered heavyweight champions. Only when one takes the time to study him and examine his record do we see how special Charles really was. He defeated several outstanding champions and all-time great fighters. He went 4–1 against Jimmy Bivins, 3–0 against Joey Maxim, 1–0 against Gus Lesnevich, 1–0 against Anton Christoforidis, 3–0 against legendary all-time great Archie Moore, 2–0 against Charley Burley, and 2–1 against Lloyd Marshall. Burly and Marshall, along with Moore, were part of the famous "Black Murderer's Row" fighters. These fearsome fighters were avoided by nearly everyone. Furthermore, Charles went 2–2 against Jersey Joe, beat an older Joe Louis, and was also the only fighter to go the full fifteen rounds with the hard-punching Rocky Marciano. Charles also defeated a number of outstanding top contenders including Lee Oma, Elmer "Violent" Ray, Rex Layne, Harold Johnson, Harry "Kid" Matthews, and Joe Baksi, to name a few.

Today, most experts typically rate Charles among the three greatest light-heavyweights of all time. In 2009, *Ring* magazine rated Charles the number one greatest light-heavyweight of all-time. Boxing historian Herb Goldman rated Charles the number three greatest light-heavyweight of all-time. And the International Boxing Research Organization (IBRO) placed Charles at two on their all-time list at light-heavyweight.

Not only was Charles an outstanding middleweight and light-heavyweight, he was also a excellent heavyweight. Among the big boys, Charles is typically rated somewhere among the top twenty. The IBRO ranks Charles at number 17 at heavyweight, no small accomplishment for a fighter that was best at light-heavyweight. In 2006, the IBRO named Charles as the 11th greatest fighter of all-time on their pound-for-pound list.

Ezzard Mack Charles was born July 21, 1921, in Lawrenceville, Georgia. He was named after the doctor who delivered him. His middle name came courtesy of his grandfather. When Ezzard was nine, his parents split up and he went to live with Maud Foster, his grandmother, and Belle Russell, his great grandmother, in Cincinnati, Ohio. Charles started boxing in high school as a featherweight. He had an extremely successful amateur career, going 42–0 and winning several amateur championships. In 1938 he won the amateur diamond belt. He followed this up by winning both the Chicago tournament of champions and the national AAU middleweight championship in 1939. After he turned professional in 1940, he began his career with a fourth-round knockout of Melody Johnson. Ezzard ran his record up to 15–0 before losing his first fight, to the vastly more experienced ex-middleweight champion Ken Overlin. Putting the loss behind him,

Charles continued on up through the middleweight ranks by facing and defeating some great fighters, including the much-feared and avoided Charley Burley, all the while developing his extraordinary skills and building a record of 30 wins, 4 losses and 1 draw.

Besides boxing, the soft-spoken and humble Ezzard had many other interests, including reading, hunting, fishing and rooting for his favorite baseball team, the Brooklyn Dodgers. He was also a very talented painter and bass fiddle player, good enough to regularly play with famous jazz and blues musicians.

World War II interrupted Ezzard's boxing career in 1945. He was drafted into the U.S. Army and served in Italy. As a result the "Cincinnati Cobra" was out of ring action for all of 1945. Once the term of his service reached conclusion, Ezzard returned to boxing. But during the time he spent in the military, he matured physically and was no longer a middleweight. On February 18, 1946, the Cincinnati Cobra entered the ring as a light-heavyweight. He scored an easy second-round knockout of Al Sheridan. He continued on, defeating the best light-heavyweights and heavyweights in the game. His conquests included a number of impressive opponents such as Jimmy Bivins, Archie Moore, Elmer "Violent" Ray, and Lloyd Marshall.

In 1948 Ezzard's march toward a title was halted by an unfortunate tragedy. Charles fought a fighter named Sam Baroudi and knocked him out in the tenth round. Sam never regained consciousness and died six hours later of a cerebral hemorrhage. Ezzard was devastated by the death and nearly quit the ring. He was eventually talked out of quitting and resumed his career. First, though, he fought a charity bout with all the money going to Sam Baroudi's family. Charles continued on after the death of Baroudi, although some say that he was never quite the same, never quite as aggressive. It has been said that Charles had lost a little of the killer instinct. By the time he and Walcott met, Ezzard had amassed an impressive record of 60-5-1. The Cobra was 27 years old and at his peak. Jersey Joe, at age 35, would have to be in top condition to beat him.

To get in top condition, Walcott began training on May 1 at Grenloch Park, which was now Jersey Joe's regular training spot. He did road work and chopped tree trunks and logs for a couple weeks. During this time Felix and Florio made some trips to Chicago to scout for prospective training sites. They eventually chose Peaceful Valley Country Club near Momence, Illinois. The club was about 12 miles from where Charles had set up his camp, at the Sunset Hill Golf and Country Club. On May 20,

Walcott and his entourage arrived in Chicago and began setting up camp to prepare for the June 22 fight.

About a week after Walcott began training, Bocchicchio decided to pay the Cincinnati Cobra's camp a visit. On a sunny Saturday afternoon, he caused quite a stir when he showed up at the enemy's training site to watch Ezzard spar. Upon noticing Felix sitting in the stands, Charles' manager, Jake Mintz, a balding, middle-aged, excitable ex-pug, accused Felix of spying. A heated verbal exchange between Bocchicchio and Mintz commenced as the two criticized each other's fighter. Mintz told Felix, "See that you're Walcott quits his fancy stepping and dodging so my boy can get this fight over in a hurry."[3] Bocchicchio snorted his reply, "Your boy Charles is too light to be fighting for the heavyweight title."[4] Felix was subsequently run out of the camp. A few days later, possibly in retaliation, Mintz stole into Walcott's camp. After observing Jersey Joe workout for a while, Mintz began taunting Walcott, boasting that Charles would win easily. Mintz's snide remarks eventually angered Felix, who was known to be hot tempered. Infuriated, Bocchicchio jumped out of the ring and grabbed hold of Mintz. The two struggled for a moment but were separated by spectators before any serious punches were thrown. Mintz stormed out saying, "I'm going back to see a good workout."[5]

As if a near fistfight between the managers wasn't enough, ticket sales for the fight were selling at a snail's pace. This led to the fight being dubbed the "Slim Pickens Heavyweight Championship." In fact, about a week after the fight was announced, sportswriters asked Joe Louis how ticket sales were going. Instead of the usual promoter response of "ticket sales are great!" or "I've got orders for hundreds of tickets from Chicago and New York," Louis, being green and honest, responded, "I don't know. We ain't sold none yet."[6] His response shocked everyone.

To further add to the drama, a few days later a series of huge summer thunderstorms ripped through the Chicago area. The storms lasted for several days. Walcott and his sparring partners were forced to conduct their matches in the hayloft of an old barn. Across town, Ezzard was forced to work out under a large tent. The two camps rode out the storms, and eventually the weather cleared. A few days after the wild weather, Joe Louis stopped by Walcott's camp. After watching Walcott spar a few rounds, Louis got the itch to pull on some gloves and go a few round with his old rival. Bocchicchio, thinking it would not be a good idea, refused, saying that he thought that Walcott would "drop Louis on his panties."[7] Not long after Louis' visit, former heavyweight contender "Two Ton" Tony Galento visited both camps and picked Walcott by a knockout. "Charles is fast but give me a puncher anytime," said Tony.[8]

Even with the near fistfight between Felix and Mintz, the bad weather, and slow ticket sales, it was a good training camp. Walcott worked himself into great shape. He had jogged over 300 miles and boxed over 131 rounds; he was, as one reporter described, as solid as a bull and rarin' to go. A few days before the fight, Dr. J.M. Houston, chief physician of the Illinois Athletic Commission, examined both fighters, declaring them to be in excellent shape. The doctor said, "I'm not sure how old Walcott is but whatever his age he is in perfect condition; he is an amazing specimen."[9]

How Jersey Joe Walcott and Ezzard Charles compared physically for their first fight, in 1949.

With the doctor's physical examination out of the way, the fighters broke camp; all that was left was the official weigh-in.

At noon on the day of the fight, over one hundred photographers showed up for the weigh-in ceremony. This caused a slight delay to the weigh-in proceedings. After clearing all the photographers out of the way, Walcott stepped on the scales and weighed in at a ready 195½ pounds, Charles at a lean 181¾. During the weigh-in, both fighters expressed their confidence in winning the match. Walcott said to the large group of reporters: "I'll be trying for a knockout in the first and if it takes fifteen I will be in there punching. I'm sure I will beat Charles. He's a good fighter but I'm bigger and can punch harder."[10] Charles said: "I'm in good shape and I will be in there giving my best. I'm not underrating Walcott, he's a smart fighter and can hit with either hand. If I win the title I hope to be a popular champion."

It was a cool, clear summer night when Jersey Joe Walcott and Ezzard Charles faced off on June 22 to do battle for the heavyweight crown. Despite the sluggish ticket sales, there were 25,932 fans at Comiskey Park on fight night to witness the battle. When the two warriors entered the ring, the odds were nearly even. Though Walcott held an edge in weight and strength, Charles was still a slight 6-to-5 favorite because of his age. Ezzard was only 27, eight years younger than Jersey Joe.

Another aspect that shifted the odds in Charles' favor was the fact that Jersey Joe had not fought in a year; some thought he might be rusty, although Jersey Joe denied that he would be. He insisted that he had kept busy training and sparring and that he was in great shape and would carry the fight to Ezzard. Charles, on the other hand, said his plan was to smother Jersey Joe's punches, keep on top of him and do all of his fighting at close quarters. Charles didn't want to give Walcott an opportunity to land his overhand right, the punch that was so effective against Louis. It sounded like the recipe for a great fight. While the fight was generally entertaining, some reports say it was at times dull due to both fighters being a little too cautious. Moreover, it slowed in the later rounds with Walcott doing a lot of running. Still other reports described the fight as a see-saw affair in which neither fighter was able to win more than two rounds in a row.

At about 8:30 P.M. the fighters made their way to the ring. After the customary pre-fight instructions, the two fighters returned to their corners. Moments later the bell rang to signal the start of round one. Jersey Joe came out aggressively and, like he had said, took the fight to Charles. He looked determined to score an early-round knockout over his lighter opponent. Walcott landed some telling blows to Ezzard's chin and body and won the round by outfoxing and outfighting Ezzard. Walcott was again the aggressor in the second round. He beat Charles to the punch and pressed the fight. Despite losing the first two rounds, however, Ezzard hung tough. Now warmed up, the advantage switched to Ezzard in the third and fourth rounds as he became the one to force the fight. The Cincinnati Cobra began landing sharp, stinging lefts to the head and hard rights to the body. Walcott returned fire and frequently landed left hooks, but they seemed to lack steam. It was apparent that Charles was a little sharper than Jersey Joe in the third and fourth rounds; Walcott was obviously feeling the effects of his year-long layoff.

In the fifth round, Walcott seemed to shake off some of the rust and enjoyed a great round. He caught Ezzard with a smashing left to the chin that drove the Cincinnati Cobra into the ropes. He then connected with a pile-driver of a left hook that landed on Ezzard's chin, followed by an overhand right that sent Charles reeling and momentarily shaken up. In the sixth, Charles was still a little groggy from the shellacking he received in the previous round. The Cobra was penalized for low blows and was outboxed by Jersey Joe. Ezzard recovered for the seventh and was a bit more aggressive during this round. He came right at Jersey Joe and brought the fight to him. The two warriors exchanged punishing blows at center ring. Then they began to wrestle and hold. Walcott, perhaps angry over the low blows in the last round, threw Charles to the canvas. An angry Ezzard rose and viciously attacked Walcott, landing a powerful right to the jaw. The blow rocked his bull-shouldered opponent and sent Jersey Joe into the ropes. Charles then landed three more hard rights to the head. The combination of punches sent Walcott staggering around the ring. It seemed Jersey Joe was close to being stopped, but his experience and ring savvy saved him from a knockout.

Charles continued his assault in round eight, hurting Jersey Joe and winning the round with fast, sneaky punches. In round nine, Jersey Joe battled back. He landed several effective counter punches and out-muscled Charles for most of the round. The tenth was Ezzard's best round. He drove a hard straight right into Walcott's jaw that wobbled Jersey Joe. Several more blows forced Walcott to the ropes. Ezzard then let loose a barrage of fast punches to Walcott's head and body. The vicious attack left Jersey Joe bleeding from his nose and had ripped open his upper lip.

The eleventh round saw Charles again outfight and outland Walcott. Jersey Joe enjoyed some success in the twelfth when he began side-stepping, backpedaling and using his "Walkaway." He repeatedly beat Charles to the punch and opened a cut under the Cincinnati Cobra's left eye. A follow-up right-hand punch split Ezzard's lip. The crowd, not appreciating Walcott's boxing ability, loudly booed his retreating tactics.

Between the twelfth and thirteenth rounds, Joseph Trainer, chairman of the Illinois State Athletic Commission, ordered referee Davey Miller to advise Walcott's handlers to tell him stop his retreating tactics and make Walcott fight. These orders certainly did not go over well with Walcott's seconds, especially Bocchicchio.

Walcott continued his side-stepping, backpedaling tactics in the thirteenth and fought an even round with Charles. Jersey Joe took round fourteen by again doing a lot of feinting, counter punching side-stepping and backpedaling. These tactics once again evoked some loud boos from the crowd. In the fifteenth and final round, the two men fought a close give-and-take battle and ended the round on even terms.

When the final bell sounded the two fighters headed to their corners and awaited the official verdict. The fight had been a hard-fought contest. Both fighters carried the marks to prove it. Charles was cut above and below his swollen left eye. His lips were puffed and split and his left cheek was severely enlarged. Walcott had a long gash and a hole that went completely through his upper lip. His right hand was injured and his right cheek was swollen. Moments later, as both fighters were having their wounds attended to, the decision was read. Judges Frank "Spike" Adams and Harold Markowitz both voted 78–72 for Charles. Referee Davy Miller had it 77–73 for Charles. With all three in favor, the new N.B.A heavyweight champion was Ezzard Charles! The Charles fans roared. The Walcott fans booed. A second later, the ring was swarming with a mass of photographers, radio microphone bearers, as well as friends of Charles and Walcott. Ezzard's manager, Mintz, was so overcome with excitement and emotion that he fainted in one of the neutral corners seconds after the decision was announced. His wife, seeing her husband lying on the floor, became hysterical. She clawed her way through dozens of people, eventually making it into the ring so she could be with her husband. Mintz was quickly revived by Dr. Houston of the State Athletic Commission and eventually left the ring under his own power.

Moments after the decision, Ezzard was interviewed. He was very happy with his win: "He's a cutey and very tricky. I hurt him with three different right hands in three different rounds. I didn't want to chase him because of his hard right hand, though."[11] The Cobra then added that he wanted to be a fighting champion like Louis. And like Louis he wanted to play golf. Louis, who was in attendance, was also interviewed and said that he was happy with the fight and felt Ezzard deserved the win since he was the aggressor and forced most of the action.

Disgusted and angry, Walcott and his handlers left the ring shortly after the decision was announced. Back in his dressing room, Jersey Joe was fuming as he answered question about the fight from a dozen reporters: "I thought I won all the way, I thought I won nine rounds."[12] He then went on to complain about the low blows that Ezzard had landed. Walcott also added that Ezzard hit him on the break several times. "He's not a great fighter," said Walcott.[13] But he then added some derogatory remarks about Charles, saying, "He's a sneaky puncher who hit coming out of the clinches. When the referee broke us I stopped fighting, but that dirty fighter kept banging away."[14]

Bocchicchio then spoke up by saying, "Charles kept hitting low every round; they were punches that hurt my boy."[15] One reporter asked why Jersey Joe was unable to drop Charles as he had done with Louis. Walcott explained: "He wouldn't exchange with me like Louis was willing to do. All he wanted to do was counter. He's not tough, he just rolled with the punches and he was in to last the distance."[16] Jersey Joe then went on the offensive for a rematch, saying, "I think Louis should force Charles to fight me again. I think I'm entitled."[17]

A member of the press asked if Jersey Joe thought the year long layoff had any effect on his performance to which he replied, "Yes, my timing was off. I only did gym work until I began training for this bout and the long layoff after the Louis fight hurt."[18] When asked if he would continue on even though he was 35 years old and a father of six, Walcott said he "had to." The reporter then asked, "Why? Do you need the money?" "No," replied Jersey Joe, "I gotta win that title."[19] Walcott then said that he would fight Charles next week if a match could be arranged, "but right now I'm going back to Camden to rest and then I will be ready for anyone."[20]

—12—

Sweden, Omelio and Johnny Shkor

Jersey Joe didn't have much time to rest once he got back to Camden. Just a few days after his fight with Ezzard Charles he was signed to fight Swedish heavyweight champion Olle Tandberg. The fight was scheduled take place in Stockholm, Sweden, on August 14, 1949. This didn't give Walcott a lot of time to train and get everything ready for the trip. Jersey Joe was extremely confident about his upcoming fight. After seeing the fight between Tandberg and Joey Maxim at Madison Square Garden, Joe said: "Olle is a good rough fellow with a hard punch, but he is not hard to hit. I expect to win by a knockout and plan to finish him as quickly as possible. I'll get back into the title picture by beating Tandberg; he will be the first victim in my new drive to get another crack at the heavyweight title."[1] In fact, Walcott and Felix had indeed come up with a plan to get back into the title hunt. The first step of the plan was for Jersey Joe to defeat the Swedish champion. Bocchicchio would then try to match his charge with as many of the top contenders as they could get while in Europe. "That way," said Walcott, "there will be no question as to who is champion when I get another chance at Charles."[2]

Walcott and his team, along with Mrs. Bocchicchio, boarded a Scandinavian Airlines plane bound for Sweden on Saturday, June 23. It was Walcott's first time traveling overseas. It must have been exciting for a poor boy from New Jersey to be able to travel and see the world. About twelve hours later Jersey Joe arrived in Stockholm. Walcott and his team stayed in a nice hotel. The first few days were spent setting up a training camp and getting accustomed to their new surroundings. News of the American's arrival and his impending fight with Olle had spread like wildfire. Walcott and his contingent soon found out that they attracted a lot of attention wherever they went. A few days after his arrival, Walcott awoke early one morning and headed out to get a newspaper at the corner stand. Several citizens instantly recognized the American fighter and asked for his autograph. In a matter of moments Jersey Joe was surrounded by a crowd of autograph seekers so huge that it stopped traffic on Vasa Street. After the local police quickly broke up the mob, they asked Walcott to return to his hotel, no doubt after getting their own autographs. It's unclear if Jersey Joe ever got his newspaper.

Once his training camp was set up, Jersey Joe had about a month to prepare for his Swedish opponent. This wasn't a lot of time. Luckily, he was still in great shape from all of the training he had done for his recent fight with Charles. He had also continued to do road work and hit the gym nearly every day since the fight, so he wasn't too far from peak condition. Walcott almost immediately discovered that it wasn't just at the newspaper stand where he drew a crowd. His daily workouts, which were open to the public, drew thousands of observers. At one point, over ten thousand people showed up to watch the American train, and most wanted autographs. Autograph hunters chased the boxer everywhere. Being a gracious fellow, he tried to get to everyone. After his workouts, he would spend time signing hundreds of autographs. After days of signing his name thousands of times, Walcott complained that his right hand was shaky and sore, saying that "I've had to sign my signature too often."[3]

Meanwhile, back in the United States, Ezzard Charles was preparing for his first title defense against Gus Lesnevich. The fight was scheduled for August 10, just four days before Walcott's fight with Olle. However, the New York State Athletic Commission still refused to recognize Charles as the legitimate heavyweight champion. Furthermore, they refused to even recognize the fight as a "championship bout." Their reasoning was that they wanted to put on more heavyweight tournaments and then a championship fight. "With who?" asked an angry Abe Green of the National Boxing Association. "Charles is the champion, recognized as such in every state except New York."[4]

Walcott ended heavy training on August 10. There is little doubt that later that evening he sat around with Florio and Bocchicchio and either watched or listened to Charles defeat Lesnevich by a seventh-round technical knockout. It was a solid win for Charles but did little to further his claim as "world heavyweight champion." Just a few days after the fight, Ezzard's manager made it publicly known that Charles wanted to fight Joe Louis. Mintz had asked Louis to come out of retirement, saying, "I explained to Louis that the public never would recognize Charles as a genuine world heavyweight champion until he has the chance to prove his ability against Louis."[5] According to Mintz, Louis said he would take the proposal "under consideration."[6] Mintz then brazenly told reporters, "I believe Louis will come back."[7]

A huge crowd of 43,000 excited fans showed up at Raasunda Football Stadium on August 14, 1949, to witness Walcott and Tandberg slug it out. It was the largest ever Scandinavian boxing crowd. The fans paid 640,000 Swedish crowns, the equivalent of 175,000 U.S. dollars, to watch the fight. Since betting was illegal in Sweden, there were no odds on the fight. But most people felt that Walcott would beat Olle by decision since the big Swede had never been stopped. Bocchicchio said that he expected Jersey Joe to knock out Tandberg in seven or eight rounds. When a reporter pointed out that Olle had never been knocked out, Bocchicchio replied that he didn't think that Tandberg would be able to stand up against Joe's attack. Olle's Swedish fans were, of course, hoping for another upset victory like the one he pulled off against Joe Baksi in 1947.

If Olle's Swedish fans were hoping for an upset, they were quickly disappointed. From the opening bell it was obvious that Walcott was the superior fighter. The 6'6" 209 pound Tandberg was too slow and had nothing to match the speed, skill, and power of the 194-pound American. Olle tried to make a fight of it, though. He used his long left jab effectively and looked to find an opening in Walcott's defense during the first two rounds, but was unable to get through. In the third round Jersey Joe floored the blond Swede for a count of eight with a counter left hook to the jaw. Olle recovered quickly from the knockdown and put up a good fight for the remainder of the round. In the fourth the two fighters fought on even terms, each giving as much as they took. Walcott turned up the heat in the fifth round and went on the offensive. He knocked down Olle with a short right hand that sent the sweat spraying from Tandberg's head. Olle rose unsteadily at the count of eight and was met by a vicious two-fisted attack from Walcott. The crowd, loving the excitement, went wild and roared their approval. Jersey Joe's assault sent Tandberg back down to his knees, courtesy of another hard right hand; he then pitched forward onto his face. Showing the heart of a champion, Olle staggered to his feet as referee Andrew Smyth counted. The big Swede pulled himself up, only to slump back into the ropes. Having seen enough, Smyth stepped in and ended the fight. He turned to Walcott, raising the American's hand in victory at 2:30 of the fifth round. Both fighters were given loud cheers for their efforts as the official outcome of the fight was announced. Moments later, as he left the ring, the popular Walcott waved to the crowd and was heartily cheered. Back in his dressing room, dozens of reporters waited to interview and praise him. Along with the reporters, Walcott received a special visit from the United States ambassador to Sweden, Harrison Freeman Matthews, a big boxing fan, who had sat ringside and came to congratulate Jersey Joe on his victory.

The next day back at his hotel, a happy Jersey Joe was all smiles as several reporters interviewed him. He lay stretched out on his bed, grinning from ear to ear. The veteran fighter told the journalists that he wanted another crack at Charles and that he felt certain that he would beat Ezzard next time. Bocchicchio readily nodded in agreement.

Jersey Joe continued his European vacation for about another two months, as Bocchicchio tried to negotiate several fights. One of the contenders Bocchicchio was hoping to get a match with was "Fearless" Freddie Mills, the light-heavyweight champion. Born in Bournemouth, Dorset, United Kingdom, Freddie was a very popular fighter and a crowd favorite due to his aggressive style and willingness to get in close and mix it up. A match between Jersey Joe and Mills was a guaranteed money-maker. Unfortunately, the fight never happened. There was also some talk of matching Jersey Joe against Bruce Woodcock, another popular British fighter, or Lee Savold for the British version of the heavyweight championship. Although they tried, Walcott and Felix were unable to carry out their plan to take on as many top contenders in Europe as they could. Most of the top contenders already had fights scheduled or flat out refused to fight Walcott. Not able to secure a fight, Jersey Joe and his handlers spent time visiting tourist attractions. They spent several days visiting Italy, including Rome. One day they visited the Roman sports stadium where ancient pugilists wearing metal-studded leather gloves once fought in bloody battles. On September 17, Walcott, along with forty pilgrims, met with Pope Pius the XII at Castle Gandalfo in Italy. Jersey Joe knelt before the pope and kissed the fisherman's ring on the pontiff's left hand. The deeply religious Walcott said it was like being "close to heaven. I feel very humble."[8]

Although Europe was a lot of fun, Walcott and his team eventually had to get back to America. They arrived in New York on October 4. While the trip and the fight had been a big success, Jersey Joe was happy to be home with his family. Once back to work, Felix wasted no time trying to get a match for his fighter. He quickly went to work with matchmaker Charles Pinto. Together the two tried to set up possible fights with Gus

Lesnevich, Joe Baksi, or Lee Oma. For one reason or another, none of these fights could be arranged. This mattered little since a better match against a young contender soon materialized.

On December 23 it was officially announced that the "veteran" 36-year-old Jersey Joe Walcott would fight the young upcoming 22-year-old Harold Johnson. The fight was penciled in for February 8, 1950, at the Philadelphia Arena. Ironically, Harold was the son of Phil Johnson, a fighter Walcott had fought and knocked out way back in June 1936 when Walcott was, just like Harold now, 22 years old. Facing the son of a fighter he had knocked out some 14 years previously, Walcott must have reflected on how long he had been in the fight game.

At 22 years old, Harold was 14 years younger than Walcott. The fact that he was so much younger, and hungry, seemed to provide him with a significant advantage. The Philadelphia fighter was no soft touch and considered to be a very good prospect. In just three and a half years of fighting, he had amassed an impressive record of 28–1. His lone defeat was to the vastly more experienced Archie Moore. The fight was promoted by Harry Steinman and was appropriately billed as "Youth Versus Age." It was thus far Harold's most important fight, and was a big step up in competition for the young pugilist. Harold knew a win over the well-known Walcott would vault him into boxing prominence. When asked by the press if he would be making a personal issue of the fight to try to avenge his father's defeat, Harold said such a thing never occurred to him.

The year 1950 started off with a lot more rumors of a possible Joe Louis comeback. In a poll taken of 90 sportswriters, 59 believed that Louis would return. Thirty-one believed he would stay retired. The rumors really started to pick up steam when the Brown Bomber reentered the exhibition circuit and knocked out his opponent, Pat Valentino. During an interview after the Valentino bout, Louis was evasive when asked if he would make a comeback. No doubt some of these rumors were discussed at the annual New York Boxing Writers Association dinner held in New York on January 12. It was at the dinner that a very gracious Ezzard Charles was presented with the Fighter of the Year award for 1949 by owner and editor of *Ring* magazine, Nat Fleischer. Ezzard was also presented with the Edward J. Neil memorial plaque, an award given out by the Boxing Writers Association of America to the boxer who was, irrespective of weight class, judged by the membership of the association to have done the most for boxing in the given year.

Even though Walcott had the upcoming fight with Harold, Bocchicchio was thinking ahead. Since their recent overseas tour was such a success,

12 — Sweden, Omelio and Johnny Shkor

and fun, Felix planned another one. He informally agreed to a fight with undefeated (18–0) German heavyweight champion Hein Ten Hoff. Felix and Walcott were anxious to get back to Europe, not just for another fight but because they still had several thousand dollars tied up in a Swedish bank account that they were having trouble getting their hands on. Once there, it would be much easier to withdraw the money and bring it home. The fight was tentatively set for May 7, 1950, in Mannheim, Germany. But first Jersey Joe had to get past a hungry young lion.

At about 9:00 P.M. the "Youth Versus Age" fight was about to begin. The veteran Walcott, who had just turned 36 years old nine days before, shuffled into the ring, a 2-to-1 favorite. Moments later Harold made his entrance as well. Walcott came into the fight weighing 197 pounds. Harold, standing two inches shorter than Jersey Joe at 5'10", weighed in at a rock hard and cut 180 pounds. Both fighters knew this was an important fight. A loss here would almost certainly derail Walcott's dream of another title shot. A win would place him near the top of a short list of the contenders that were considered worthy of a title fight. Likewise an upset win over the highly ranked Walcott would help Harold get a shot at Joey Maxim's light-heavyweight title.

After receiving their pre-fight instructions from referee Dave Belofl, the bell rang to start round one. Harold came out of his corner fast and went straight at Walcott. He surprised Jersey Joe with his aggressiveness. The younger fighter took the first round with sharp jabs and solid right hands that caught the Camden fighter several times. In the second round Walcott's experience began to tell. The cagey veteran seemed to figure out Harold's style. Jersey Joe began using his signature "Walkaway" move and the "Walcott shuffle" to confuse the young fighter. He stepped back, drawing Harold in and caught the youngster several times with vicious rights that shook Johnson up. Nevertheless, Harold kept coming forward and was willing to mix it up with the stronger fighter. During one of their many exchanges in round two, Walcott dropped his young opponent with a sharp counter left hook for a count of three.

The third round was much the same as round two. Both fighters were willing to mix it up and were battling on even terms. After a particularly brisk exchange, Walcott danced back four or five feet in an attempt to draw his younger opponent into a sneaky right hand. Suddenly, to Jersey Joe's surprise, and everyone else's, Harold collapsed to the canvas without being hit. His face was a mask of pain as he lay on the ring floor clutching his back, unable to rise. The crowd, assuming that Harold had been knocked down, shot to its feet. It soon became apparent that it was not a knockdown at all, since Walcott was several feet away from Harold at the time of the collapse. Doctors and ring officials hurried into the ring as they realized that Harold was seriously injured and in a lot of pain. The young boxer lay on the canvas for ten minutes writhing in pain while being examined by state athletic commissioner, John "Ox" Dagrosa, and ringside doctors. Eventually a stretcher was brought in and Harold was rushed to the nearby Presbyterian Hospital. Once at the hospital, Dr. Joseph L. Levy examined the prostrate fighter and took over a dozen x-rays. The x-rays revealed that Harold had suffered a serious injury to the vertebral disc located in the small of his back. The injury was so bad, in fact, that there was some talk that it could end the up-and-coming fighter's career.

During a post-fight interview, shortly after Harold was rushed to the hospital, Walcott said that he thought the injury was caused in the second round when Harold twisted his back as he went down from a left hook. Following his interview, Commissioner Dagrosa announced that both fighters would have their purses held pending an investigation. "I'm sure that there was nothing irregular in the fight," said Dagrosa.[9] "But just to be on the safe side I'll talk it over with all concerned," he added.[10] The next day, after a short hearing, both fighters were cleared of any foul play and their purses released.

As for Harold, despite talks that his back injury may be career threatening, he went on to make a full recovery. Although it took nearly a year before he could climb back into the ring, he went on to enjoy a long and successful boxing career, one that saw him win the N.B.A. light-heavyweight title and the light-heavyweight championship of the world. He retired in 1971 and was inducted into the International Boxing Hall of Fame in 1993.

Only a few days after his fight with Harold, Walcott agreed to take on a tough Cuban fighter named Omelio Agramonte for a March 3 tilt at Madison Square Garden. Omelio, a wild swinging fighter with a good punch but little finesse, hailed from the mean streets of Camaguey, Cuba, where he worked as a carpenter and learned how to box. When he was a young boy, his favorite sport was baseball. "I was the good baseball player," Omelio said.[11] And sure enough, he could play center field fine and was a good hitter, too. He added, "Only I figured out I hit better in the box."[12] Indeed, Omelio did hit better "in the box." He had scored 25 knockouts in 35 wins. He may have been a bit crude, but he was a hungry fighter and hungry fighters are always dangerous. Omelio knew that fighting Jersey

12 — Sweden, Omelio and Johnny Shkor

Joe was a huge opportunity. A win would catapult him into the top ten and bring big-money fights.

The upcoming fight between Walcott and Omelio was not the first time these two met. In 1946 they sparred several rounds during an exhibition match. In fact, Agramonte expressed some anger during the buildup to their fight when Walcott claimed to have knocked him out during the sparring session, while wearing heavily padded 16-ounce gloves. Omelio fiercely responded to Jersey Joe's claim. "She's never happened," he growled in his broken English.[13] Omelio continued, "That Walcott, he's put me down but I am up again and finish the box. At the finish he is having so much trouble as he can handles."[14] Omelio then shook his massive fist and added that this time it would be Walcott on the receiving end, saying: "A man that old should be retired. He should be leaving the box to younger and better men. Walcott says he is 36. At 36 he is, the legs can't be what she used to was."[15] Omelio then vowed that he would retire old Jersey Joe Walcott for good.

While in training for Omelio, Walcott, and Bocchicchio received a message from Benny Baum, the American agent for the German fight promoters that represented Hein Ten Hoff. The message said that it would be impossible to meet the financial demands that were initially agreed upon. Felix wired back that the fight would be called off if the original terms were not met. Initially, Walcott was to be paid 40 percent of the gate with a minimum of $17,500 guaranteed, $2,500 for traveling expenses and $3,500 for training and living expenses. A few days later, Felix and Walcott met with Baum in New York in an attempt to work out the fight's money issues. Baum was instructed by the German promoters to offer a $15,000 guarantee plus traveling expenses for a party of five and free training. Since this meant that Walcott would make a few thousand dollars less than originally agreed upon, Walcott and Felix were not happy. As far as they were concerned the fight was off for the time being.

During the trip to New York, Walcott stopped by the famous Stillman's Gym, one of the most legendary gyms of the golden age of boxing. It was run by owner and fight trainer Louis Ingber, better known as Lou Stillman. Stillman, a former beat cop and detective, became involved in the fight game shortly after World War I when he began managing Stillman's Gym; eventually he became the gym's owner. Patrons that came to the gym assumed that Lou's last name was Stillman and greeted him as Mr. Stillman. After a time Lou became fed up with having to correct people so he legally changed his last name to Stillman. Lou was famous for keeping his gym as unsanitary as possible. He allowed the public to smoke in the gym and NEVER opened the windows or cleaned the hardwood floors. Even when heavyweight Gene Tunney wanted to train at Stillman's for his 1927 fight with Jack Dempsey, Lou refused to open the windows. Lou's response to these conditions was that he kept the place like that for the fighters' own good, since if he cleaned it up they'd catch a cold from the cleanliness. Lou was also famous for being moody and mean. He carried a loaded .38 revolver in open display and was not afraid to throw a boxer or visiting celebrity out of his gym. Despite its grimy conditions and the abrasive personality of the gym's owner, some of the greatest fighters of all time trained at Stillman's, such as Jack Dempsey, Joe Louis, Willie Pep, Rocky Marciano, Rocky Graziano and Primo Carnera. While visiting Stillman's, Walcott spent some time with Freddie Beshore. Freddie, who owned the title "Heavyweight Champion of the Battleship New Jersey," a title he gained during the war, was in training for his upcoming title fight with Ezzard Charles. Walcott and Freddie hung out for a while as the press took photos of Jersey Joe holding the heavy bag while Freddie pounded away.

Meanwhile over in England, Jack Solomon was busy promoting the rematch fight for the British heavyweight title between Lee Savold of New Jersey and Bruce Woodcock of England. The winner was hoping to face Joe Maxim and the winner of that fight was rumored to possibly face Joe Louis. The N.B.A. had Ezzard-Beshore. Jack Solomon had Woodcock-Savold for the British version of the heavyweight title and the I.B.C. headed by matchmaker Al Weil had Walcott-Omelio. The 20th Century was no doubt planning some kind of tournament to crown its own champion. With all the different heavyweight fights going on, particularly fights for different versions of the heavyweight title, it's no wonder that the heavyweight division was in a state of growing confusion.

Jersey Joe made his return to the square circle at Madison Square Garden on the night of March 3, 1950. It was Walcott's first appearance at the boxing Mecca since his disputed loss to Joe Louis on December 5, 1947. The event turned out to be somewhat of a homecoming, since Philadelphia was practically Jersey Joe's home and most of the 8,000 fans were there to cheer for the New Jersey fighter. When interviewed shortly before the fight, Walcott said he hoped to use the Agramonte fight to keep his comeback momentum going for a fourth title shot. "Who else is there?" he asked.

Climbing into the ring, the 36-year-old Jersey Joe came in at 198 pounds and was a 3-to-1 betting favorite. Omelio, at 25 years old and 5'11", entered the ring a lean, yet muscular, 183½ pounds. The fight turned

12 — Sweden, Omelio and Johnny Shkor

out to be wild slugfest with seven knockdowns. The headlines in the sports section of the newspapers the next day read "Jersey Joe Mops Floor with Omelio Agramonte." Although Omelio tried, the Cuban looked like an amateur compared to the slick Jersey Joe. Agramonte's punches were wide and he was often off balance. In the first round, Jersey Joe floored the wild swinging Cuban with a barrage of blows for a count of nine. Moments later Walcott dropped Omelio again for a one count. He then floored Omelio for a one count in the fifth round and counts of nine and eight in the seventh round. Having seen enough, referee Jack Watson stopped the fight to save Omelio from further punishment at 2:11 of the seventh round.

In his dressing room immediately following the fight, Walcott started clamoring for a fourth shot at the heavyweight title. He told reporters: "I want Ezzard Charles or Joe Louis, soon. Look, Louis gave me two shots and we made a lot of money. Charles ought to give me another crack. Who else can he fight that could bring a decent gate? If anyone thinks he deserves a shot let's hear from him. If Louis is serious about coming back then I am the guy for him."[16]

Walcott followed up his match with Omelio by jumping right back into the ring just ten days later on March 13. This time he was taking on 6' 4" 216 pound Johnny Shkor, "the fighting sailor." Johnny, a Polish American, earned his nickname during the war when he won the Pacific Ocean heavyweight title while stationed in Hawaii. Shkor's manager, Johnny Buckley, who at one time managed former heavyweight champion Jack Sharkey, hoped that Walcott would elect to slug it out with Johnny. The confident manger said that his fighter was the better and stronger boxer and if Jersey Joe stood toe-to-toe with Johnny, he would get waffled like Joe Louis did. Buckley was referring to the no-decision exhibition match that Louis and Johnny had fought. During the match, Johnny dumped Louis to the canvas in the eighth round during a heated exchange. Buckley also claimed that he offered Ezzard Charles $30,000 to fight Shkor, but Ezzard wanted no part of Johnny. At 29 years old, Johnny was seven years younger than Walcott and by all accounts would be a tough test for the aging veteran.

As it turned out, the fight was no test at all, but for the 3,500 fight fans in attendance at the Philadelphia Arena it was exciting, if only for a few brief seconds. Both fighters came out cautiously in the opening round, feeling each other out. They jabbed and boxed for about a minute. The end came suddenly. Walcott, fighting out of a slight crouch, threw several straight right hands to Johnny's belly. He then feinted to throw a left hand punch to the Baltimore fighter's stomach. Johnny dropped his left to ward off the blow, which never arrived. Instead, Jersey Joe shot over a fast overhand right that landed flush on Johnny's exposed chin. The newspaper the next day described the punch as "picture perfect." The force of the blow instantly knocked out Johnny. Shkor, unconscious as he fell, landed hard on the canvas, his head hitting the ring floor with a dull thud. Referee Jack Watson began his count as a visibly stunned Johnny tried to rise but sank back down and out. It was five minutes before Johnny could be fully revived. Officially, the end came at 1:34 of the first round. It was Jersey Joe's fourth straight knockout win since losing to Ezzard Charles. He and Felix were now more vocal than ever about getting another shot at the title.

—13—

Germany and Rex Layne

Three weeks after his one-round annihilation of Johnny Shkor, Walcott saw his dreams of a fight with Ezzard Charles nearly disappear. On March 28, 1950, news broke that Charles had suffered an injury while training for his upcoming fight with Freddie Beshore. The fight had to be canceled. The injury, thought to be a bruised rib, was found to be much more serious; Charles had actually damaged one of his heart muscles. After further examinations and tests, it was reported that the injury might even be serious enough to force Ezzard into early retirement.

Bocchicchio, being a shrewd businessman, quickly laid claim for Walcott to hold the title in the event that Charles was unable to return to boxing. "Who else is there to claim the championship but Walcott?" asked Felix.[1] Walcott's enterprising manager then added that Jersey Joe was "the only heavyweight to go the distance with Charles and has knocked out his last four opponents."[2] Luckily for Ezzard, after going through several more tests and examinations, doctors said he would probably be able to fight again as long as he rested and gave the damaged muscle time to heal. This meant that the champion would be sidelined for at least a few months. Walcott and the other contenders would have to wait to see if the muscle healed and whether or not Charles would be cleared to fight again. The possibility that Ezzard might not be able to return to the ring caused further confusion in an already muddled heavyweight division. For the time being, though, Jersey Joe had a fight in Germany to prepare for.

During the month of April, Felix and Walcott were busy trying to work out the details of their upcoming fight with Hein Ten Hoff. In early April, Felix was expecting an advanced payment of $21,000 to be deposited in a New Jersey bank. The money never arrived. As it turned out, the German promoters were running into a lot of red tape that hindered the transfer of the money. On April 12, Felix sent his representative, George K. Bruns to Frankfurt, Germany, with instructions to accept the best offer available. Bruns met with fight promoter Leo Koenig to try to clear up the confusion surrounding the fight and its financial issues. Koenig was willing to put up a guaranteed $17,000 (some sources report $25,000) as well as $6,000 for expenses. After seeing the written agreement and permission from financial officials that Walcott could collect his advance pay in dollars, Bruns telephoned Felix for approval. Bocchicchio accepted the terms.

It seemed that the fight had finally been finalized. In fact, tickets went on sale April 17. Cheap seats started at $4 and became progressively more expensive with ringside seats going for $16. But just about a week after tickets went on sale, reports came out that the fight might possibly be moved to Stuttgart, Germany. As a matter of fact, the American fight promoter who was working with Bocchicchio, James Friedman, said under no circumstance was Walcott going to fight Ten Hoff in Mannheim. Friedman said he was going to stage a fight in June at Stuttgart's Neckar Stadium, featuring Jersey Joe and an unnamed opponent.

Other reports were saying that Walcott might try to dodge the fight altogether and stay in the U.S. because of a possible title fight with Ezzard Charles, or Joe Louis. Indeed, Bocchicchio even went as far as to confirm that talks with Louis had been going on for months. Promoter Koenig denied the claims that Walcott would "dodge the fight" and said that he had spoken with American representative Bruns and that Walcott had already booked plane reservations to Germany on April 24. Koenig further added that he was backed by Heinz Schneider, president of the Wurttemberg-Baden-Hohenzollern-Pfala Boxing Commission. Schneider said, "Walcott either fights Hein Ten Hoff at Mannheim May 28, or he never fights in Germany." Philip Lorber, an American attorney representing Koenig, also warned Walcott's representative at a conference that Koenig held a valid contract for the bout that must be honored. When Bruns did not disagree from this view, the fight was indeed on. It would be Germany's first big international boxing match since the war. The official date was May 28, 1950.

With the fight details finally worked out, Jersey Joe was ready to go to Germany. For this trip he decided to bring his 17-year-old son, Arnold Junior, who was no doubt excited to be going. Walcott arrived in Hamburg at Rhine-Main Airport on May 9, 1950. A U.S. military escort awaited the fighter and his group. Following his arrival, Walcott and his party made a quick motor tour through downtown Frankfurt, then journeyed to Mannheim where the 427th Army Band greeted them with a stirring

13 — Germany and Rex Layne

"There'll Be a Hot Time in the Old Town Tonight." This was followed by a meeting with the mayor of Mannheim, Paul Riedel, who extended Walcott his best wishes. Joe and his group then made their way through the large group of people who had gathered for the ceremony and drove over to their hotel in Heidelberg.

Wasting no time, Walcott was up early the very next morning. He did several miles of road work through the numerous Heidelberg hills. After a short nap, Walcott, along with Felix and their American promoter, spent the rest of the day scouting for a suitable spot to set up a training camp. Jersey Joe was shown two possible sites. One of them was the Ice Arena, the other a facility in the small town of Schwetzinger, about nine miles southeast of Mannheim. After two days of scouting, Walcott chose the town of Schwetzinger, and officially opened training camp the next day.

Walcott started his daily workouts at 7:00 A.M. His early morning runs took him near the beautiful flower-covered gardens located next to the famed fourteenth century Schwetzinger Castle. After a five-mile run, Jersey Joe returned to camp to begin the sparring phase of his workout. There was only one problem: Team Walcott had no sparring partners. Jersey Joe was promised, by the German promoter Leo Koenig, that several experienced sparring partners would be provided, but none showed up. To try to find some sparring partners, announcements were sent out via a loudspeaker to the large crowds that gathered to watch Jersey Joe work out. Although there were hundreds of spectators that showed up daily to watch Walcott work out, by quitting time of the third day there were still no takers to be a sparring partner. The situation grew desperate. A few days later, several fighters were rounded up that were willing to work with Walcott, although none of them seemed overly anxious to get in close and mix it up with the hard-hitting American. The first fighter Felix could find was a fast middleweight from France named Robert Charron; the second fighter was Sherman (Sandy) Overton. Sherman was a member and light heavyweight champion of the United Sates European Command, better known as EUCOM. Two brave GI sluggers from constabulary units also volunteered to do their best as sparring mates for Jersey Joe. Another man agreed to spar with Walcott for 25 marks a round. But after going a few rounds with the hard-hitting American, he demanded double that amount, which he received. After three more rounds, he left camp and was not seen again.

Although two of the sparring partners were decent, Walcott still needed to get some top-notch professional fighters to spar with. Plans were soon made to import a couple of skilled fighters from Sweden, but before it came to that three professional heavyweights from Germany were found. The three fighters were just what Joe needed. He began sparring two rounds with each fighter every day and impressed the hundreds of spectators that gathered each day with his speed and power during these sparring matches. Jersey Joe also retained the services of Robert Charron and Sherman Overton and boxed a few rounds with each of them daily as well. After his sparring sessions, Jersey Joe had a medicine ball tossed at his mid-section several dozen times while he shadow boxed. Following the medicine ball, Walcott worked the speed bag and heavy bag. Occasionally when punching the speed bag, Walcott would get sand in his eyes. This was because sand from a sand-filled burlap bag, which rested atop the speed bag platform to help steady it, would occasionally seep through and rain down on to Jersey Joe's face. Following his bag workouts, Walcott spent several minutes skipping rope and then doing push-ups and sit-ups. He would then get a rubdown and take a warm shower.

After his daily workout was done, Jersey Joe spent some time each day writing letters to his five children who remained at home. He would write one letter a day to each of them. At the end of the week, he would mail them out. Between the letters and regular phone calls, he was able to keep a close eye on his family's activities back home in Camden. The rest of Jersey Joe's free time was taken up with promoting the fight, making guest appearances and visiting American soldiers who still remained in Army installations and hospitals. On May 19, Walcott was a guest of honor at a review held at the 28th Transportation Battalion at the Turley Barracks in Mannheim. On May 20 Jersey Joe threw out the first pitch to open the 1950 EUCOM baseball season in a game between the Heidelberg Hawks and the Wurzburg Warriors at Mannheim Stadium. The following Sunday Walcott was a big hit with the Heidelberg post's American children, when he addressed a Sunday school class at Providence Church in Heidelberg and spoke about a Mother's Day theme.

Meanwhile, over at the Ten Hoff training camp, all was quiet. The German fighter and his team went onto seclusion in the forest-covered spa town of Bad Durkheim, near Weinhelm. They stayed there for a few weeks until the noise from the town started to bother Hein Ten and kept him awake at night. They eventually relocated his training site to the nearby town of Weinhelm. About the only people that were allowed to see Hein while he was in training were reporters. When asked by visiting reporters about his predictions on the fight, the German champion was silent. His trainer Frank Mueck was a little more outspoken. When he was asked what he thought his fighter's chances were of beating the hard-punching American, Mueck replied, "As I see it the question should be what chance does Walcott has of beating Ten Hoff? I'd say its 50–50."[3] Mueck then went on to say that Hein was in perfect condition and training very hard. He claimed the German champion was perfectly relaxed, since he was taking Finnish sauna baths and falling asleep each night to the sounds of a nearby stream. Apparently Ten Hoff was content to stay isolated at his training camp. In fact, since Jersey Joe had arrived, Hein had made no attempt to meet him. Ten Hoff and his trainers were also a no show at a pre-fight meeting. This mystified the Walcott contingent.

Eventually Walcott and Ten Hoff did meet on May 17, at a spring festival held at Heidelberg Castle. The two were all smiles and very cordial towards one another as they were photographed shaking hands. The 6'6" German towered a full head over the 6'0" American. When asked about the size difference, Walcott said it mattered little, and that he actually preferred fighting taller, bigger fighters, since he had an easier time with them.

As the fight approached, a problem arose concerning the selection of the referee. At first the job was allegedly offered to former light-heavyweight champion and boxing legend George Carpentier. Carpentier claimed that he had a verbal agreement with the Mannheim Boxing Association to referee the match. The Frenchman accused Walcott of "influencing" the boxing association to break the verbal agreement. Carpentier then filed a breach of contract lawsuit for 19,000 German marks. Felix was quick to retaliate, saying that the suit was ridiculous and denied that Carpentier's name had ever been specified in any pre-bout negotiations. As it turned out, the job of referee was eventually given to Arthur Koch just a few days before the fight.

On May 28, the day of the fight, the weather was cold. Gray clouds covered the sky and rain and hail fell all morning. At about noon, both fighters showed up for the official weigh-in. Walcott stepped on the scales first and weighed in at a career high of 201 pounds. Ten Hoff, looking to be in great shape, weighed 219 pounds. Later that afternoon the weather hadn't cleared up at all and it was still cold. At around five o'clock, Walcott entered the ring wearing a heavy white robe with his name inscribed on the back. He reinforced the robe with a thick gray blanket to keep warm and wore slacks over his white trunks to keep the chill off his legs. Moments later Ten Hoff and his seconds climbed through the ropes. The towering

German was likewise covered up to keep warm, wearing a tan robe that was pulled tightly over a blue sweatshirt and matching sweatpants. Both fighters quickly made their way to their respective corners after a brief handshake. Despite the terrible weather, 30,000 rain-spattered fans showed up to witness the fight, although this was about half the number expected by the promoters. Most of the spectators wore plastic raincoats or hid under umbrellas to stay dry. Along with the civilian fans, several thousand American servicemen also braved the rain and came out to cheer for Jersey Joe.

Before the main event got underway several ex-fighters were introduced at ring center, the most famous being former heavyweight champion Max Schmeling. The popular former champion received a thunderous round of applause and loud cheers from his countrymen. Shortly after the introduction ceremonies, the bell sounded to begin round one.

Walcott came out aggressively and landed several hard right hands to the German's face as he moved inside Ten Hoff's longer reach. Hein tried to use his long jab to hold off Jersey Joe, but had little success. Midway through the round, the hard-punching Walcott caught Ten Hoff with a smashing right hand, the same kind of right hand that had floored Joe Louis. The punch broke Ten Hoff's nose and caused blood to drip throughout the fight. Despite the pain and blood, Hein toughed it out and put up a competitive battle in rounds two and three. The giant German was surprisingly agile, as he boxed on his toes and used his longer reach, which was 10 inches longer than Walcott's, to keep Jersey Joe at bay. In the fourth round, Walcott slipped in a neutral corner where spray from the rain had dampened the canvas. Even though a large tarpaulin covered the top of the ring, some of the rain and hail had made it onto the ring floor to make the footing treacherous. The slip seemed to raise Walcott's ire and a moment later he staggered Ten Hoff with a hard right to the jaw. Seeing that his opponent was hurt, Walcott poured it on and started bombing his taller opponent with punches. The 6,000 American servicemen that came to cheer for Jersey Joe screamed "timber" as they waited for the towering German to fall like a chopped-down tree. Luckily for Ten Hoff the bell sound to end the round before Walcott could land a finishing blow.

In round five, the German champion enjoyed his best round. Hein used his longer reach effectively and forced Jersey Joe into a neutral corner, where he landed several hard body blows. After the fifth round, it became apparent that whatever advantages Hein had because of physical measurements Jersey Joe was more than making up for with twenty years of ring experience and savvy. Walcott kept Hein on the run during rounds six and

13 — Germany and Rex Layne

Walcott fights Hein Ten Hoff in Mannheim, Germany, in May 1950.

seven with hard right hands and looping lefts. In the later rounds, Walcott switched his attack to Hein's body and slowed the German down with half a dozen bruising shots to the mid-section. By the tenth round it was all Jersey Joe, as he went all out for a knockout. Using his fancy footwork and "Walkaway" move, Walcott confused Hein and caught him with several clubbing punches and sneaky right hands. Walcott's attack forced Hein to keep moving. At one point the big German slipped to the rain-soaked canvas but was quickly up and retreating. Seconds later, the bell sounded to end the fight. In spite of Jersey Joe's best effort to put the German champion away, Hein managed to finish the fight on his feet. Moments later the official decision was announced that proclaimed Jersey Joe to be the winner. Walcott had won every round except for round five. To symbolize his victory, Walcott was presented with a large wreath that was placed around his neck as dozens of photographers took pictures of a smiling Jersey Joe.

After the bout Ten Hoff smiled broadly among friends in his dressing room while being interviewed. Even though it was his first professional defeat, the big German gained a lot of prestige by going the distance with Walcott. "Joe really hits hard," Hein said, delighted with his performance and happy that he held up in the match.[4] Hein added further evidence that he was tough, saying, "In the first round he broke my nose."[5] When asked what his next plans were, Hein said that he hoped that he had done well enough to be invited to America for some fights.

Over in Walcott's dressing room, Jersey Joe was happy with his victory and had nothing but praise for his German opponent, saying, "He a fine fighter, and should go a long way."[6] However, when asked why he failed to knock out Ten Hoff even though he had the German staggered, Walcott blamed the rain, saying, "The canvas was so slick I couldn't get set."[7]

Immediately following the fight, it was announced that Walcott would face the hard-punching Conny Rux, Berlin's blond boxing idol, at Cologne on July 9. But just days after both fighters agreed to meet, the fight was cancelled. Conny's promoter, Joachim Goettert, cancelled the match because he said he only wanted Conny to perform in Berlin. The reason actually went even deeper than what Conny's promoter had said. Jersey Joe wanted a guaranteed $50,000, all of it up front so he could get his hands on it. "The promoters and I want the fight," said Walcott.[8] However, business was business, so "the $50,000 guarantee is a must," Jersey Joe said.[9] Around this time talks were also underway for a possible match with newly crowned "British and European Heavyweight Champion" Lee Savold. There were several different options available for Walcott at this time, but what he really wanted was another crack at Ezzard's heavyweight title. Since Ezzard's heart muscle had healed and he had been cleared by his doctor to fight again, it looked as though the two boxers would eventually meet.

After returning home to New Jersey in mid–June, Walcott and Felix immediately began working on negotiations for a rematch with Charles. By late June the International Boxing Club announced that they had accepted an offer for a Charles-Walcott fight. And that the word from the Charles camp was that Ezzard was fine with a rematch. Of course, the fight depended on Ezzard getting past Freddie Beshore, whom he already had a fight scheduled with, and Joe Louis, whom Charles was expecting to get a fight with. Ezzard and Louis had nearly concluded negotiation for a match. And Louis was expected to announce his return to the ring within the next few weeks.

The Walcott-Charles fight, although not officially set, was tentatively scheduled for some time around March 1951. This gave Walcott about eight months of time to prepare for the fight. Not wanting to get rusty, Walcott and Felix began looking for a tune-up fight. But first there was another pressing matter that Jersey Joe had to deal with. Walcott had not yet been paid for his fight with Hein Ten Hoff. The German promoters told Jersey Joe that he would receive his money about a week after his return to the United States. The money never showed up.

In July, Walcott flew back to Germany with his son Arnold Junior to help clear up the technical difficulties that were holding up his money. Apparently, the fight promoter never had the German Financial Ministry approve Walcott's purse to be converted from marks to dollars before the fight was held. This was making it difficult to change the money from German marks into American dollars. The sum of $27,000 (some reports say $16,000) was now tied up in a German bank. On the day that Jersey Joe departed for Germany, he said he did not expect to have any difficulty in getting the money, and believed it was just a matter of being present to sign some papers. Felix did not accompany Walcott on the trip since he was not needed and Walcott's lawyer was already there. Instead, Felix stayed behind and continued negotiations for the Charles fight and a possible tune-up fight with Rex Layne. By this time, Jersey Joe was a little tired of traveling. When it was suggested that he should bring his wife and six kids, Walcott sighed and said, "I'm a hometown man myself; I've been traveling a lot lately, fighting wherever I can, but I like it at home a lot better."[10]

Trying to get his money was a lot harder than Walcott had anticipated. On July 21 Jersey Joe met with the German Allied Bank Commission. The commission blocked Walcott from converting the West German marks over to dollars or even taking the money out of Germany. This meant that Walcott would be forced to spend the money only in West Germany. That was the rule for all foreigners earning marks in Germany, said a commission official. Walcott was not happy with the ruling and neither was his American lawyer, Milton J. Teiger. "Joe's gotten a raw deal," said Teiger.[11] The lawyer tried to put a positive spin on the matter, saying: "I think this red tape is merely a temporary setback. I feel confident that when responsible officials examine the facts they will make a justifiable exception in Walcott's case. So far Walcott has got nothing out of his ring victory except a few thousand dollars for traveling expenses and the admiration of German fight fans."[12] After about a month of fighting to get the money, the Allied Bank Commission came to the conclusion that "the fight contract was never submitted to us and I doubt if it was to the proper German officials either. All foreign earnings in Germany are blocked just like Walcott's."[13] Jersey Joe did win one small consolation though; the German commission dismissed an $18,000 damage suit filed against Jersey Joe by the original Walcott-Ten Hoff fight promoter who claimed that Walcott reneged on a previous contract to fight Hein. Basically, it looks as though the whole ordeal may have been a financial bath for Walcott, as the records do not say if Jersey Joe was ever paid or not. Walcott and his son Arnold continued their stay in Europe for about another month. While there, they visited Rome and Walcott once again met the pope. On September 19 Jersey Joe returned to the United States and was soon home in Camden.

Right around the time Walcott was spending time in Germany, his ex-manager, Joe Webster, was filing a lawsuit against Joe and the Camden Athletic Corporation for the sum of $9,500. Webster claimed that the money was back pay due to him for services while he managed Jersey Joe between May 1, 1945, and July 15, 1948. Webster was eventually paid and the suit was settled.

In August 1950 Joe Louis made it official, he would attempt a comeback. He signed to meet Ezzard Charles for the heavyweight title on September 27, 1950. The ex-champion didn't have much of a choice. He was in massive debt and needed the money. He was fighting because he had to. The money he earned would go directly to pay off his tax debt. Louis, now thirty-six years old, had not fought for two years except for exhibitions. His enthusiasm for boxing was gone and he had only six weeks to prepare. Charles saw the fight with Louis as an opportunity to finally prove himself. Since Ezzard had won the title, the public had not fully accepted him as heavyweight champion because he had not won the title from Louis. Ezzard may have been champion, but Louis was still king. Ezzard figured if he beat Louis the public would finally accept him and give him the respect he deserved. He would now get his chance to prove that he was a worthy champion.

On the night September 27, 1950, Ezzard Charles buried the ghost of Joe Louis. The younger, faster fighter won an easy fifteen-round decision over the ex-champion. Louis, entering the ring at 218 pounds, about ten pounds over his prime weight, was too slow and shaky in his timing to catch Charles. The once-feared Brown Bomber did manage to swell up Ezzard's eye, but in return he absorbed a bloody beating and was nearly knocked out in the fifteenth round. It was only out of respect for his childhood hero that Charles held back to allow Louis to finish the fight on his feet. When it was over, an exhausted and bloody Louis cried after the announcer declared Charles the winner by unanimous decision. After his win over Louis, Ezzard was universally recognized as heavyweight champion of the world. But even though he had defeated Louis, his victory did little to gain him the respect he so desperately sought.

On October 27 matchmaker Al Weil announced that Walcott and young 22-year-old heavyweight prospect Rex Layne had agreed to a ten-round bout at Madison Square Garden on November 24. Walcott had found his tune-up. Layne, one of the better young upcoming heavyweights, was born June 7, 1928, in Lewiston, Utah, and started boxing in the Army during the war. During his time in the service, Layne was a staff sergeant with an airborne division stationed in Soporo, Japan. While in Japan, Layne won the heavyweight championship of the U.S. troops in Nippon. When the war ended, Layne returned to Utah. The young man had two choices as far as jobs went. He could continue to follow in his father's footsteps as a sugar beet farmer or pursue a career as a fighter. Eventually Layne chose boxing.

Rex began his amateur career in 1947. As an amateur, Layne dropped a close decision in the Olympic tryouts to Jay Lambert, who went on to win the United States Olympic title. Layne then lost another close decision to Utah State's Dale Panter in the Utah Golden Gloves, but earned a trip to Boston and won the intermountain championship by winning four bouts, three by knockout. In 1949 Rex won the AAU heavyweight championship. Shortly after winning the amateur heavyweight title, Layne turned pro on May 23, 1949. In just a short year and a half, Layne had run up a record of 25-1-2 and was being touted as a real prospect.

The Walcott fight would be the first step into the big time for Rex. The young fighter knew that this was an important fight and a win could get him a fight with Ezzard Charles, so he trained very hard. He did six miles of road work every morning over mountain roads. The young fighter then boxed five rounds each with several fast middleweights to sharpen his reflexes and footwork so he would be prepared for the clever and fast Walcott. To help his young charge get ready for his fight, Layne's manager, Marv Jensen, got hold of the movies of Walcott's two fights with Louis. Together, fighter and manager examined the fights and were confident of victory. Just a few days before his battle, Layne told reporters at his training camp, "I'm ready for Walcott, and I think I can beat him. I know he's tough and a cutie. I've gone over the movies of his two fights with Louis. But don't worry, I won't be frightened."[14]

There is little doubt that Jersey Joe was looking past Layne and took him lightly. Wanting to stay sharp, Walcott took the fight with the stocky, curly-haired westerner as a tune-up for his upcoming fight with Charles. Not thinking much of the inexperienced slugger, Walcott underestimated Layne and came into the fight in less than top shape. Jersey Joe's lack of committed training was disastrous.

On November 24, Walcott came into the ring at Madison Square Garden weighing 200 pounds. This was about five or six pounds over his best fighting weight. Most of the press and knowledgeable boxing people felt that Layne was being grossly overmatched at this point in his short career. As a result, Walcott was a 5-to-1 betting favorite. A small crowd of 5,995 people showed up at the Garden and paid only $19,676 to witness what turned out to be the most surprising upset of the year. The 192-pound Layne earned a hard-fought ten-round decision over Jersey Joe. "I went out to bust his guts," said Layne, "and I guess that's what I did."[15] Layne worked Jersey Joe's body with vicious straight right hands and hard lefts throughout the fight. On several occasions, Layne knocked Joe into a corner or onto the ropes with hooking barrages to the head. In rounds six, nine and ten, Rex had Walcott wobbly and holding on. Walcott, on the other hand, was not at his best. His jabs were not sharp and neither was his vaunted right hand. Walcott did manage to seriously cut Layne's left eye in the first round, which required ten stitches to close. And he landed several hard right hands during the bout, but Layne showed unexpected ruggedness and took the blows with little effect. In the eighth round a frustrated Walcott back-handed Layne and was penalized for the foul. When it was over, the decision was unanimous. Referee Rudy Goldstein had it six rounds for Layne, two for Joe and two even. Judges Bert Grant and Frank Forbs voted in unison, six rounds for Rex, three for Walcott and one even.

Following the fight, an unhappy and exhausted Walcott sat in his dressing room, soaking his bruised right hand in a bucket of ice water. The hand had been injured sometime during the third round when Walcott punched Layne on top of his head. Not very impressed with his conqueror, Walcott had little praise for Rex and said, "He's a rough, strong kid, but he's definitely not a fighter. He's about a year or a year and a half away. It's too bad he got past me, now he'll be in trouble."[16]

Over in Layne's dressing room, the scene was quite different. The young fighter and his manager were happy and excited about their win over the veteran Walcott. Both of them knew that the win would lead to bigger fights. Manager Marv Jensen said, after Layne rested for at least two months to let his cut eye heal, "Then he'll be ready to accept the best deal offered. Whether the opponent is champion Ezzard Charles or any other top-ranking heavyweight, this boy can beat any of them."[17] After his win over Walcott, there were many who believed Marv might be right.

The surprising upset loss to Layne did little to keep Walcott from getting another fight with Ezzard Charles. As a matter of fact, most people viewed the loss as a fluke. Since negotiations had been going on for months and the fight was practically set, plans to get the two fighters back in the ring continued on. But first Ezzard had to get past one more opponent before he was clear to face Walcott: "Loose Leaf" Lee Oma.

Although 1950 ended on a low note for Jersey Joe, a new year was right around the corner. For Walcott, 1951 would prove to be the pinnacle year of his boxing career. His dreams were about to become a reality.

—14—

Winning the Title

"This is my last chance. I've got to win this time or I'm through."
— Jersey Joe Walcott

Ezzard Charles defeated Lee Oma on January 12, 1951, to retain his heavyweight championship. Immediately following the fight, a bitter Cincinnati Cobra was irritated because of the boos and catcalls yelled at him after the fight, and because he felt that he was not getting the credit that he deserved, even after his convincing win over Joe Louis. In truth, Ezzard was not getting the credit he deserved, primarily because he was fighting in the shadow of the great Joe Louis. "I'll keep on fighting and I'll keep on winning and then maybe the people will give me full recognition as champion. Maybe I'll show them more next time," Ezzard said.[1] That next time would be against Jersey Joe Walcott.

Despite Jersey Joe's recent upset loss to Rex Layne, he was getting another shot at Ezzard's title. There were several reasons for this. First, Jersey Joe was a big name and a big draw. Even though Layne had beaten Walcott, Charles could make a lot more money fighting Jersey Joe. Second, Walcott was still a top contender, and most people felt that his loss to Layne was a fluke. At this time, the heavyweight division was a little thin when it came to worthy contenders. Most of the top men like Lee Oma, Lee Savold, Joe Louis, Gus Lesnevich and Joey Maxim were getting old, or had already lost to Charles. As far as the new up-and-comers were concerned, fighters like Rex Layne and Rocky Marciano really needed more seasoning and required a few more big bouts on their resumes before challenging for the title.

The last details of the fight rematch were ironed out at a conference held at the offices of at the International Boxing Club on January 13. The next day it was announced that the second meeting between Ezzard Charles and Jersey Joe Walcott was all set. The bout would take place on March 7, 1951, in Detroit. Ezzard would receive 40 percent of the gate, about $30,000, and Jersey Joe would get the challenger's customary 17½ percent, or about $13,000.

In mid–January, Walcott once again set up his training camp at Grenloch Park. On January 31 "Pappy" Walcott, as the newspapers were frequently calling him, celebrated his 37th birthday. Of course, nearly everyone continued to believe Jersey Joe was much older. Training at the park went as usual until the morning of February 9. Walcott along with trainer Dan Florio and several sparring partners were eating breakfast before the daily workouts began. They were unaware that a fire had started in the building that Jersey Joe used as his gymnasium. Separated from the gym by a building, Walcott and his team were unable to see the blaze. They became aware of the fire only after hearing the approach of loud sirens. Apparently a passing motorist, seeing that the building was on fire, had called the local fire department. By the time Jersey Joe and his group raced out to investigate, it was too late. The gym was engulfed in flames and the sky was filled with black smoke. All Walcott and his team could do was watch helplessly as the fire department fought to get the fire under control. After the fire was extinguished and an investigation was done, it was found that an overheated stove used to warm the gym that morning had caused the fire. Wilson J. Thorp, one of the park's owners, estimated the damage at about $15,000 along with $2,500 for the boxing equipment.

With the gym and his training equipment destroyed by the fire, Walcott had no place to train and no equipment to train with. Luckily for Jersey Joe, the firefighters that put out the blaze were fans, so the fire captain offered Jersey Joe the use of his spacious firehouse as a temporary gym. Walcott and Bocchicchio accepted. After making a trip to New York to purchase some new boxing equipment, Walcott and several firemen put together a makeshift boxing ring and Jersey Joe was soon sparring as usual. "Now we will have a boxing show every day, you can't beat that," said one of the firemen.[2] For the next four weeks Walcott worked out at the firehouse. Not wanting to be one-upped, the local Camden police station also offered Walcott their gymnasium to work out in. Jersey Joe didn't want to play favorites, so he spent a week sparring at the police station and entertaining the police officers. After five weeks of preliminary training, Walcott and his team headed for the Motor City on February 26. Ezzard had already arrived on the 25th.

Although his fighter was preparing to fight Walcott and could very well lose, Charles' manager Jack Mintz was looking ahead. He had Ezzard's next few fights already mapped out and was working on putting the details together. First up would be Joey Maxim, and then possibly Rex Layne. But what the champion really wanted was a final showdown with Louis. In fact, Ezzard was upset with the Brown Bomber for talking down to him. Ever since Ezzard beat Louis in September 1950, the ex-champion had been making little cracks about Charles. The Brown Bomber said that he had fought a lot of fighters that were better than Ezzard. He placed Ezzard number six on his personal top ten list, behind Billy Conn, Max Baer, James J. Braddock, Max Schmeling, and Tommy Farr. Incidentally, Louis put Walcott even further down on that list at number eight, right behind Primo Carnera. Louis also said that he was sure he could whip Ezzard if they fought again, especially if he could get to Charles early.

It wasn't just Louis' words that angered Ezzard. He was also upset at the lukewarm reception he continued to receive as heavyweight champion. He wanted to retire Louis so that people would accept him as a worthy champion, saying, "I thought Joe would retire after I beat him the first time; now it looks like I'll have to do it again."[3] Indeed it looked like Ezzard would get a second chance to face Louis, as plans were under way for a potential rematch in April. Of course, a loss to Jersey Joe would put an end to Ezzard's plans and maybe Louis' as well.

After he arrived in Detroit, the bulk of Walcott's training was comprised of sparring sessions. More specifically, he worked on developing a new style. In a pre-fight interview at his training site the challenger said, "I'll have to fight straight and tag Charles if I'm going to beat him. I've been working hard on developing a new style and I think my surprises will do the trick."[4] Walcott said he was in far better shape than when he faced Ezzard the first time. He added that he was definitely in better shape than when he had fought Rex Layne, saying, "I took Layne too lightly and didn't train properly. I was up to 200 (pounds) and should have been 194."[5]

On March 1, Walcott and Charles, accompanied by their managers, were examined by Dr. Joseph Cahalan, physician for the Michigan State Boxing Commission. Both fighters were found to be in great shape and the exam went smoothly until the two fiery managers became involved in a loud verbal argument along with state athletic commissioner Floyd Stevens. Mintz wanted to be provided with a list of the possible fight officials so he could conduct a private investigation of them. Felix wanted the officials to be picked from a hat "to be fair to the commission, fighters, and public."[6] Stevens, finally fed up with the argument, told the managers that he would personally pick the officials and that they wouldn't be announced until an hour before the fight. Angrily, the two managers parted with their fighters in tow.

At noon on March 7, the two fighters weighed in. Both looked to be in excellent condition and were in high spirits. Jersey Joe was a svelte 193 pounds, the lightest he had been in four years, and looked rock hard. Ezzard was a fit 184 pounds. The odds on the fight favored Ezzard 4-to-1. The oddsmakers felt that Charles was too young and too fast for the aging veteran. They saw no reason why Walcott would do any better than he did two years earlier. However, not everyone thought Charles would win. Joe Louis predicted a possible Walcott upset: "Walcott has just the stuff to upset the dope wagon. He hits much harder than Charles, which I know from experience. He knocked me down three times and Charles never even staggered me. Walcott's good right hand could catch the champion off guard."[7] Likewise, during the weigh-in ceremony, Bocchicchio predicted that his fighter would knock out Charles. He then told reporters that the International Boxing Club "can forget about a Joe Louis-Charles rematch for the championship because Walcott is going to be champ by Thursday, by a knockout."[8] Walcott agreed and predicted that he would knock out Charles within seven rounds. Said Felix, "That's no idle boast. Walcott knows that he must shoot the works and win by a knockout."[9] Ezzard on the other hand said he would concentrate on outpointing his opponent instead of going for a knockout. "I know the fans are clamoring for a knockout but I figure I will keep my title by out boxing him."[10] Ezzard then pointed out that the New Jersey fighter was a much tougher opponent than indicated, but that he was still confident of victory.

Surprisingly, as the fight neared, the people of Detroit started showing a lot of interest and tickets really began to sell. Some believed the reason for the attention was that the Detroit fans were eager to witness the prowess of the fighter that had defeated their hometown idol, Joe Louis. Others believed that the Detroit fans wanted to witness Walcott avenge Louis' defeat by knocking out Charles. Whatever the case, Lew Cromwell, the box office boss for the Olympia Stadium, reported just a few days prior to the fight that ticket sales had exceeded the $50,000 mark and "if the weather stays good we should sell out."[11] Although the fight didn't sell out, ticket sales were high and a crowd of 13,852 showed up and paid $75,502. This was despite the fact that the bout was broadcast on television, radio, and places such as Rose's Tavern where a person could go and watch the fight on what was then a huge 20" television while enjoying authentic Italian food like spaghetti, ravioli and Italian tomato pizza pies.

When Jersey Joe Walcott climbed into Detroit's Olympia Stadium ring at about 9:45 P.M., he made history. He had the distinction of being the first fighter ever to get four tries at the heavyweight title. Most people figured it would be his last chance. Some felt that because of his loss to Rex Layne he didn't even deserve it. As with his fight with Louis back in 1947, several sportswriters felt that "Pappy" Walcott was too old. They even went as far as to give him a new nickname, the elderly sounding "Father of Camden." Little did the sportswriters realize that despite his age Walcott had plenty of gas left in the tank.

The rematch turned out to be similar to their first one for the first three rounds. The two master boxers came out and circled each other, throwing sharp jabs. For the most part, it was a tactical battle with occasional flurries of punches. When they got close, they would hold and pound away on each other until the referee pulled them apart. Walcott tried feinting and using shoulder movement and his "Walkway" to try to sucker Ezzard into sneaky right hands. But the Cobra wasn't falling for any of Jersey Joe's tricks and boxed cautiously. Even though both fighters were wary, the fight did offer up some great action.

In the fourth round, Walcott nearly toppled Charles off his throne when he landed a sneaky fast right hand on the Cobra's chin that buckled the champion's knees. Ezzard was hurt and immediately started holding, at which point the two fighters pounded away on each other's head and body. After his head cleared, Charles let go and danced away with Jersey Joe in hot pursuit. Walcott threw a left hook that Ezzard blocked and the two fighters clinched again and fought at close quarters in a neutral corner. Referee Clarence Rosen separated the fighters and Charles danced back on his toes. Walcott, fighting more aggressively as per his plan, walked right into Ezzard and blazed away with lefts and rights. His willingness to walk straight into battle brought the crowd to its feet, cheering loudly. The challenger caught Ezzard with a looping left hook and two rights, and then crashed another left into the side of the champion's face. The punches were thrown as hard as the challenger could throw them and wobbled Charles for a second time in the round. Seeing the champion momentarily shaken, Jersey Joe let the punches fly, throwing lefts and rights, some landing, some missing. The punches again wobbled the champion and again Charles was forced to clinch. He clung to Walcott for the last sixty seconds of the fourth round and managed to survive.

After the shaky fourth round, Charles got very cagey and boxed more carefully and gradually regained control of the fight in rounds five and six.

The champion boxed beautifully and forced Walcott back with his rapier-like jab, and hard body blows. Ezzard continued to outbox Walcott in the seventh but the round turned ugly as both fighters resorted to low blows, hitting on the break, throwing elbows, and head butting. In the eighth, the fight slowed to a crawl as the two fighters circled, jabbed, and looked for openings. The fans, obviously not impressed with the display of cautious boxing, booed loudly throughout the round. Thankfully the ninth round offered up a lot more excitement. After again starting off cautiously, the champion caught Walcott with a powerful right to the head, followed by a left hook to the jaw that knocked Jersey Joe down. Seriously hurt, Walcott remained on the canvas for a count of eight to give his head time to clear. He then rose to his feet, barely making it up before the referee said ten. It was so close in fact that Ezzard's handlers screamed that Walcott had been down for ten seconds and should be counted out. The referee yelled over to the champion's corner, assuring them that Walcott had regained his feet in time.

Once Jersey Joe was up, Ezzard was all over the challenger trying to end the fight. The champion opened up and scored effectively at close

Jersey Joe (left) takes a trip to the canvas courtesy of a punch thrown by Ezzard Charles in their second fight in March 1951.

range with short punches to the body and head. It looked like Ezzard was starting to wear down Walcott with his steady attack. But Jersey Joe had been in this type of situation before and knew how to survive when hurt. It took all of his savvy but Walcott managed to make it out of the round before being stopped. Despite nearly being knocked out in the ninth, Walcott got his second wind and battled back in the tenth. He landed a hard right to Ezz's left ear about halfway through the round. Immediately the ear began to swell up and drip blood. Jersey Joe kept things fairly even in rounds eleven, twelve and thirteen. In the fourteenth, Charles nearly floored Walcott again when he caught the challenger with a right to the jaw that sent Jersey Joe staggering into the ropes on rubbery legs. Seconds later, before the champion could take full advantage of his stunned opponent, the bell came to Walcott's rescue. Jersey Joe came out for the fifteenth round determined to put Charles away; he nearly succeeded. Despite being hurt in the fourteenth round and the fact that he was 37 years old, Walcott was surprisingly fresh. He belted the champion with a couple of hard rights to the chin, followed by a left hook that obviously hurt Ezzard. Walcott then went on to knock Charles around the ring for most of the round with lefts, rights, and upper cuts. Several times he had Charles in trouble, but he was unable to put the champion down. The action of the round had the fans on their feet cheering for Jersey Joe. Charles, abandoning his slick boxing, chose to stay close and slug it out with Walcott for the last thirty seconds. The fight ended with both fighters throwing punches as the crowd cheered loudly.

Jersey Joe had tightened things up by coming on strong late in the fight and winning the fifteenth round. But it was too little too late. Referee Charles Rosen had it 80 to 70 for Charles, Judge Jack Aspery had it 84 to 66 for Charles and Judge Joe Lenahan had it 83 to 67, all in favor of the champion. The Associated Press scored it 8-5-2 for the champ.

After hearing the decision, most of the 13,000 fans roared their disapproval. They booed for a full six minutes. Felix, mad as hell, stormed all over the ring, yelling, "We wuz robbed! What must we do to get a decision? It's the third time he has been robbed."[12] As Walcott and his handlers left the ring, the fans gave Jersey Joe a terrific round of applause and booed the champion Ezzard Charles as he made his exit. Likewise Joe Louis, who had sat ringside, was given a massive standing ovation as he made his way out of the arena. When asked what he thought about the fight, Louis merely shrugged his shoulders and said he would be glad to fight Charles again.

Back in his dressing room, Walcott complained about the decision and felt that he was again robbed. "I landed the cleanest punches," said the unhappy challenger.[13] "I just don't know how they could score it that way," he added before vowing that he would keep fighting until he won the title.[14]

Across the hall, the champion iced his blood-engorged ear. Charles' handlers couldn't understand why the crowd booed. Mintz thought Charles won easily. Ezzard's only comment on the jeers was, "I'm used to that."[15] Although claiming that the loud booing didn't bother him, it was obvious that it did. The Cincinnati Cobra wore a sad expression and went on to say: "There were fewer boos this time than when I beat Lee Oma so that's a good sign. I'm catching on as champion. The more I win the more the fans will get used to my being champion and then the cheers will follow."[16] He added that Walcott had given him a tough fight. "I thought he was done when I put him down in the ninth but the Jersey man has a lot of fight in him. His punches hurt but I never felt in danger of going down," Charles said with a smile.[17] Charles insisted that he was certain of victory at all times, even in the fourth and fifteenth rounds when he was hurt.

Following the fight, the champion was taken to a Detroit hospital to have his swollen ear looked at by Dr. Ray Clark. An examination revealed that Charles had suffered a ruptured blood vessel as well as a ruptured eardrum. The swelling to his ear was so severe that he had to have it lanced open so the blood could be drained out. A few days later Ezzard's co-manager, Tom Tannas, said, "The champ is OK but he'll have to give the ear time to heal before he does anything else."[18] Ezzard was ordered by his doctor to let the ear heal for at least two months. This meant that the proposed fight with Joe Louis in April would not happen. The Brown Bomber was extremely disappointed since he was expecting to fight Charles and was in great shape, having trimmed down to 207 pounds. Once the ear healed, Charles said he would face anybody the I.B.C. offered, including Louis.

The fight was an unexpectedly heroic effort from Walcott and virtually guaranteed him a fifth crack at the heavyweight title. As a matter of fact, two days after the fight, president for the International Boxing Club Jim Norris said that the managers for Louis and Charles were at such a wide disagreement on terms that a Charles-Louis match would be impossible before September. Mintz wanted 40 percent of the gate while Marshall Miles, Louis' manager, wanted a 50–50 split. However, Norris said that Walcott certainly deserved another fight with Charles after his tremendous showing against the champion.

Not sure if they were going to get an immediate return fight with Ezzard, Walcott and Felix went into negations on March 10 for a rematch with Rex Layne, who was fresh off his win over Bob Satterfield. There were also some talks about Walcott facing Lee Savold, who held the British version of the heavyweight title. Jersey Joe was also offered a June match in Germany to fight Hans Neuhaus. But Felix wound up turning down these fights when it became apparent that Walcott and Charles would fight again, as long as Charles got past Joey Maxim in April. With the fight all but signed, Walcott relaxed a little and spent some time training his 10-year-old son, Vincent, who had aspirations of following in his father's footsteps as a fighter.

On May 30, Jersey Joe was in attendance at the Chicago Stadium for the Ezzard Charles–Joey Maxim fight. After watching Charles' decision over Maxim in fifteen rounds, he immediately flew home the next day to begin preparations for his third fight with Charles.

On Thursday, June 7, 1951, Walcott and Charles, along with their managers, met in Pittsburgh to sign the official contracts for their title fight. Because of traffic, Walcott and Felix showed up an hour and a half late; otherwise the signing went as usual. The fight would be held at Forbes Field on July 18, the first heavyweight title fight ever fought in Pittsburgh. It was quickly realized a few days later that the fight date coincided with that of Rex Layne's fight with Rocky Marciano. The Layne-Marciano fight date was eventually moved back to July 12. Since Layne had failed to secure a fight with Walcott, he accepted one with undefeated up-and-coming Marciano. It was a big mistake for Layne. Rocky knocked out Rex with an overhand right that sheared off four of Layne's upper teeth and sent his bloody mouthpiece flying into the crowd.

After the signing was concluded, Walcott expressed his belief that he would beat Charles: "I just hope Ezzard starts to tear in and rip away. Ezz is a great champion. But all I hope is that he fights me the way he fought Maxim. If he bears in, well maybe there'll be a new champion because I'm ready for him."[19] Ezzard, perhaps not in a talkative mood, simply said, "It's just another fight."[20] The next day when the fight was officially announced, tickets went on sale starting at $2.95 for general admission. Ringside seats were a bit more expensive at $25 apiece.

Walcott went into serious training for his unprecedented fifth shot at the heavyweight title, in early June at a training site located in Pleasantville, New Jersey. One report went as far as to say that if Walcott lost again he would be the most successful failure in boxing history. He spent a total of three weeks training at Pleasantville. Then on June 29 he and his team left New Jersey and drove to McKeesport, Pennsylvania, where a reception awaited the fighter. The group then drove over to a local drive-in movie theatre located at Rainbow Gardens. The spacious theatre grounds offered plenty of parking, a makeshift boxing ring, and seats for spectators. Walcott began training in earnest on July 2. Just a few days after training began, a local boy named Jimmy Slater began hanging around Walcott's training camp. Walcott was Jimmy's favorite fighter. The boy showed up every day to watch his hero train. He even accompanied Walcott at times on his morning runs and the two became fast friends. A day before the fight, Jimmy gave Walcott a lucky rabbit's foot and Jersey Joe promised to take Jimmy to dinner if he won the title.

Much like in Germany, Team Walcott ran into problems getting quality heavyweight sparring partners and had to resort to using local talent, mostly middleweights. However, Walcott's handlers told visiting reporters not to worry about Jersey Joe's condition. Bocchicchio stepped in and said, "Joe's fit right now. We've been trying to get Joe some good sparring partners and still may get some, but there's no sense in putting on actual fights and running the risk of cuts or other injuries. And we don't want to leave the fight in the training camp. That's happened often enough to good fighters. Joe is no kid and he knows best what he needs and how hard to work."[21] Jersey Joe agreed. "I feel great," exclaimed the confident challenger.[22] "I hope to wear the crown. I don't know what round I will knock Charles out but I know I will be trying in the first. If it takes all fifteen rounds I'll still be in there punching."[23] He sparred four rounds with Pittsburgh middleweight Art Swiden, went five fast rounds with two other sparring partners, and polished off the day's drill by skipping rope and working the heavy bag.

After watching his fighter, Felix thought Jersey Joe looked exceptionally sharp, too sharp in fact. "He looks too fine," Felix said to the interviewing reporters.[24] He planned to have Jersey Joe take a few days off until after the Fourth of July holiday was over, saying, "It's a long way off until July 18 when he meets Charles and a short rest will do him a lot of good."[25]

Across town at the champion's training camp, Ezzard's trainer, Ray Arcel, said they were ready for Walcott and any cute tricks he tried to pull. Mintz was a little less optimistic, saying, "If it wasn't for the promise made in Pittsburgh about a good match, we'd never meet Walcott again, he is the toughest of the challengers."[26] Grumbled Mintz, "But Charles wants to fight him, so here we are."[27] When asked what his fight plan would be, the champion said he really had no plan and conceded, "I really don't know how I'll fight Joe until after that opening bell sounds."[28]

Up to this point, talk between the camps had been polite. But just a few days before their showdown, gossip between the two camps began to heat up. Word got back to Ezzard's camp that Walcott had said that he was robbed of decisions on two occasions when he had fought Charles. Ezzard shot back that he had beaten Walcott twice before and had him in trouble and had him down in both fights: "If he's going to pop off like that I'll be sure and kayo him early in the bout. If I have to knock him out to prove my two previous decisions weren't phonies then I'll do it. But regardless, I'll win."[29] Jersey Joe fired back, "If he carries it to me I think he'll change his mind pretty fast. I had him in serious trouble the last two times we met."[30] Joe added that he intended to be more aggressive and wanted a quick knockout so there would be no doubts about his legitimacy as champion.

The morning before the fight, both fighters were examined by E.C. Krug, the Pennsylvania boxing commission physician. Krug announced that both men were in excellent condition and added that the 37-year-old Walcott was in better shape than most men 10 to 15 years his junior. Following the examination, Charles stepped on the scale and weighed a trimmed-down 182 pounds, four pounds less than the last time he had fought Walcott. Jersey Joe came in at a ready 194 pounds.

It was a superbly conditioned Ezzard Charles that "Pappy" Walcott climbed into the ring with on the night of July 18, 1951. A record turnout of 28,272 fans showed up at Forbes Field to see if the old guy could pull off the upset to win the most coveted crown in sports. To accomplish his goal, Walcott would have to defeat a prime champion. At 30 years of age (his birthday was eleven days earlier), Ezzard was at his best and making the ninth defense of his title. Walcott again made history by fighting Ezzard. This time he broke his own record for attempts at the heavyweight title, this being his fifth try. Also, at 37 years old, he was the oldest man to ever challenge for the heavyweight title. The great father of Camden was given little chance to defeat a prime Ezzard Charles; the odds against his victory were as high as 7-to-1.

At home in Camden, Walcott's six children gathered around the TV at about nine o' clock and prepared to cheer for their dad. Lydia, being too nervous to watch, only caught bits and pieces as the fight unfolded. It started off like a typical Walcott-Charles fight. The two fighters came out jabbing, circling, and looking for openings. Each fighter had a healthy

14 — Winning the Title

respect for the other's counter-punching ability and didn't want to get caught, so both were wary. As they circled each other, both sent out fast stinging jabs to the head and body, after which they would usually come together, clinch and fight on the inside until the referee broke them apart. At times, Jersey Joe would tap his gloves together before initiating an exchange of punches. He won the first round by landing the harder blows and being the more aggressive fighter. Round two was a continuation of one, with the fighters circling, jabbing, and clinching.

In round three, Walcott started to come on and was even more aggressive than he had been in the two previous rounds. He landed the harder blows, including several digs to the champion's body and bloodied Ezzard's mouth. Ezzard managed to nail Walcott with an overhand right. But a second later Jersey Joe smashed his own right into the champion's jaw. The two clinched and referee Buck McTiernan separated them. Walcott finished the round by landing a couple of body blows as the bell rang. Walcott got the better of the champion in round four, especially during the infighting, by landing some good body shots and upper cuts. Both fighters landed

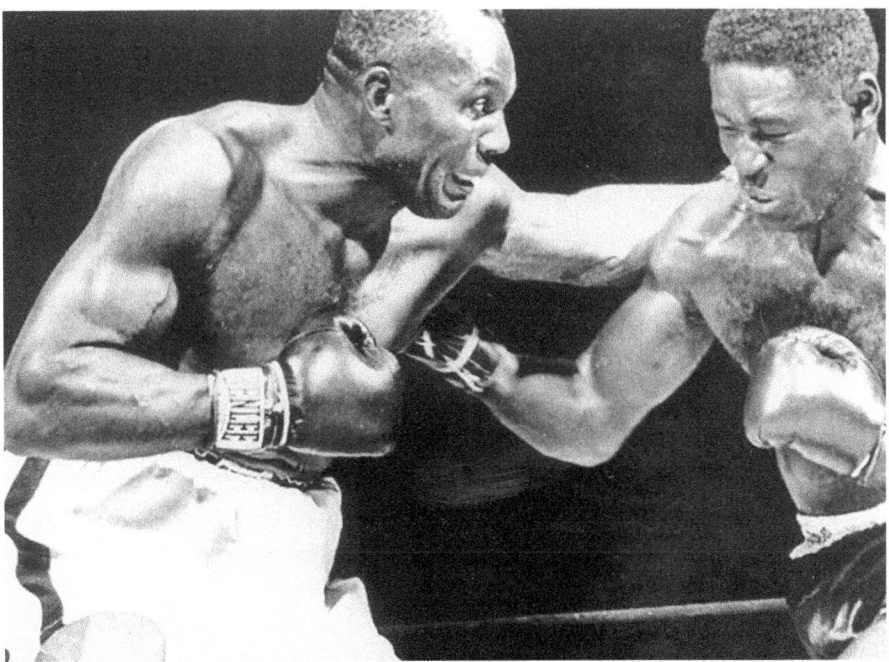

Walcott battles Ezzard Charles (right) in action from their third fight in July 1951.

hard punches during round five, particularly with their right hands. Ezzard was a little more aggressive and effective with his jab and kept Walcott off balance and backing up.

Round six started slow but the challenger stepped up the pace and was the aggressor. He forced the champion to give ground. Walcott looked to land his right hand and missed the first two that he threw. For much of the round, the two boxed and clinched. Jersey Joe tried several times to land sneaky left hands but the champion blocked or avoided most of the blows. Walcott managed to land one right hand that caused the champion's right eye to swell. Charles tried for a late-round rally, but Walcott nailed him with two jolting lefts to the jaw just as the bell sounded. It was a good round for the challenger, who was now ahead on two of the three judges' scorecards while even on the third.

The two fighters came out for round seven, circling, firing jabs, and then clinched. Referee McTiernan quickly separated the two. Walcott tapped his gloves together as Charles came in swinging. The veteran Walcott easily blocked the champion's punches as the two clinched in a neutral corner. The referee again separated the two fighters and Ezzard danced back on his toes out to the center of the ring. Almost casually, Walcott walked after the champion. The moment Charles stopped bouncing back he shot out a quick jab that Walcott easily avoided. Jersey Joe then countered with a perfectly timed left hook/uppercut into the right side of Ezzard's chin. The punch was devastating and landed with crushing force. All the strength and power of Walcott's muscular shoulders was behind the blow. The champion crashed to the canvas face first as cameras began flashing by the dozens and the crowd rose as one with a mighty roar. Walcott's first thoughts, as Charles fell, were "Thank God, this is it."[31]

Referee McTiernan waved Walcott to a neutral corner. He then got on his hands and knees next to the fallen champion and began counting loudly. Ezzard had been motionless on his stomach for about five seconds. At about the count of nine, Ezzard miraculously willed himself up. But his punch-rattled brain couldn't control his body. He stumbled backward, landing in a neutral corner. Charles was counted out at 55 seconds into the seventh round. Jersey Joe Walcott was the new heavyweight champion of the world!

A second later the ring exploded into chaos as the referee helped the dazed ex-champion to a sitting position. In an instant, Walcott was surrounded by police officers, trainers, boxing commissioners, ringside physicians, managers, the press, friends and relatives. Felix and Florio did their

14 — Winning the Title   145

best to protect their fighter from the growing mob of excited people by pushing the crowd back. Walcott, overcome with emotion, fell to his knees in his corner. The new champion gave thanks to God for giving him the strength to win the fight. At that moment he remembered the words that his father had spoken all those long years ago, the words that he had carried in his heart since he was a boy: "Let me tell you one ting, if this boy gets the right trainer and manager he could become a champion."[32] As Walcott recalled his father's words, tears of happiness streamed down his face and he said to his father, "We did it, Dad, we did it."[33]

Moments later, surrounded by a group of policemen, the new champion and his team pushed their way through swarms of people to get to their dressing room. Once there, the scene was pandemonium. There was shouting and screaming and everybody, including Walcott's sisters and brothers, was hugging and pounding the new champion on his back as camera bulbs flashed. Dozens of excited reporters waited to interview Jersey Joe along with the mayor of McKeesport, Charles Kinkaid, who had fought his way through the throng to congratulate the winner.

Choked up and nearly unable to talk, with tears and sweat still running down his face, Walcott told reporters, "I want to be a fighting champion and a credit to the ring. I tried for twenty-one years for this night. Now I feel like I'm 16 years old. I read my Bible before every fight and I prayed between every round. I asked God to help me."[34] In response to the question of the punch that felled Charles, Walcott replied, "It was a left hook that did it, just a left hook and no follow up."[35] As to how he felt after winning the title, Jersey Joe said, "I feel fine, I was never hurt, I knew I was in command right from the start. I could have gone fifteen rounds, I could have gone and gone and gone."[36] The new champion then phoned home and spoke to his excited wife and children. Walcott quickly found out that all the neighbors and the press were at his house and were sharing in the excitement with his family. When asked by the press what she thought about the fight, Walcott's 12-year-old daughter Ruth summed it up best when she said, "We knew it all the time."[37] After hanging up, Walcott told reporters, "I sort of knew I would win. I knew this was going to be my night."[38] And indeed it had been.

Over in the devastated ex-champion's dressing room, the scene was quite different and a lot more subdued. A crestfallen Ezzard Charles sat with his weeping wife and told reporters, "All I remember was the count of five," he moaned. "I never saw what hit me. Then I was getting up, and that's all. I'm terribly disappointed. I can't believe it, I just can't believe it."[39] When asked if he thought the punch that Walcott had knocked him out with was a lucky one, Ezzard said, "No, it was no lucky punch that he caught me with. He was in there to win."[40] The Cobra then went on to say, "I don't know what it was tonight but he seemed more aggressive than ever. He was taking chances with haymaker punches and leaving himself wide open but I couldn't seem to do anything about it. I guess I was waiting for later when he would tire out."[41] Charles then looked over at Mintz and asked, "Did they really count me out?"[42] Mintz sadly nodded yes.

Winning the title from Ezzard Charles was one of the most truly amazing accomplishments in sports history. The victory was in the cherished American tradition where the poor boy gains fame and fortune through perseverance and clean living. It was a true rags-to-riches story, perhaps more so than any other, and one of the greatest upsets in boxing history. After 21 grueling years, Jersey Joe Walcott had finally triumphed!

—15—

Bringing the Title Home

When Jersey Joe Walcott won the heavyweight title in July 1951, there was only one heavyweight champion and one heavyweight title. The championship was still something very special and according to sportswriter Red Smith was "the most glittering bauble in sports."[1] To possess it meant that you were the greatest fighting man on the planet and one of the most recognizable figures in the world. The man that was fortunate enough to win the coveted crown was bestowed with fame, fortune, prestige, and glory. The heavyweight champion was royalty and occupied the ultimate position atop the sports world. There were few, if any, that could rival his fame. Sadly, in modern times, the once great boxing crown has lost nearly all of its luster. The modern championship is a poor representation of the once great title. Nowadays, there are several third-rate fighters running around with numerous heavyweight championship belts, each one claiming to be "the heavyweight champion."

Following Walcott's win over Charles, Felix booked the ballroom on the 17th floor of the William Penn Hotel, where they had been staying during training camp. The new champion and his friends celebrated the victory late into the night.

In the early morning hours, Walcott was finally able to get to bed secure in the knowledge that he possessed the greatest prize in sports. His nap, however, was brief. After only two hours of sleep, Felix, Dan and several reporters were knocking on Walcott's hotel door. Although he was tired and a little sore from the fight, Jersey Joe welcomed the interruption and was eager to begin his day. After all, he was the new heavyweight champion of the world. And as the new champion he had things to do, places to go, people to see, and promises to keep. As he prepared for his day and answered questions from the reporters, he and Felix started going through the dozens of congratulatory telegrams that had arrived during the morning. One of the first ones Jersey Joe read was from ex-champion Joe Louis: "Congratulations, it was a great fight. Wishing you continued success."[2] By the end of the day the telegrams numbered in the hundreds.

Jersey Joe's first stop was a visit to Ezzard Charles' hotel room. The new champion and the ex-champion sat and visited for a while as they were interviewed and photographed. Walcott and Felix then drove over to their training site at Rainbow Gardens, where hundreds of fans waited to greet and cheer the new champion. Among the fans was Walcott's young friend Jimmy Slater. Jimmy had watched his hero win the title and had fashioned a crown out of paper that read "Champion" across the front. The boy presented Walcott with the crown and placed it on the new champion's head as cameras photographed the happy moment. Walcott then signed autographs and he and Felix filmed a short interview. During the interview, Walcott demonstrated the punch that he had used to knock out Charles.

After the interview Walcott and Felix headed over to Mayor Charles Kinkaid's office where the champ was presented with the key to the city of McKeesport and made the honorary mayor for a day. From there, Walcott and Felix traveled 160 miles to Harrisburg, Pennsylvania, where Jersey Joe had a prior commitment to speak at the Elks lodge. Thousands showed up to hear the new champion speak and to congratulate him. With the visit to the lodge done, Jersey Joe motored back to McKeesport, where he made an appearance at a minor league baseball game. He gave another speech, finishing it up with, "I hope I'm the same guy you used to know."

After his appearance at the baseball game, the champ then drove over to Jimmy Slater's house along with a full police escort. The young boy ran out excitedly saying, "Gee, champ, thanks a lot for coming out to see me."[3] As promised Walcott took Jimmy out to dinner that evening. It had been a very busy day for the new champion, a day that he compared to the grind of a training camp. Later that evening as he was being interviewed again, for about the tenth time, Walcott said he was eager to get home to see his wife, six kids, and all his friends.

The new champion arrived home at the Camden Airport at 4:15 P.M. on July 20 to the cheers of more than 5,000 excited fans. The crowd chanted "Welcome home champ" as Walcott exited the airplane and posed for a battery of news photos.[4] Jersey Joe's wife Lydia and his six children waited among the fans. As the police pushed the crowd back, Walcott was able to greet his happy family and embrace them. With the police pushing back the excited mass of fans, the Cream family along with Felix piled into a

Walcott, the new heavyweight champion, receives a homemade crown from his young admirer Jimmy Slater (left) in July 1951, as manager Felix Bocchicchio (right) looks on. (AP Photograph)

large green Cadillac convertible. They drove over to City Hall followed by an eleven-car motorcade surrounded by police on motorcycles. The drive took about thirty-five minutes. Along the way more than 100,000 people (some reports estimate 200,000) from all over New Jersey, Philadelphia, and surrounding areas lined the streets of Camden to watch the new champion drive by. The scene was carnival-like as vendors circled the crowds of people selling "Jersey Joe Walcott buttons" and "Jersey Joe Walcott golden cups" at anywhere from $.50 to $1.00 and everyone was eating peanuts and popcorn out of big red bags that read "Welcome home champ."

Mayor George E. Brunner, who had attended the fight in person and had arrived home only a few hours before, awaited the champ at City Hall along with thousands of fans. As soon as Walcott arrived, a crowd of people patted him on the back as they surrounded him, asking him to say some-

Jersey Joe enjoys the victory parade in his hometown of Camden, New Jersey, after winning the heavyweight title in July 1951. (AP Photograph)

thing or just yelling and howling. When the excited crowd finally settled down, Walcott spoke. In a rather hesitant voice, obviously overwhelmed by it all, he thanked God for his victory and repeated what he had said in Pittsburgh about trying to be a worthy champion. He then said to the crowd, "Thank you, thank you." Mayor Brunner then proclaimed the day Jersey Joe Walcott day! The crowed went nuts and cheered their hometown hero. Shortly thereafter Walcott was in the mayor's office. Mayor Brunner gave Walcott an official welcome home and presented him with the key to the city. It had been another incredibly hectic day for Jersey Joe, but eventually he made it home. He spent the remainder of the evening with his family and some friends and finally was able to get a full night's sleep.

Jersey Joe Walcott slipped into the role of heavyweight champion easily and he proved to be a very popular champion. The press delighted in painting a picture of Walcott as a dedicated family man, a religious man, and a devoted husband. To attest to his popularity, Joe received hundreds of letters a week from fans all over the world. The champion did his best to answer them all, especially the ones from U.S. servicemen stationed in Korea during the Korean conflict of the early 1950s.

Just a few days after winning the title, Walcott had amassed about 25,000 letters from clergymen, priests, rabbis, and heads of organizations concerned with youths. Most of the letters asked the new champion to make an appearance and bring the message of clean living to young people. Apparently, these people and groups viewed Jersey Joe as a formidable weapon against juvenile delinquency. Walcott agreed and wanted to make as many appearances as possible.

There was only one problem with making those appearances. As quickly as one day after the fight, there were talks of a rematch. By August 1, negotiations were under way. Ezzard's managers wanted an immediate return as stipulated in the contract, which said the champion was required to give Charles a rematch within ninety days. Ezzard, anxious to regain his title, insisted that the contract be honored. Walcott and Bocchicchio were in no hurry and wanted to wait until next summer. Bocchicchio gave several reasons why he wanted his fighter to wait to defend his title. First, he said that Walcott needed time to make some of the thousands of requested appearances so that he could deliver the message of a clean life to the nation's youngsters. Second, Bocchicchio said that a champion should only defend his championship once a year, to make each defense a classic. He believed that the twenty-five defenses made by Joe Louis and the nine made by Charles "cheapened the title."[5] Third, a delay would permit Walcott time to cash in on the hundreds of offers for exhibition fights and refereeing jobs that were being offered. "Joe and wife Lydia and their six kids could use some fast money to build a nest egg for the future," Bocchicchio emphasized.[6] Of course, none of these reasons went over too well with the Charles camp, as Mintz pointed to the contract that provided for a return fight by October 16.

The discussions continued at the headquarters of the International Boxing Club. On August 2 it was finally decided, after much arguing, that Walcott should be given time to cash in on the fame and fortune that the title could provide. Jim Norris and Ezzard's co-managers, Mintz and Tom Tannas, were all in agreement that Walcott would be allowed to postpone his first title defense until June or July in 1952. "We're not trying to cut anyone's throat here," said Mintz.[7] "If we try for Walcott to fight within 90 days we would be putting promoter Norris in the middle. If Charles suffered an injury or ailment a week before the fight, Norris would be out a lot of promotion money and we would be out of training money."⁸ Instead, Charles and his team would seek another match, maybe with Louis or Marciano, while Walcott was on tour. Jersey Joe was now free, for the time being, to enjoy the crown and the glory that came with it.

After hearing the reports that Walcott would not immediately fight Charles, Joe Louis turned soothsayer. It was reported on August 9 that Louis predicted Walcott would be a sorry man if he waited to defend his title. The ex-champion said that Walcott would not be able to stay in condition without some fights under his championship belt, and that he would suffer for it.

Beginning in early August, Walcott began an exhibition and guest appearance tour that took him all over America. First off, he made several guest appearances, beginning with a stop at a sandlot-title baseball game at the Polo Grounds in New York. The champ then made stops at the Philadelphia Naval Hospital and Valley Forge General Hospital, where he spent several hours visiting and cheering up patients. The following Sunday he was a guest speaker at a church in Norristown, Pennsylvania. Walcott then attended the Louis-Bivins fight at Memorial Stadium in Baltimore on August 15. A few days later, Jersey Joe was refereeing a ten-round welterweight clash between Johnny Saxton and Tommy Clario. On the 17th Walcott officially began the "fight exhibition" portion of his tour in Marshalltown, Iowa, where he fought a four-rounder with sparring partner Jackie Burk of Brownsville, Pennsylvania. His next stop was the Toledo State Juvenile Home on Saturday the 18th. Walcott handed out pins with his picture, shook each boy's hand and spoke of clean living and trust in God. On the 21st Walcott and Burk were back in Philly putting on another four-rounder in front of several thousand fans. By the 25th Walcott was in Louisville, Kentucky, refereeing the grudge match between wrestlers Wild Bill Logson and the mighty man of the Ozarks, 260-pound Ray Eckert. The champ then boxed four fast rounds with Burk. Tickets for the wrestling show were $3 for ringside and $2 for general admission. Tickets for the Walcott portion of the show were $.50 more, with the additional charge going to charity.

For the next several months, Walcott's hectic schedule pretty much followed the same pattern. The champ made dozens of guest appearances, which included refereeing, visiting churches, fighting exhibitions, speaking on the radio and appearing on television. On October 19 the champion took a break from touring and drove to New York along with his manager, trainer, and family. He was the guest of honor at a luncheon put on by the

An emotional Jersey Joe Walcott receives the heavyweight championship belt from Nat Fleischer in 1951.

New York Boxing Writers Association and Nat Fleischer, the president of the association and editor of *Ring* magazine. Nat presented Jersey Joe with the official *Ring* magazine heavyweight champion belt. Reflecting on the years and all the struggle it took to win the belt, Jersey Joe was overcome with emotion. He wiped away tears of happiness as he put the belt on.

While Walcott was on tour and enjoying being "the champion," events were unfolding in the world of boxing. On October 10 Ezzard Charles made his return to the ring against Rex Layne, in the very same Pittsburgh ring where he had lost his title. The Cobra scored an eleven-round technical knockout in what was called an unimpressive victory. After the fight, Charles said that he wanted a few more bouts before facing Walcott again. On October 26, Rocky Marciano knocked out Joe Louis at Madison Square Garden and ended the Brown Bomber's comeback and career. The knockout was sensational and had the boxing community buzzing about a Walcott-Marciano match. Bocchicchio, being a shrewd businessman, knew that a fight with the undefeated Rocky would make a ton of money, so Felix moved quickly. By November 2, Bocchicchio was in talks with Jim Norris about a possible bout in February against Marciano instead of the previously agreed upon match with Ezzard in June. Norris quickly reminded Felix that Charles had a contract and was next in line to fight Walcott, so he would not attempt to bypass Charles to give the first chance to Marciano. Norris then added that Charles' co-manager Tom Tannis would gladly oblige a February fight in place of a June match but would absolutely refuse to step aside for Marciano. For now, Rocky would have to wait. As Jim Norris said, talk of a Marciano-Walcott match was just wishful thinking by Bocchicchio.

On January 17, 1952, at a dinner at the Waldorf-Astoria Hotel, Walcott was again a guest of honor. He was awarded the Edward J. Neil plaque for 1951. Walcott earned the plaque for having contributed the most to boxing during the year, with his upset win over Ezzard and for his crusade against juvenile delinquency. Along with Jersey Joe, two other sports figures were recognized for their outstanding achievements. The first was amateur sensation Gil Turner, who won the prize of rookie fighter of the year. The second was former New York State Athletic Commissioner Eddie Eagan, who received the James J. Walker Memorial Award for his six and a half years of meritorious services to boxing. During the ceremony Walcott gave a speech. When asked when he would defend his title, he said he had no plans to fight until at least June and did not know for sure who his opponent would be. These remarks got back to the ears of Bob Christenberry, head of the New York State Boxing Commission. The Commission quickly targeted Walcott by saying that everyone connected with the commission was "burned to a crisp" at Walcott's words.[9] Christenberry made it public that he expected to have Walcott on the New York carpet shortly after his 38th birthday on January 31. He also made it very clear that if Jersey Joe did not agree to a title defense soon, he would be stripped of his title and banned from boxing.

In February Bocchicchio was back in the offices of the I.B.C. to discuss Walcott's future plans with Jim Norris. Felix was angling to make as much money as he could from Walcott's first defense and wanted a $250,000 guarantee from the I.B.C. He told Norris that he was offered a quarter million dollars by Harry Hunt, a Los Angles promoter, to fight Harry "Kid" Matthews in Las Vegas. Felix then threatened to take the fight. After the half-hour meeting, agreements had not been reached and both parties were upset. A few days later Felix and Norris were at it again. This time Norris reported that he and Felix were closer to an agreement but were certainly not done negotiating. "We're certainly no further apart," said Norris.[10] Norris told reporters that he thought a Walcott-Ezzard Charles match was the only possibility. "I don't blame Felix for trying to get all the money he can get. We're still talking, taking up different propositions. Sometime this week we have to reach a deadline. Mr. Christenberry, Chairman of the New York State Athletic Commission is serious about the mid–February deadline he set for Walcott to sign."[11]

It took two more meetings, four in all, before Felix and Norris eventually came to an understanding. The simple fact was that no matter how much Felix tried to finagle or how much step-aside money he offered the Charles camp, Walcott would have to fight Ezzard before they were free to take on one of the other top contenders. By February 16 it was official that Walcott would defend his title against Ezzard. The stage was set for a June match.

On April 1, Walcott and Charles met in Philadelphia to sign the contract for their fourth meeting. The bout was scheduled for June 5, 1952, at Philadelphia's Municipal Stadium. At the signing, Ezzard was confident that he would be the first fighter to succeed in winning back the title. The former champ said that all the other champions that had tried were too old and usually hadn't fought in a few years. He wasn't in that fix and was only 30 years old. Since his last fight with Jersey Joe, Ezzard had kept himself sharp by having three fights. The ex-champion had also added a little weight, he was up to about 192 pounds, and felt great. Walcott and Florio, on the other hand, were happy as well and expressed the opinion that the added weight would slow Ezzard down.

A couple of weeks before the fight, all was quiet as the fighters dedicated themselves to serious training, Charles at Pleasantville, New Jersey, and the champion in Atlantic City, New Jersey. It was reported that both fighters looked good in training. And even though Walcott was 38 years old and had not fought in nearly a year, he was "punching sharply, stepping lively and his endurance seemed endless."[12] When asked by a visiting reporter if he had learned anything about Charles in their last fight, Walcott replied, "He doesn't like a left hook."[13] The calmness of the camps was broken when Felix and Mintz, as usual, got into an argument. The feud traced back to the last fight when Bocchicchio then protested that there were too many officials from the Pittsburgh area, Mintz's native hometown. This time they argued over who would referee the fight. Bocchicchio wanted Joe Louis to referee the fight; Mintz wanted a list of referees and wanted to personally screen them and then let the boxing commission know which ones he did not want to have as officials. The commission calmed the two feisty managers and assured Felix that it would even things up this time.

Both fighters wrapped up their training on June 3. One of the last reports said that that despite his age and year-long layoff, the champion looked terrific during his last workout and was indeed a miracle man. "It's really surprising," said veteran journalist George Barton of the *Minneapolis Star Tribune*. "He appears to be just as good as he was a year ago. He's just as sound and just as fast and seems to be hitting just as hard."

At about noon on June 5, the two fighters officially weighed in. Walcott tipped the beams at 196 pounds. This was one pound more than he wanted to weigh. Ezzard came in at a career-high of 191½ pounds. The odds on the fight favored the younger challenger. In fact, most experts felt that Charles would be the first ex-champion to regain the crown. Former lightweight and welterweight champ Barney Ross predicted Charles would win back the title saying, "Old Papa Walcott can't keep bouncing around on the same old legs forever."[14] Likewise, ex-light-heavyweight king Tommy Loughran predicted a Charles victory.

Before 21,599 fans at Municipal Stadium, the two boxers resumed their rivalry. They met face-to-face at ring center. Referee Zack Clayton, a former basketball player for the Harlem Globetrotters and the first African American to referee a world heavyweight title fight, gave the instructions. Just a moment later the fight began.

The long-awaited rematch turned out to be a typical Walcott-Charles boxing match, which meant for the most part that both fighters were cautious. The newspapers described the bout as tame, although at times the action was brisk, particularly during the first half of the fight. Walcott managed to stagger Ezzard in the second, third, fifth and ninth rounds. In return, Ezzard hurt the champion on more than one occasion as well, staggering Jersey Joe in the twelfth and bouncing him off the ropes several times during the thirteenth round. But neither fighter could score a knockdown, or follow up an advantage. Charles suffered cuts over both his eyes and a cut under his right eye that required three stitches to close. He also suffered bruises above each cheek. The champion, having taken a solid right from Charles in the twelfth, bled from his nose during the last three rounds, but was otherwise unmarked.

When it was over, Jersey Joe was pronounced the winner. Referee Zack Clayton had it 9 rounds to 6 for the champion. Judge Buck McTiernan scored it 8 to 7 Walcott. Judge Pete Tomaso had it 7 to 6 with 2 even for Jersey Joe. Of the 41 sportswriters polled after the fight, 24 voted for Ezzard and 17 for Walcott. As the scoring showed, it had been a close fight. And many observers felt that Charles deserved the nod. If he had been a little more aggressive, he would have certainly gotten it. The Walcott supporters, however, pointed out that the Cincinnati Cobra had failed to "go get him," especially in the last few rounds when Walcott rallied. McTiernan may have summed it up best when he said, "You can't take a man's title away on such a close fight as that."[15] In general, most people were divided about 50/50 as to the outcome of the fight, but the decision was basically seen as fair.

Shortly after the fight in the champion's crowded dressing room, Jersey Joe expressed happiness over the decision victory to the dozens of reporters that huddled around him. "I really was glad I won a decision instead of a knockout. I planned to win a decision and that's what I did. Naturally I wanted a knockout if I could get one but I knew that a decision would be more satisfying. It proves that I'm really Charles' master, not a guy with a lucky punch. I hope this fight proves to the world that I'm the rightful heavyweight champion. People have been asking if I was lucky in Pittsburgh. Some didn't even ask, they just said the old man landed a lucky punch. They ought to know better now."[16] Walcott then posed for photos with his arm around his good luck mascot, 11-year-old Jimmy Slater. Walcott hadn't forgotten about his good luck charm. He had Jimmy and his family come over from McKeesport and gave them ringside seats to the fight. As the cameras flashed, the questions continued. When asked if Charles ever hurt him during the fight, Walcott said, "When you get hit they all hurt. Charles is a good fighter and a good, hard puncher. He doesn't kiss you when he hits."[17] In response to another question, the champion said, "I was never in any trouble at any time. I thought I had him all the way."[18]

Meanwhile over in the challenger's dressing room, Charles was expressing his dissatisfaction at not regaining the title. He was deeply disappointed, but did not criticize the officials. "I thought I had it won but they didn't vote for me, so I have no alibis. I'm just another fighter now," he said, adding, "Maybe I'll never get another chance. I guess I've had it."[19] Ezzard Charles couldn't have been more wrong.

With the Charles fight out of the way, Team Walcott was now free to pursue any fight they wanted. Walcott's next one would prove be a classic. At an age when most fighters had long since hung up their gloves, "Old Pappy" Walcott was about to fight the greatest fight of his career, a titanic give-and-take battle that would go down in boxing history as one of the greatest-ever heavyweight title fights.

—16—

Walcott-Marciano I: The Build-Up

If 1951 was the defining year of Walcott's career, then his fight with Rocky Marciano in 1952 was his defining fight. Just a few days after his successful defense against Ezzard Charles, it was reported that Walcott would put up his title against the winner of the Marciano-Mathews fight. On July 28, 1952, Marciano crushed Mathews in the second round with two left hooks. The win prompted Marciano to say, "I'm ready for Walcott. I can lick anybody that I step into the ring with."[1] Jersey Joe, who attended the fight, said afterwards, "He's a pretty good puncher, a hard puncher. But I thought that Mathews was careless. I hope we can get together."[2] The next day, negotiations were underway for a Walcott-Marciano clash. The International Boxing Club, Al Weil, and Bocchicchio were really pushing this fight. Everyone involved knew that it was big money and predicted the gate could reach a million dollars. Since the heavyweight division was currently at a low spot, the International Boxing Club felt that this fight with the popular young knockout artist was just what boxing needed to spark fan interest.

Former heavyweight champion Gene Tunney put it perfectly when he said that boxing needed someone to give it a boost, "The ring loves new faces. Rocky has a new tough face and a touch of ring greatness."[3] Tunney went on to say that Marciano hit harder with two hands than any fighter he had ever seen, including Jack Dempsey. Gene predicted that Rocky would defeat Walcott. Dempsey himself eventually got around to giving his prediction on the fight, saying it would be a good one, and that it could be another Dempsey-Firpo. The fight that Jack Dempsey was referring to was one of the most exciting heavyweight title fights in history; a wild two-round brawl that had eleven knockdowns, with Dempsey being knocked completely out of the ring, landing on typewriters and members of the press, in round one. Jack refused, however, to predict who would win. Former lightweight champion Lew Tendler predicted that Walcott would win by a knockout inside of six rounds, saying, "Walcott will upset the odds and his younger opponent."[4] Former heavyweight champion Joe Louis also predicted that Walcott would knockout Marciano within six rounds, stating, "Walcott is smart and tricky and has a good left hand with which Marciano can be hit."[5]

While ex-champions were making predictions and fans were eagerly awaiting a fight date, negotiations were moving along slowly. As usual there were disagreements from managers, promoters and boxing commissioners. For the most part, the arguments were over money, and where the fight would be held. Jim Norris and promoter Herman Taylor were offering Bocchicchio 40 percent of the gate and wanted to have the fight in New York. But Bocchicchio was playing hard ball, insisting on 45 percent of the gate and wanting the fight to be held any place other than New York. Apparently, because of his past criminal activities, Felix was not licensed to work as a fight manager in New York. Furthermore, the New York State Boxing Commission said it would not issue Felix a license. This meant Bocchicchio would not be allowed in his fighter's corner on fight night. Angered, Felix refused to have a fight if he were not allowed in Walcott's corner. The feisty manager then threatened to pull out of the negotiation and take Walcott on a European tour unless another location was found.

On August 12 the I.B.C officials and fight managers gathered once again to continue talks as to where the fight would be held and how the money would be divided. Although it was not yet official, the newspapers were reporting that the fight would be held in Philadelphia on September 23. In fact, both Walcott and Marciano had already started to train. Rocky opened up shop at a new training site, an airplane hangar located at Grossingers, in the Catskills region in New York. Jersey Joe began his preliminary training at Pleasantville, New Jersey. He later relocated to Bader Field in Atlantic City and trained in the same building that Jack Dempsey had once used as his training headquarters.

Finally by mid–August, after weeks of tiring meetings and long discussions, everyone came to their senses and agreed upon the terms and location of the fight. It was officially announced on August 18 that the I.B.C and the fighters' managers had come to an agreement at Herman Taylor's summer home in Atlantic City.[6] The fight would be held at Philadelphia's Municipal Stadium on September 23, 1952. It was the same stadium where Jack Dempsey and Gene Tunney had battled it out in front of 120,757 fans who paid over $1,800,000 to see the action. The champion would receive 40 percent of the gate; the challenger would get 20 percent. Each fighter would also receive a percentage of television, movie, and radio rights. The official signing for the fight followed two days later at the office of Mayor Joseph S. Clark, Jr., where both fighters posted the $5,000 bond to guarantee that they would show up and give a faithful performance.

Jersey Joe's partner in this dance of destruction was Rocco Francis Marchegiano, otherwise known as Rocky Marciano, the Brockton Blockbuster. Rocky, an Italian-American, was born on September 1, 1923, and grew up in Brockton, Massachusetts. As a boy, Rocky was active and enjoyed sports. He excelled at both football and baseball, even going as far as to try out for the Chicago Cubs as a catcher in 1947. Unfortunately for the young man, he wasn't good enough to make it in the big leagues. But he soon found out that he had another talent, boxing. At the relatively advanced age of 24, Rocky got his start in the fight game. At first he was so crude and clumsy that nobody gave the young pugilist a second look. However, it was soon realized that the 5'10½" 190-pound slugger was extremely strong and carried dynamite in his fists. As fate would have it, Rocky came under the guidance of master trainer Charley Goldman, an ex-pug with a crooked nose. Over the course of the next few years, Charley would mold Rocky into a great fighter. In fact, Marciano would become Goldman's greatest creation.

To begin, Charley taught Rocky the fundamentals of boxing and how to punch correctly. The tough old trainer also helped Rocky develop his crouching, bobbing and weaving style of fighting. It was a style that was necessary since Rocky had a reach of only 67". Because Rocky's arms were too short to box effectively at long range, Goldman trained Rocky on how to slip his opponent's punches so he could get close. Once inside his adversary's reach, Rocky would pound away with sledgehammer blows and ripping uppercuts. It mattered little to Marciano where his punches landed, just as long as they landed.

The one thing Goldman didn't tamper with was Rocky's natural leverage and punching power. The stocky, short-armed, thick-legged heavyweight was able to infuse a tremendous amount of power into his punches. Guided by Charley's expert teaching, Rocky improved with every fight and developed some underrated boxing skills. The young slugger also became one of the most destructive hitters in heavyweight history. His punches were so hard that he broke blood vessels in one opponent's arms and sheared off four teeth in another fighter. By the time Walcott and Rocky met, the Brockton Blockbuster had amassed an impressive record of 42 wins, with 37 knockouts and no losses. His destructive fists left knockout victims all over Rhode Island and New York boxing rings.

Despite the fact that Marciano had built an impressive record and was a feared puncher, Jersey Joe didn't think much of Rocky's abilities. At the official signing of the fight, Walcott, usually the most respectful of gentlemen, started to talk a little smack. "Rocky is an overrated fighter. He isn't as good as they make him out to be, and he doesn't hit like they think, though he does hit pretty good," Walcott said, adding, "He's always coming at you; I won't have to look for an opening. It will be one of my easiest fights."[7] Later in the month the smack talk continued as the two fighters exchanged boasts. Walcott said that he planned to open up in the fight and be aggressive and that he would pitch and Rocky would catch. Rocky came back with: "I hope he doesn't lose his nerve. Hope he really means to make an aggressive fight. If he does he will be playing my game. Let him pitch one of his wild throws and I'll knock his head off pegging back to second."[8]

The talk continued through the build-up for the fight, with the champion saying that he had fought several fighters who had styles similar to Marciano. "Years ago I fought three who were like Marciano. They were 'Wild' Bill Kent, Pat Roland, and Al Blake. I handled them without trouble." When asked if he thought that any of the fighters he had fought hit as hard as Rocky, the champion replied, "I think perhaps that Curtis 'The Hatchet Man' Sheppard hits harder."

Walcott went even further when he said, "I want to repeat, if Rocky beats me just take my name out of the record books. I won't deserve the title of heavyweight champion of the world." And then he said that he was sick and tired of hearing how great Marciano is. "He didn't lick Joe Louis; he just beat the name of Joe Louis. Marciano licked Joe when he was all through."

By September both fighters were well into their training regimen. Al Weil, who had recently quit as matchmaker for the International Boxing Club to become Marciano's full-time manager, reported that Rocky was well ahead of schedule and working as hard as he did when he trained for the Louis fight.

The champion, having finished his preliminary training in New Jersey, arrived in Atlantic City on September 1. For the next three weeks he would spar over fifty rounds at night with Oakland Billy Smith and Freddie

16 — Walcott-Marciano I: The Build-Up

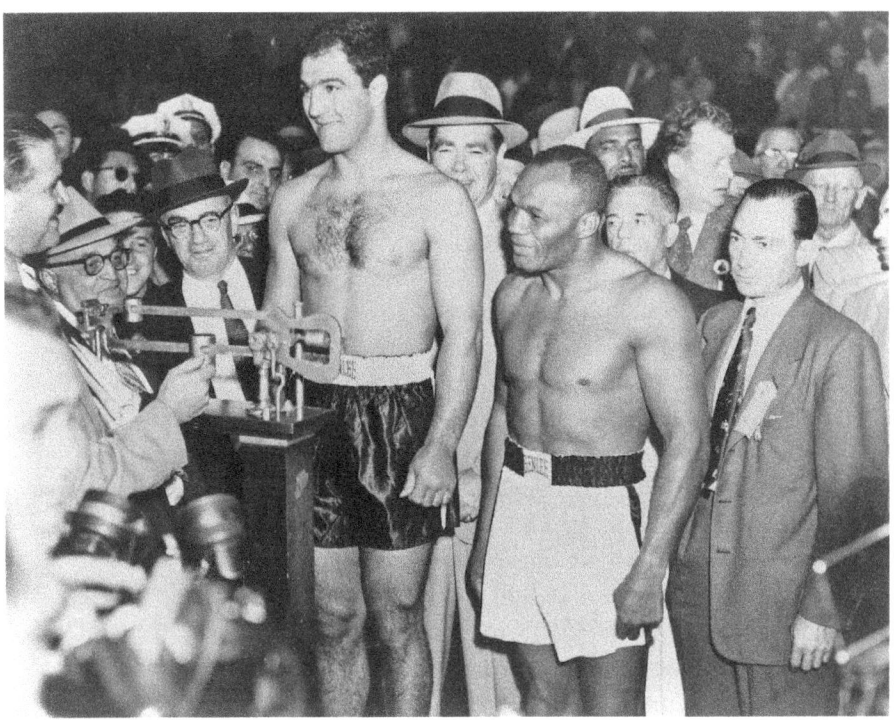

Rocky Marciano and Walcott weigh in for their September 1952 heavyweight title fight, as Felix Bocchicchio (at Jersey Joe's left shoulder) watches the proceedings.

Newhall. Bocchicchio reasoned that since the fight was at night and outdoors it would be a good idea to have the champion train at night to condition his body to the cool night air. "The fight is going to be at night," said Felix, "and I think it is good experience for Jersey Joe to work out in the night air."[9] As an added training routine, Walcott started playing tennis every afternoon with sportswriter Harry Hoffman as a way to sharpen his eye and make himself mentally alert.[10] To further toughen his body, Jersey Joe would get into the ring without his gloves and let Pete Nelson, one of his sparring partners, hit his body and stomach while he tried to avoid and or block the blows.

Walcott trained diligently, even as events that threatened to cause a cancellation of the fight were unfolding. A dispute over the contract, concerning a rematch in the event of a Marciano win, had Felix threatening to pull out of the fight just days before the bout if Marciano and his manager didn't sign a return-bout contract by weigh-in time. Fortunately, the matter was resolved quickly when promoter Herman Taylor and Jim Norris stepped in and straightened everything out. From there on, preparation for the bout proceeded on course.

The dispute over the contract had little effect on the build-up to the fight, which had been growing since its announcement. It was the first heavyweight title fight in years that had really captured the public's imagination; from the start, ticket sales were brisk. By fight night the city of Philadelphia was energized as 40,379 fans packed into Municipal Stadium to see what promised to be a thrilling fight. The atmosphere was reminiscent of the old days of boxing when a heavyweight title fight was more than a fight, it was an event.

Those who couldn't make it to the fight gathered in movie houses across America to watch on the most extensive closed-circuit television network ever. Over fifty theaters in thirty-one cities from coast to coast showed the fight live from Philadelphia. In fact, just across the river in New Jersey, the fight was causing quite a lot of commotion. A rampaging mob estimated between 20,000 and 30,000 descended on the Route S-3 drive-in movie theatre. Cars were double and triple-parked on and off the two main highways and surrounding streets, causing a traffic jam that lasted for hours. The mob of movie-goers built bonfires to keep warm, swigged beer and played poker as they anxiously waited for the fight to begin.

—17—

Walcott-Marciano I: The Fight

It was a cool night with just a touch of autumn in the air as Jersey Joe made his way into the ring at Philadelphia's Municipal Stadium on September 23, 1952. He received loud cheers from his fans as he climbed up the wooden steps, slipped under the middle rope and went to his corner. Moments later the pre-fight ceremonies began with the playing of the national anthem. At the song's conclusion, Rocky and his team entered the square circle. Ring announcer Phil Calabrese then introduced several fighters, including Archie Moore, Sugar Ray Robinson, who wore a loud checkered sportsjacket, George Benton, Sandy Saddler, Bob Satterfield, Benny Bass, Tony Galento, Joey Giardello, Lew Tendler, Joe Louis, Gene Tunney, Jimmy Braddock, Barney Ross and the light-heavyweight champion Joe Maxim.

With the ring ceremonies finished, Calabrese introduced each fighter. His voice resounded loudly over the loud speaker: "The main attraction, fifteen rounds for the heavyweight championship of the world, from Brockton, Massachusetts, wearing black trunks with a white stripe, weighing one-hundred-and-eighty-four pounds, the challenger, Rocky Marciano."[1] Rocky stood and waved to his cheering fans. "From Camden, New Jersey, wearing white trunks with a black stripe, weighing one-hundred-and-ninety-six pounds, the heavyweight champion, Jersey Joe Walcott."[2] Jersey Joe likewise stood and acknowledged his screaming fans.

With the introductions out of the way, the fighters and their seconds were called to the center of the ring where they were given instructions by referee Charley Daggert. For about a minute, the handlers of each fighter questioned the referee concerning rules and fouls. Finally, Daggert put an end to the questioning and said, "I ask both youse boys give me no kidney or rabbit punches. I'm gonna call 'em if you do. I wan' both of yas to give me an honest, clean fight."[3] With that admonition, the fighters returned to their respective corners where they disrobed and received last minute advice from their handlers.

With his robe off, the champion looked fit. Despite the fact that Jersey Joe was 38 years old, he was still in splendid condition and could have outboxed most fighters ten years his junior. At 38, Jersey Joe was the oldest heavyweight champion to defend the heavyweight crown. Jack Johnson and Jess Willard were both the second oldest, each at 37 years of age. As was usual for Walcott, the odds on the fight favored the much younger challenger. Rocky, having just turned 28 years old only a few weeks before on September 1, was an 8-to-5 favorite to take the crown from the champion. Seconds later, the bell for round one rang loudly, and the two fighters came out for battle.

From the start Jersey Joe surprised everyone. He didn't come out fighting like he usually did, boxing, dancing and using his patented "Walcott shuffle." Instead he went straight at the Rock and they collided like two locomotives in the center of the ring. The champion began to bomb the challenger with a barrage of hard blows. Rocky, caught off guard by Walcott's fast start, didn't know what hit him. He desperately tried to fight back against the champion's onslaught, but there was little he could do as Walcott landed a hard right to his chin that momentarily wobbled him. Shaken by the punch, Rocky grabbed hold of Jersey Joe to steady himself, but referee Daggert quickly stepped in and pushed the two apart. And then it happened. As the two fighters came back together, Jersey Joe threw a beautiful left hook that found its mark on Marciano's chin. The punch sent Rocky to the canvas. Amazingly, it was the first time that Rocky had ever been put down in his forty-two fight career. Walcott turned and walked to a neutral corner as the crowd screamed in excitement and the referee started the count. He didn't get far. Rocky, being inexperienced when it came to finding himself on the seat of his pants, jumped up at the count of three instead of taking the full eight count. "I wasn't hurt," Rocky would later say.[4] "I wasn't even dazed."[5] One ringside observer claimed to have heard Marciano angrily say to Walcott, as he rose from his knockdown, "I'll get you, you son of a bitch!"[6]

A second later, the battle was back on. The champion came in with a hard left hook, a right and another left, all three landing on Marciano's face. The punches hurt Rocky and he held for a few seconds until he was told to break by the referee. The two then fought at close proximity until separated by Daggert. Walcott continued to be aggressive and came back with a looping left that the crouching challenger ducked under. While down low, Marciano hit Walcott with a left and right to the body as Jersey Joe grabbed the Rock and pounded the side of his ribs. Walcott then released his adversary, danced back a few feet, reset, and threw a long hard right that just missed. At the same time, Rocky threw a right of his own that hit Walcott on the side of his face, followed by a left hook that Jersey Joe avoided by ducking. The two fighters then exchanged hard rights and Rocky missed a left. The relentless attack of lefts and rights continued for the remainder of the round. Every punch was thrown with the intent to end the fight. Both men were putting the full weight of their bodies behind every blow, as could be seen when they twisted their shoulders into the punches. When the bell sounded to signal the end, it was the champion's round. "Pappy" Walcott had outslugged and dropped his younger opponent. He had also drawn first blood by cutting the inside of Rocky's lip. Maybe Jersey Joe's prophecy about an easy fight was coming true.

When the fighters met in the center of the ring for round two, neither one seemed willing to back up. Instead they circled each other. The champion flicked out a jab and Rocky returned with a quick left right-left combo that Jersey Joe mostly avoided with quick head movement. The champion jabbed again and barely avoided a fast right hand from the crouching challenger. Another jab from Walcott and Rocky came in low, throwing a wild left that missed by a mile. The two then clinched and pounded away on each other's body. Stepping back, Jersey Joe dug a left to Rocky's belly and a hard right to his temple that shook the challenger and had him holding for a second. The champion started the next exchange by landing a right. Rocky retaliated with an uppercut inside. The two then went back to circling and jabbing. Marciano suddenly leaped in with a left uppercut to Walcott's stomach and Jersey Joe tied him up. They fought on the inside until the referee broke them apart, at which point Walcott came back with two rights to the side of Rocky's head.

Marciano evened things up by landing a right of his own, and then opened up with a combination of lefts and rights to the champion's body. Walcott fired right back with a hard left, right, and left. He then held the back of Rocky's head and landed a solid uppercut as Rocky landed two rights to Jersey Joe's rib cage. Walcott then pushed Rocky away, circled, and began using his "Walkaway" move. He took several steps back and let the challenger come to him. Rocky obliged and came right in. Walcott threw a right hand that hit Marciano's head as Rocky landed a left-right to the body. Jersey Joe then drove home a powerful left that smashed into

Rocky's face just as the bell sounded ending the second round. It was another good round for the champion.

Round three marked the first momentum shift of the bout. Up to this point it had been the champion's fight. It was now the challenger's turn to take the fight to the champion. The action started with the fighters circling and jabbing. Rocky dug a left to Walcott's body and they clinched. Marciano jabbed and Walcott fired a counter right that landed, followed by two lefts, each landing flush. Jersey Joe then backed off and Rocky missed an awkward left-hook swing, but got in a good right hand to the body and a right that grazed Walcott's face, and the two men clinched. Once separated, Walcott landed a jab and a hard right to the challenger's body and pushed Rocky to the ropes. Walcott then slammed a left to Rocky's body. Marciano missed a left-right combination, but landed two rights to Walcott's midsection and then a right to his head along with a left, and another right. Jersey Joe then danced away and threw a right hand as both fighters opened up, each landing several punches. Walcott circled and fired a quick right that caught the challenger square just as Rocky landed a left and right to Walcott's face. The champ then threw a quick left, right, left that landed on Rocky's head. Both men attacked with vicious punches just seconds before the bell sounded, Walcott with a left-right combination and Rocky with a pulverizing right to the champion's face that staggered him as the bell was ringing. It was Marciano's best round.

The fourth round was more of the same from the challenger as he slowly started to turn the fight into a typical Marciano brawl. Continuing to be the aggressor and backing the champion up, Marciano rushed in and threw a left-right combination that hit nothing but the cool night air. Again Rocky charged the dancing champion, throwing a sweeping left that Walcott avoided with his fancy footwork. The two clinched briefly. Walcott then found a home for his right hand on Rocky's face and tried to land a jab, but the challenger ducked under it as he landed a hard right to the champion's body that hurt. Perhaps angered, Walcott came alive and attacked with a five-punch combination of lefts and rights to Rocky's head, but Rocky battled back with a left and right of his own as Walcott threw another left and right. They held for a split second and then commenced fighting at close quarters, each ripping fierce punches on the inside until Daggert pushed them apart. But they came back together immediately. Rocky shot a right that missed as Walcott threw a left, right, left that landed. Both fighters tore into each other at this point with lefts, rights, and uppercuts as they once again fought at short range.

As the infighting slowed down, Daggert stepped in and parted the fighters. The champion set off the next exchange of punches with a fast left-right combination that Rocky crouched under. Walcott kept throwing and landed a left hook on the side of Rocky's face. Marciano answered back with a short left hook that Walcott ducked, but the follow-up right smashed into Jersey Joe's face and wobbled the champion, causing him to grab hold of Rocky. Marciano then forced Jersey Joe back against the ropes while landing hard uppercuts. Although he was hurt, Walcott fought back with a hard left to Rocky's body. The two then engaged each other in close, landing lefts and rights as Rocky again forced Walcott to the ropes. Both men pounded away, but it was Rocky who was getting the better of the infighting as the bell rang.

Round five followed much the same pattern as round four. Rocky continued to be the aggressor and backed Walcott to the ropes several times. The two would fight at close quarters with Rocky generally getting the better of the infighting. Near the end of the round, Walcott found Marciano's chin with a hard left. But it was the challenger's round by virtue of his aggressiveness.

By the sixth round, Marciano was controlling the tempo of the fight. He was backing the champion up and at times trapping him on the ropes. To begin the round, Jersey Joe danced back and threw out a jab. Rocky swung a left that missed and a right that grazed the top of Jersey Joe's head. The champion then threw a volley of lefts and rights, catching the Brockton Blockbuster on his head and neck as he was rushing in. The two then moved around the ring with Walcott backing up and Rocky in pursuit. The champion jabbed and Rocky winged a wide left as he came in bobbing and weaving. He forced the champion to the ropes again and landed a hard right. The two men held momentarily, but were quickly told to break. Jersey Joe backed up and jabbed as Rocky came in landing a looping right to Walcott's rib cage. The two then fought on the inside with Rocky landing bruising uppercuts and Walcott connecting with stinging lefts and rights to the challenger's head.

Separated after the fierce infighting, Rocky came right back with a rush and landed a hard left and a chopping right proceeded by a right, left, right as Walcott stormed back with a few of his own that forced Rocky to take a couple of steps backwards. Crouching low, Rocky jabbed his way back in and landed a sledgehammer right to Walcott's body and then a few light uppercuts. The champion returned with a fast right as Rocky landed another right to the body that drove Walcott to the ropes.

Walcott takes a massive right from Rocky Marciano in their first fight, in September 1952.

After the two men brawled on the ropes in a fierce exchange of leather, suddenly there was blood everywhere. It showed brightly on Jersey Joe's white trunks and was all over Rocky's hairy chest. At some point during the violent infighting, the two fighters had banged heads. Jersey Joe was cut badly over his left eye and Rocky sported a jagged cut on the top of his head near his hair line. Despite the blood, Rocky opened up for the last few seconds of the sixth round with a series of blows that the slick veteran Walcott either slipped, rolled with, or ducked. The ding of the bell put an end to Rocky's attack. The bloody fighters headed to their corners where their cut men quickly went to work trying to stop the flow of blood. As Walcott walked to his corner at the round's end, he appeared tired. As novelist and writer for *The New Yorker* A.J. Liebling saw it, "Rocky was slowing him down. The old man would go in a couple more rounds."[7]

To start round seven, Rocky came out pursuing the backpedaling champion. Jersey Joe shot out two jabs, snapping the crouching challenger's head back. By then Walcott was wiping at his left eye and having a little trouble seeing. Rocky then crouched and attacked. He rushed in with a hard left-right combination that had the full weight of his body behind the blows as they landed on Jersey Joe's stomach. The two then held, but Daggert was quick to part them. The action slowed for a few seconds as the two men circled each other and then Walcott drove in a solid left to Rocky's face and a fast right to his jaw. Rocky threw two rights, the first one missed; the second landed flush on Walcott's cheek and rocked the champion for a second. Seeing that Jersey Joe was hurt, Rocky went on the offensive, throwing a left hook and a right uppercut, both blows impacting solidly. Walcott retreated, circled, and jabbed. Just as Rocky jabbed, Walcott landed a thudding right under Rocky's heart. They exchanged jabs and Rocky caught Walcott with a clubbing left hook and smashing right hand. But the champion got in his own hard right to Rocky's face, which was becoming a crimson mess from all of the blood flowing from his cut that had reopened. Through the mist of blood which veiled his eyes, it became clear that the challenger was having a difficult time seeing as he continuously blinked and wiped blood away. Rocky was also starting to miss his punches. As Liebling wrote in his book *The Sweet Science*, "He (Rocky) seemed to be coming unstuck. It was, unaccountably, Marciano who was beginning to flounder."[8]

Through the gore, the two fighters continued their battle. The champion missed with a wide left that Rocky ducked under. He then shot out long jabs as the two came together and fought in close and clinched. Pushed apart by the referee, Rocky waded back in and threw a right that missed big. Walcott jabbed and tried to stay away from the swarming Marciano, but the challenger jumped in and landed a left as Walcott caught Rocky with a powerful right to the jaw that brought a roar from the crowd and sent drops of blood splattering. Quickly the champion followed up with another right that connected solidly and a left hook that Rocky rolled with. Walcott then leaped in with a sweeping left hook to the body and a right to Marciano's neck. The bloody challenger grabbed to steady himself as the bell rang. The tide of the fight had once again changed. Walcott had battled back to take command.

It was pandemonium in Rocky's corner between rounds seven and eight. It was evident near the end of round seven that Rocky had something in his eyes and was fighting blind. But what was it? Was it blood? Was it the concoction that his corner men had applied to his cut after round six to stop it from bleeding? Had the concoction run down his face and into his eyes? Was it possibly the medication that Walcott's corner had put on the champion's cut that had gotten into Rocky's eyes during a clinch or while the two were fighting on the inside? Or was it something more diabolical? Like chemical warfare as Marciano and his team later alluded to, fingering Bocchicchio as the prime suspect. Whatever had gotten into Rocky's eyes, naturally or unnaturally, he was in serious trouble, blind and vulnerable.

Lucky for Rocky, Freddie Brown, a cut man hired on the morning of the fight for $50, was there to save the day. Among all the screaming and confusion, Freddie was calm. He worked on cleaning out Marciano's eyes and spoke to him saying, "Now listen, you don't have to see. Don't worry about it. Just get your hands on the guy's body so you know where he is and fucking pound."[9] And that's what Rocky tried to do in round eight. But he was mostly ineffective. Despite Brown's attempt to clean out Marciano's eyes, it was noticeable that the challenger was still having difficulty seeing as he threw wild punches, looked clumsy, and blinked continuously. This caused Al Weil to scream at the referee several times concerning his fighter's vision problems. Al's rants were enough to attract the attention of John "Ox" DaGross, one of the Pennsylvania state athletic commissioners. John told Weil to shut up or he would have him thrown out. This, of course, did little to stop Weil, who continued to relay instructions to Rocky throughout the round, via Rocky's bodyguard.

If there was foul play afoot, Jersey Joe failed to capitalize on it. Instead of going out for the kill in round eight, the champion decided to box at long range and keep Rocky at bay, which he did for most of the round with his stinging jabs and slick boxing skills. It was fortunate for Rocky that Walcott decided to box cautiously, content with circling and jabbing. Rocky did manage to land a thudding right hand to Walcott's body during the opening seconds of the round, but from then on it was all Jersey Joe. Every time Rocky charged in, Walcott would tie him up or easily duck Rocky's clumsy telegraphed swings. Near the end of the eighth round, Walcott jabbed Rocky twice and landed a hard right to Marciano's face that stunned the challenger and had the crowd roaring at the bell.

Between rounds the champion's corner went to work on Jersey Joe's cut, which was bleeding again. Rocky's corner concerned themselves with cleaning out Marciano's eyes and stopping the bleeding from a new cut that their fighter had gotten over his right eye. Weil was nearly hysterical at this point, having just watched his fighter lose another round because he was half-blind. Out of desperation, Al approached referee Daggert and pleaded for an investigation of Walcott's gloves, believing that they were tainted with a chemical that was blinding Rocky. The referee promptly waved Al back to his corner.

Rocky came out jabbing to begin round nine and it looked as though his vision had cleared. As he resumed his pursuit of the champion, he leaped in with a left that Walcott avoided by dancing out of range. Jersey Joe then shot out a fast jab as Rocky threw a right uppercut. Neither punch landed. Rocky swung a right that was short as Walcott backed out of range. Swarming in behind his jab, Rocky pushed the champion up against the ropes and threw a right uppercut that just missed followed by a left hook that found its mark on Walcott's face. Escaping from the ropes, Walcott boxed and circled as Rocky came in behind a left hook to the body and a right to the head. At the same time, Jersey Joe landed his own right to Rocky's body and then danced away. The champion circled his opponent, jabbed and landed a thudding right to the body underneath Rocky's jab. Marciano came back with an uppercut that snapped back the champion's head. The two were giving their all and exchanged a succession of hard lefts, rights, and uppercuts, each fighter scoring equally in the exchange. A quick clinch ended the fierce brawl and a second later the two were again circling and jabbing each other. Rocky sprang in with a left to Walcott's body as Jersey Joe countered with a right to Rocky's head. They exchanged left hooks and Walcott jabbed and connected with a right to the Rock's body. Rocky then pushed Walcott to the ropes and the two bombed away with lefts and rights. Once he was off the ropes, Walcott was content to backpedal and jab until Rocky connected with a hard right. Walcott avoided Marciano's follow-up punch and shot over his own right that grazed Rocky as he ducked. The two attacked each other with murderous blows and continued to wage war for a few seconds after the bell rang.

It had been a brutal ninth round. With his vision restored, Marciano had resumed command and had caused yet another momentum shift in the fight. But it was the old champion who was amazing everyone with his incredible stamina. As Liebling observed, "Somehow the calculations had gone awry; the old fellow looked further from collapse now than he had six rounds earlier. It might go the distance after all."[10]

The champion came out backing up in round ten. The two fighters exchanged jabs and Rocky jumped in with a left that grazed Jersey Joe's ribs just as Walcott backed out of the way. Rocky then jabbed as he stalked Walcott around the ring. The challenger again jumped in and dug a left to Walcott's body and just missed with a right to the face. The champion could be seen laughing as he backed up and jabbed. Walcott then shot a right that barely missed Rocky's face as Marciano threw a looping left hook that Walcott easily avoided. The Rock followed up his missed punch with a crunching left uppercut to Walcott's stomach that landed hard. After a brief clinch, the two started to fight on the ropes. Rocky caught the champion with a clean right to the head that brought a grin to Walcott's face. He continued with a quick left and right to the midsection. Walcott slid off the ropes, jabbed and turned up the heat with a hard left right combination that landed as Rocky landed a right to the body. Rocky then landed a right to Walcott's head as Jersey Joe put his full weight into a left to Rocky's body and then retreated with Rocky in pursuit. Catching up with the champion, the challenger once again shoved him to the ropes.

Thus began another furious exchange of leather-covered lefts, rights, and uppercuts. Rocky threw a four-punch combination, but missed with most of his punches because of Walcott's quick head movement. Separated by the referee after the violent exchange of blows, Walcott walked straight into Rocky and drove in a left to the body. They held briefly and again Walcott walked right into Rocky and landed another left to the body. The force of it literally lifted Marciano off his feet and brought a cheer from the crowd. The two clinched and traded hard lefts. The crowd roared loudly as the fighters swapped lefts and rights with Rocky landing a big right hand at the bell. As hard as the ninth round had been, the tenth had been harder. According to Liebling, it was "the hardest fought round of all."[11] Both fighters had taken some massive punches. Jersey Joe continued to impress everyone with his stamina and ability to absorb punishment. But it was now Rocky's turn to find out how much pain he could take, as the fight inevitably shifted back into the champion's favor.

Rocky came right at the champion and landed a jab and a right to his face to start round eleven. He continued with a left to the body while Walcott landed two lefts to the side of Rocky's head. After a quick trade of jabs, the Rock swarmed in, landing a left to the body and a right to the head but missed a left-right combination that Jersey Joe slipped. Walcott jabbed twice, snapping Rocky's head back with the second jab. Marciano tried to catch Walcott with a left to the body, but the elusive champion quickly moved out of range. The two went back to circling and jabbing and just when the pace seemed to be slowing Rocky went back on the attack, slamming a right to Walcott's body proceeded by a left and right to Walcott's face that the champion rolled with to keep from taking solidly. Jersey Joe stopped Rocky's attack by holding and then moved back away from the challenger, throwing out a jab as Rocky tried a right. Marciano ducked under a Walcott left while hooking a left to Jersey Joe's jaw that missed, but landed a left and right as well as an uppercut to Walcott body. Jersey Joe then jabbed and landed a devastating right to Rocky's body. The resounding thud was said to be heard by all who sat ringside. Rocky grimaced in pain, sagged, and doubled over. The challenger was hurt badly.

The champion sprang in for the kill with a sustained attack of brutal lefts and rights. Rocky bobbed and weaved to try to avoid the punches but there was little the injured challenger could do but hold on. The champion pushed Marciano away and kept punching, landing a right to the side of Rocky's head. Once again the shaken challenger grabbed and held. Daggert stepped in and pushed the two apart. Walcott came right back with a hard left hook, catching Rocky flush on the side of his face. Marciano tried desperately to put up some kind of a fight, but his punches lacked power and he couldn't keep the champion away. It was now Walcott who was pushing Rocky back, landing lefts and rights as Rocky poured blood from a fresh cut that had opened up under his swollen right eye.

As Rocky held, wiping the blood from his eye, Walcott drove in another left to Marciano's body and pushed Rocky away. Rocky punched back with a weak left to Walcott's body, but the blow lacked any real clout. The champion jabbed and kept his arm out, using it to measure his adversary. With his range fixed, Walcott guided in a crunching right to Rocky's face that buckled the challenger's knees and nearly sent him to the canvas.

As the crowed screamed in a frenzy, Rocky grabbed hold of Jersey Joe and hung on, just trying to survive. Walcott again pushed Marciano away and landed yet another left and right to Rocky's face. Marciano tried a feeble jab, but was again hit in the face by a counter left hook and right-cross combination. Marciano managed to get in a right to Jersey Joe's body as the champion shoved the challenger to the ropes and landed a terrific left hook that caused Rocky's head to turn from the impact and sent a shower of blood raining down on press row. The crowd was now on its feet and roared every time the champion landed a punch. Jersey Joe, now completely overcome with the fighting spirit, continued to rip into Rocky by landing two more solid lefts to the body. At this point Marciano was just about ready to go down and was clearly hanging on for dear life. Daggert pushed the two fighters away from each other, but it was like trying to pull apart two magnets. Walcott stormed back in and landed a left to Rocky's body. Rocky fired a couple of frail jabs as the bell sounded, putting an end to the pounding. It was no doubt a welcome sound for the challenger who had just taken the worst beating of his entire career.

The old champion continued to astonish everyone in round twelve. The fighters came out jabbing, clinching, and circling. Rocky tried to land a left, but his punch was wide and Jersey Joe easily bounced out of the way as he jabbed the challenger's head. Rocky tried another left but was wide again and missed by a mile as Walcott used his superior boxing skills to dance out of range. Marciano did the only thing he could do at this point; he continued to follow the moving target that was the champion.

As incredible as it seemed, Jersey Joe looked fresh and was moving around like it was the first round. No doubt he had caught his second wind. Rocky, on the other hand, looked sluggish and tired. He swung and missed a looping right to Walcott's body and was having a hard time getting to the champion since Walcott constantly presented a moving target. The champion stopped his movements long enough to catch Rocky with a beautiful left jab that snapped the challenger's head back as he was getting set to throw a punch. A split-second later Walcott was again on the move, keeping Rocky off balance and out of his rhythm with piston-like jabs.

Rocky continued to go after the champion, swinging wide punches that missed by huge margins. The old champion was easily outboxing the challenger and making him look like a novice. Rocky finally succeeded in getting Walcott to the ropes and landed a ripping right to the body and a left to Walcott's head, but Jersey Joe took the punches without any apparent effect. Not wanting to be pinned on the ropes, Walcott went back to moving and boxing and as the crouching Rocky came in to attack, Walcott smashed him with a left hook that brought another roar from the crowd and stopped the Brockton Blockbuster in his tracks.

Quickly, Jersey Joe hit Rocky again with two more powerful lefts and a right to Rocky's head. Marciano gave back a light one-two that missed, and then came in low, shooting out a left jab and a left hook, neither one landing. Walcott, finding Marciano an easy target, tagged him with a left hook and right cross to the head. The punches caused Rocky's cuts to bleed once again, causing the swelling under his left eye to get worse. Marciano swung a right that missed big and threw two jabs. The two clinched and wrestled for a few seconds until the referee parted them.

Walcott went back to dancing on his toes and jabbing Rocky. The short-armed slugger rushed in and tried to land a wild left swing, but Walcott backed off and tied up Rocky. The referee yelled break, and the two fighters obeyed. Aggressively, Rocky came right back in, but the champion was waiting for just such a move. He smashed in a heavy uppercut to Rocky's body that lifted the challenger off the mat. The crowd shouted its approval after the blow landed and the two briefly fought inside, landing lefts and rights. A second later the bell sounded to end the twelfth round, but not before the champion smacked Marciano with a left hook and a right to the nose. It was another great round for the champion.

When he came out for the thirteenth round, Jersey Joe was comfortably ahead, and in control of the fight. All three judges had the champion out in front with scores of 8 rounds to 4, 7 rounds to 5, and 7 rounds to 4 with 1 round even. It appeared that the undefeated Marciano was on his way to his first loss, since the only way he could possibly win was by a knockout.

The champion started the thirteenth round by jabbing and bouncing on his toes, again looking like the much fresher fighter. Rocky couldn't do anything but follow Jersey Joe, hopelessly it seemed, and try and land a big punch. As Rocky pursued, Walcott slowly gave ground, backing up to the ropes. There has been a lot written about these last few moments of the fight, the majority of which is not correct. According to most reports, Walcott suddenly became tired, his age finally catching up with him as his legs became heavy, like lead. Other accounts claim that Jersey Joe didn't know why he backed up to the ropes. This is in direct contrast to what Walcott said in a 1974 interview and what he told his grandsons, who in turn told this author.

Going into the thirteenth round, Walcott told his grandsons that he never felt better and was not tired. He knew that Rocky was nearly finished and planned on taking out Marciano. He backed to the ropes with the intention of catching Rocky with a right hand. There was only one problem: the cut over his left eye was bleeding and running into his eye, partially blinding him. As he reached the ropes, he saw his opportunity and threw a right, and so did Rocky.[12] Although both fighters threw right hands at about the same time, Rocky's was shorter, traveling no more than a foot, and landed first. Because of his compromised vision, Walcott never saw the punch and had no chance to dodge or block the blow. Rocky's right hand landed with an incredible impact and was arguably the single hardest punch ever landed in a boxing ring. "To ringsiders, the sound of it was described as frightening," wrote Ed Pollock of the *Philadelphia Evening Bulletin*. "It wasn't the smack of gloves against flesh. It was a crack. Rocky had hit something solid, the jawbone."[13] According to Liebling, who witnessed the fight in person, "It was, according to old-timers, about as hard as anybody ever hit anybody."[14]

Rocky followed his punch with an unnecessary left that grazed the top of Walcott's head as Jersey Joe slowly sank to the canvas into unconsciousness. To sportswriter Jess Abramson, Walcott went down crumbling all the way in sections like "a slow motion picture of a chimney stack that had been dynamited."[15] Rocky turned and ran to a neutral corner as the referee gave the count, which wasn't necessary, as the champion was out cold. Rocky Marciano was the new heavyweight champion of the world.

It was a thrilling, come-from-behind, one-punch knockout by a fighter who had to score a knockout to win. As referee Daggert finished his count, the ring exploded into pandemonium. Over a hundred people, many of them Rocky's fans from Brockton, swarmed over press row, sending sportswriters diving for cover. Dozens of wild-eyed Marciano fans from Brockton resisted the best efforts of police to clear the ring as they crowded around the new champion, screaming and yelling. The official announcement came blaring over the loudspeaker at this point: "The time, 43 seconds of the thirteenth round, winner by a knockout and new heavyweight champion of the world, Rocky Marciano!"[16] Shortly thereafter, Rocky was found among all the chaos and gave a quick interview to Bill Corum:

> "Rocky, did you think you were winning?"
> "Well no, I thought I was just maybe a hair behind, I knew I had to do something, I knew I had to do something."
> "And you did do something. Did you think you were going to catch up to him?"
> "Well, I was wishing I hit him with that left hook or right hand, he surely can take a good punch though."
> "And you did hit him with a right hand of course?"
> "Yes. I hit him with a right hand and a left hook."
> "And did you think he was gone when you nailed him?"
> "Well, I knew it hurt him."
> "Well, congratulations, Rocky, you're a great fighter and game boy."[17]

Meanwhile over in Jersey Joe's corner, Felix and Dan along with several ringside physicians were attending to the fallen champion. It had taken over a minute for Jersey Joe to regain consciousness, but he was all right, that is, until he realized that he had lost his title. In the words of Matt Ring, Walcott wore "a look of such utter sorrow as to wrench the heart."[18] Moments later it was announced that Jersey Joe was clear eyed and unhurt, as he sat on his stool recovering.

In the new champion's dressing room, it was a mad house. A swarm of newspapermen surrounded Marciano, asking questions and snapping pictures. Everyone was coming up and embracing the new champ and slapping him on the back while doctors were tending to Rocky's battle wounds, of which there were several. The new champion bore the marks of one of the toughest title fights in history. He had a jagged cut on his scalp, his left eye was swollen nearly shut, his right eyebrow was gashed open, and he had a deep cut on the bridge of his nose. He was also nauseated and sick to his stomach from Walcott's powerful body blows. He was exhausted, but not too exhausted to answer questions. "He's a helluva fighter, a good tough guy," said Marciano about Walcott in response to one of the questions thrown at him.[19] When asked about the knockdown in round one, Rocky said that the punch that put him down was the hardest he had ever taken. About the knockout punch, Rocky said, "I hit him with a right up against the ropes. His head was at one side and I hooked with a left and he went down."[20]

Four years later, Rocky Marciano retired as the only undefeated champion ever, with a record of 49–0. When asked at his retirement announcement what fight had been his most difficult, Rocky replied that his championship fight with Jersey Joe was the toughest.

Across the hall in the ex-champion's dressing room, the scene was quite different. It took a half-hour before the press was allowed into Jersey Joe's room. Once in, they found the scene to be melancholy. The heartbroken ex-champion sat quietly on his dressing room table with his head in his hands and tears in his eyes, trying to cope with the loss of his title. One of his brothers came in and started to cry as he wrapped his arms around Walcott's sweaty body. The two embraced for a few seconds and then Jersey Joe answered questions from a group of reporters,

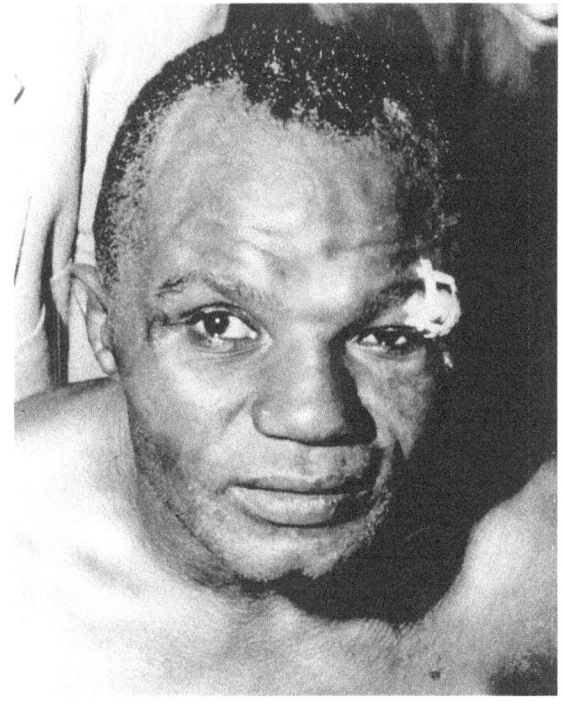

Walcott, with the look of defeat, after losing his heavyweight title to Rocky Marciano.

saying he didn't remember anything about the punch. "He caught me open and that was it. I don't know if it was a right or left. I just don't remember anything. I wasn't tired. I felt good. I was setting my own pace, then bang it hit me. Honest, I still don't know what hit me. I couldn't even try to get up. I still don't remember anything."[21]

It was obvious that Jersey Joe was taking the loss of his title hard. The ex-champion really didn't feel like talking, but every bit the gentleman in defeat that he was in victory, he answered every one of the dozens of questions tossed at him. When the subject of Walcott's future came up, a weeping Felix stepped in and said, "I won't let him fight again, he's too great a man, I won't let this happen to him again."[22] Furthermore, said Felix, "As far as I'm concerned Jersey Joe is retired. He looked pathetic against the ropes and I don't want him to get hurt. He still has all his faculties and has money in the bank. Joe has made over one million dollars in the ring, he has been a great champion and that's the way we want people to remember him."[23] Walcott sadly agreed and said, "If retirement was Felix's decision that was ok with me. Felix brought me this far from nothing. If he says I'm through, I'm through."[24]

So ended Jersey Joe Walcott's title reign. Even though Walcott had lost, he was seen as the hero of the evening because of the incredible battle he had put up against a much younger fighter. He gained new admiration and respect from the boxing world, the likes of which he had never known, and his popularity reached new heights. As far as the fight was concerned, it would go down in history as one of the greatest ever. Liebling summed it best when he wrote: "What made the fight truly great were the continuous and almost dizzying shifts in momentum. Walcott had it initially when he knocked down Marciano in the first round. Then it gradually swung to Marciano. Then it swung back to Walcott when Marciano was mysteriously blinded. Marciano regained it in the ninth and tenth, only to see Walcott recapture it in the eleventh and twelfth. And then finally and conclusively it swung back to Marciano, with his thirteenth round knockout of Walcott. You don't see many fights like that."[25]

Of course, such a great fight demanded a rematch. As far as Walcott's retirement, it was short lived. Twenty-four hours later, there were newspaper reports that a return bout was inevitable.

— 18 —

Walcott-Marciano II: The Rematch

Since the first fight in 1952 between Walcott and Rocky was so good — it was shown for several months in movie theatres all over America — there was great interest in a rematch. Even though Walcott and Felix had announced Jersey Joe's retirement at the end of the first fight, they quickly reversed that stance just twenty-four hours later.

Talks for a return bout started in October 1952. The first condition, and perhaps the only one that Bocchicchio and Weil agreed upon, was that there was no way a return fight would happen within 90 days, as was specified in the contract for the first fight. Because the fight had been extremely brutal and both fighters had suffered severe cuts, everyone involved agreed that Walcott and Rocky needed more time to let their wounds heal.

Once it was agreed the fighters would receive extra time to let their wounds mend, negotiations began in earnest. Early reports of a rematch said that the bout might take place in Miami, Florida, and apparently Felix liked the idea. By November, there were reports of an offer for a February 1953 match by West Coast promoter Jimmy Murray to have the fight at San Francisco's Kezar Stadium. Murray guaranteed a million-dollar gate if the fight were held on the West Coast. His curiosity aroused, Weil made a trip out to San Francisco and liked the looks of the huge stadium, but he balked when he found out that it would cost 10 percent of the gate to rent it.

Talks heated up mid–November when Jim Norris, Weil, and Bocchicchio spent two hours at the headquarters of the International Boxing Club discussing the fight. Norris and Weil were at opposite ends when it came to where the fight should be held. Al was leaning towards a June 1953 fight at Yankee Stadium in New York. Norris wanted a March bout at Chicago Stadium. Felix wanted a March bout as well, and of course he could not work in New York. In fact, he stated that Jersey Joe had already begun light training for a March fight. After the two-hour meeting, the details were no nearer to being ironed out.

With no one able to agree, the plans for the rematch dragged on throughout December and into January. To further complicate things, and slow the proceedings down even more, Felix suffered a heart attack on the morning of January 15, 1953, as he was getting ready to appear at a boxing commission hearing at the I.B.C headquarters. The 46-year-old manager collapsed in his hotel room and was rushed to Polyclinic Hospital. His condition was listed as critical.

With Felix laid up in the hospital after open-heart surgery, Jersey Joe and his attorney Angelo Malandra appeared before the I.B.C. commission in place of Bocchicchio. In what turned out to be a heated and highly emotional discussion, Walcott showed his loyalty to his manager. Standing before the commission, Walcott said, "Felix is more man than 90 percent of the men I meet. As far as Jersey Joe Walcott is concerned there will be no fight as long as Felix Bocchicchio is not well. I don't care whether it's six weeks or six months."[1] Jersey Joe then refused to sign any contracts until Felix was well enough to make decisions.

Finally by late February, with Felix on the mend, Walcott was given the green light to meet Marciano in a rematch at Chicago Stadium on April 10, 1953. On February 26 amid a horde of photographers at a plush restaurant, Walcott and Marciano made it official by signing the contracts. Each fighter would receive 30 percent of the gate (which figured to come to about $850,000), 30 percent of the television rights (which were expected to sell for about $300,000) and a percentage of the 3-D movie (this was the first fight to ever be filmed in 3-D) and radio rights. However, Walcott was guaranteed a flat $250,000 no matter how much money the gate took in.

After the signing, Walcott, wearing a blue suit, white shirt, and Windsor-knotted red tie, said, "I think that I'm ready for my greatest fight. He's a tough boy but maybe this time he will find it harder to tag me."[2] The champion, beaming with confidence, said, "I'm looking for a very tough fight again. I know that Jersey Joe can punch all right and this fight should be another tough go."[3] With the signing completed, only the training remained.

By late March, both camps were well into their training routine. Then,

18 — Walcott-Marciano II: The Rematch

Felix Bocchicchio (left) and Jersey Joe are all smiles as they depart for Chicago for Walcott's rematch with Rocky Marciano, in May 1953.

unexpectedly, the fight was postponed. While sparring, Rocky suffered several ruptured blood vessels in his right nostril courtesy of a punch from one of his sparring partners. The injury forced the I.B.C. to reschedule the fight to May 15. Everyone went home, Walcott to Camden and Rocky to Brockton.

The rescheduling of the fight, coupled with the long drawn out negotiations, had a very negative impact on fan interest. It also affected both fighters. Before the postponement, Jersey Joe was in great shape, feeling good and on schedule to peak by fight time. On the other hand, Rocky's training wasn't going well. The Brockton Blockbuster looked slow and seemed unmotivated to train. After a few weeks off, the fighters returned to training in mid–April. The time off had done a world of good for Rocky, who now seemed refreshed. It was a different story for the older Jersey Joe, who was having a difficult time regaining his form. Although his handlers denied it at the time, Florio would later say that the interruption hurt Walcott significantly. In fact, at the official weigh-in, it was reported that Walcott looked drawn and gave no impression of confidence like he had during the first fight's weigh-in.

At long last, after almost eight months of waiting, fight night arrived. Because of the long gap between the two fights, not many people were excited. Only 13,266 fans showed up at Chicago Stadium, far less than were anticipated. Most stayed home, turned the dial to Channel 4 and watched the fight on television. Walcott entered the ring weighing 197¾ pounds to Rocky's 184½. The champion was an overwhelming favorite at 3-to-1 odds to keep his title.

From the opening bell it was obvious that Jersey Joe had no intention of fighting Rocky in Chicago the same way he had fought him in Philadelphia. Walcott didn't come out bombing away this time; instead, he fought on the retreat, using his jab as Rocky pursued him around the ring. Rocky, on the other hand, was looking to mix it up. The champion leaped in with a left, but Walcott quickly tied him up, at which point Rocky head-butted Walcott. The two fighters wrestled and clinched until referee Frank Sikora broke them apart. Separated for a moment, the two came right back together and clinched after throwing a couple of light punches. They let go of each other and Rocky jabbed at Walcott's belly as they clinched once again.

Separated by the referee, Jersey Joe retreated. Rocky followed after Walcott and threw a left and again Walcott tied Marciano up. The two fought on the inside briefly and wrestled around. Pushed apart by Sikora,

Rocky leaped back in with an overhand right that Jersey Joe ducked. Walcott grabbed and held Rocky. It seemed at this point that Jersey Joe was a little hesitant to engage with the aggressive champion; however, he did manage to land a couple of light body blows that had no real effect. Rocky pushed Walcott away and Jersey Joe shot out a fast jab. Rocky returned with a jab of his own and again Walcott tied the champion up and held while Rocky tried to escape his grasp. Eventually the referee stepped in and pushed the two apart. Rocky came right back with a left hook that Walcott ducked under and again Walcott clinched until the referee yelled "break." Stepping back, Rocky pumped out a jab at the retreating challenger as Walcott shot out a couple of return jabs. Rocky then sprang in with a clumsy left hook that missed as Walcott danced out of the way and fired a jab as the two went into a clinch. The referee pulled the two apart and they circled briefly, each looking for an opening. Rocky spotted one and threw a right that Walcott ducked. They clinched briefly but were quickly divided by Sikora.

Continuing to force the action, Rocky came right back at Walcott and fired a low left hook that caught Walcott on the side of his face, followed by a rising right uppercut that hit Jersey Joe's chin. Walcott went down hard, landing on his back. He brought himself up to a sitting position and grabbed the middle rope. Marciano ran to a neutral corner as the referee started the count. Sitting calmly and glancing at his corner, Jersey Joe looked as though he was going to take a count of eight to regain his senses. But to everyone's amazement, Walcott made no attempt to get up at eight. Through the counts of nine and ten, he continued to sit; only when Sikora waved his arms indicating that the fight was over did Jersey Joe leap to his feet, a second too late. To everyone's amazement, the fight was over at 2:25 of round one.

At first, everyone was shocked and confused. Was the fight really over? The crowd instantly went into an uproar and started to boo, especially the ones that had paid over $50 for a ringside seat. The fans in the upper seats, unable to hear the count, assumed that Walcott had gotten up in time. They too were stunned and outraged when they realized that the fight was over so quickly. Jersey Joe turned and calmly walked to his corner. Felix, in a rage, was yelling that the referee had only counted to nine. Walcott then turned around and shot the referee a shocked look, banged his gloves together and stomped his feet. Walcott then said to Sikora, "Nine, you only counted to nine."[4] Sikora replied, "No Joe, you got a full ten count, the fight is over."[5] In a moment, the ring was flooded with boxing officials who were trying to figure out what just had happened. Felix and Walcott's handlers were quickly in the ring as well. The crowd was angry and booing loudly. Florio was talking with the referee, telling him his stopwatch showed that Jersey Joe was up at nine. Sikora told Florio that Walcott was given a full count and then yelled at Dan to get out of the ring.

As the chaos subsided in the ring, the fighters made their way to their dressing rooms. The disappointed and angry fans slowly left the arena, most of them thinking that they had just witnessed a fixed fight.

Interviewed shortly after arriving at his room, Rocky said, "At first I thought he would get up and was surprised when he didn't. Then I took a good look at him and I could see that his eyes were glassy, I knew then that he was finished."[6] After thinking it over, Rocky conceded that the blow was probably the best Sunday punch he had ever thrown, better than the head-snapping right cross to Walcott's chin that had chilled the veteran boxer in the 13th round in Philadelphia. Rocky's trainer Charley Goldman added that Rocky threw three or four loops and then ended matters by shortening his punches, and Walcott went down from a tremendous right uppercut thrown at almost the same time as a left hook.

In Walcott's dressing room, Felix was so furious that it was feared he would suffer another heart attack. "I was robbed in New York in 1948 when we beat Joe Louis and lost the decision, but I never saw no robbery like tonight," said an irate Felix to a group of reporters.[7] "The referee wanted to count Joe out so bad he counted 2-4-6-8-10, pushed him down and said the fight is over. Joe knew what he was doing. He was looking at my corner for instructions."[8] Walcott then replied, "I wasn't hurt at no time. I could have gotten up at the count of two. But I was looking at Felix and he told me to stay down. I never heard the referee count past seven; it's the most ridiculous thing I ever heard of."[9] A depressed Jersey Joe then asked to be left alone.

The next day, as thousands of angry fans jammed the switchboards of their local newspapers to complain about the fight, Jersey Joe issued a statement: "It was unfair to the entire boxing world, to those at ringside and to those who saw it on television and heard it on the radio. And above all it was unfair to me to have the fight end in this manner after the 24 years that I put in boxing."[10] With that, Bocchicchio and his lawyer filed a formal complaint, citing that the count was too fast.

An investigation into the fight began a few days later. Bocchicchio and the Illinois Athletic Commission sat down, donned 3-D glasses, and watched a three-dimensional version of the fight. The claims that Jersey

Joe was given a fast or short count were quickly disproven. The film of the fight clearly showed that Walcott was given a full ten count. Bocchicchio's claim that referee Sikora pushed Walcott down were also disproven. The simple fact was that Jersey Joe just didn't get up in time; but why?

The first and most widely believed theory why Walcott didn't get up in time was that Jersey Joe took a dive; in other words, the fight was fixed. Did Walcott and Felix have a deal lined up to fatten Walcott's nest egg? Did they place a huge bet at 3-to-1 odds, thus making a ton of money? Most casual fans felt that the fight was fixed. On the other hand, most knowledgeable boxing people didn't believe that. According to former light-heavyweight champion Tommy Loughran, if the fight had been fixed, "Jersey Joe would have assumed another posture. He would have gone down flat on his back or stomach, agonizing a bit, and listening to the full count."[11]

A second theory was that Jersey Joe was knocked out. Was Rocky's blow hard enough to knock out Jersey Joe? According to Marciano, the punch was better than the punch he hit Walcott with to knock him out in their first fight. "It was the right that got him. It traveled further and was sharper than the one in Philadelphia. I felt when it landed he had to go down. I knew he went down pretty good. I knew it hurt him. I don't think he quit."[12] Referee Frank Sikora may have said it best: "Don't let anybody tell you Walcott didn't get hit. It may not have shown on television, but believe me I was the closest man seeing that punch and it was a knockout punch. I picked up the count at three and I yelled into his ear, not even two feet away. He couldn't even get up at eleven, and he was shaky when he got up. I saw his eyes they were glassy."[13]

Another theory was that Jersey Joe misjudged the count and got up to late. "He heard the count but I think he was working too hard watching his corner to hear it," said referee Sikora.[14] Walcott stated to some reporters that he thought he had gotten up at seven, to others he said he thought he had gotten up at nine. Perhaps in the confusion of the moment Jersey Joe had lost count. Or perhaps he had received bad advice from Bocchicchio. While Walcott sat on the canvas he looked to his corner, at times. Bocchicchio waved his hands indicating to Jersey Joe to stay down. Felix said, "Walcott was ok; he was watching me for instructions. When I thought that the count had reached eight I signaled for Joe to get up, which you saw he did with no trouble."[15] The miscalculation, then, may have been Bocchicchios, not Jersey Joe's.

Yet another theory was that Jersey Joe had quit. Did the tough veteran simply quit? Did the memories of his first fight with Rocky and the brutal knockout cause Jersey Joe to abruptly become afraid to fight? It's possible. Some felt that Walcott was not mentally ready to fight Rocky again. As Florio later said, Joe froze up in the last twenty-four hours. Dan had tried all day to get him to talk fight, tactics, punches, anything. Buy Joe wouldn't talk. The guy was through before he went into the ring.

Although the talk about the fight and what really happened went on for years, the issue was never resolved. Years later, Walcott would simply say that he just lost count. As for quitting, by the following June it was being reported that Walcott would challenge the winner of the Marciano-LaStarza fight.

In a phone interview from his home in Mt. Ephraim, New Jersey, Felix said, "As for Walcott I am not retiring him. He can't quit now, not after that fiasco in Chicago. Joe's got to prove to the fight public that he was robbed."[16] When asked how ex-champion Walcott felt about fighting again, Bocchicchio said, "Well you know he has always done most anything that I've asked of him. He and I are going to discuss the matter further in the next few days."[17]

Talk of Jersey Joe fighting again went on for some time, but ultimately the second Marciano fight was his last fight. He was being pressured by his wife Lydia and his kids to honor the promise he made before the rematch that, win, lose or draw he would retire.

For a while Walcott's reputation suffered because of the fight. In the words of sportswriter Matt Ring, "Walcott sacrificed the prestige and sentimental favor he had built up with many gallant fights over the past eight years."[18] But, being the man he was, Joe quickly rebounded and in retirement Jersey Joe Walcott would achieve great things.

—19—

The 1950s and Hollywood

Before winning the heavyweight title from Ezzard Charles back in 1951, Jersey Joe Walcott made a promise to God. He promised God that if he were allowed the honor of winning the heavyweight title, he would dedicate the rest of his life to helping people after he retired, particularly youths. It was a promise that he kept. "I always wanted to get into youth works and when I won the title I promised God I would devote my life to helping youths," Jersey Joe said in 1960.[1] In fact, as far back as the late 1930s, Jersey Joe had attempted to get a job with the Pennsauken police force when he was trying to escape the uncertainties of his sagging boxing career. Unfortunately at the time, during the Great Depression, the expected job opening never came.

On January 26, 1954, Joe finally landed his long sought-after job. In a ceremony held at the Camden police station, Walcott was sworn in as a special investigation officer on the juvenile delinquent squad, by Camden's director of public safety, George Aaron. The former champion who had earned as much as $250,000 for a single fight would be paid $10 a day.

As part of the squad, it was fitting that Walcott was directly involved in the police athletic league, an organization devoted to getting kids involved with sports. In addition to athletics, Walcott worked directly with troubled youths, set up youth programs and coordinated activities with churches and other social agencies aimed at keeping children off the street and out of trouble.

It was a lot of effort keeping kids out of trouble and the days were long, sometimes 12 to 14 hours, but Jersey Joe loved the work. And the long hours eventually paid off. With Joe's help, counsel, and support, many boys with potential bad tendencies went to college instead of going down the wrong path. They became good citizens.

As a special investigator, Jersey Joe worked directly with police officers and at times his job involved more than just helping kids. On August 18, Walcott and patrolman Bernal Ford were on the trail of two boys who had escaped from the juvenile state home. The two youths, in desperate need of money, had robbed a sporting goods store for $25. Shortly thereafter, officers Walcott and Ford spotted them. After a quick foot-chase the boys were apprehended and hauled back to the state home; no doubt along the way they were given a good, long lecture by Officer Walcott. Walcott's other activities as a special investigator included patrolling the streets at night with other officers, setting up sting operations to catch muggers and helping keep the peace when racial issues arose and threatened to turn violent.

In addition to his work in Camden, the former champ traveled and gave speeches. Despite his lack of education, Jersey Joe became an excellent public speaker. In early August 1954 Joe appeared before a United States Senate committee to speak about combating juvenile delinquency.

On August 21, 1954, Walcott, along with several members of the Camden police force, including Chief Gustav Koerner, traveled to Connellsville, Pennsylvania. Before a group of people that included the mayor, city officials, and police officers, Walcott gave a speech that included the telling of his life story and what had to be done to fight juvenile delinquency. "No agency can take the place of praying, clean living, and a sound thinking mother and father in helping solve the problem of juvenile delinquency," said Walcott, who added that he blamed juvenile delinquency on parents who were neglecting their jobs.[2] He continued by saying that families that mix old-fashioned love and strap oil, a.k.a., a sound paddling, in raising their children would end delinquency. Jersey Joe then cited instances from his own childhood where turning to crime would have been an easy outlet. But instead of becoming involved in criminal activities the former champ said he had kept as his basic philosophy one given by his late father: "Live clean, be faithful, and serve God."[3] A ceremony was held after the speech and Officer Walcott was given the key to the city of Connellsville by Mayor Abe Daniels.

Along with his day job as a juvenile officer, the popular ex-champion was also in demand as a referee for both wrestling and boxing matches. Walcott began refereeing two to three matches a week shortly after his retirement and was paid anywhere from $200 to $250 dollars per match. Refereeing was a job Jersey Joe enjoyed doing and would continue to do off and on for the next 20 plus years. Often times while refereeing wrestling matches Walcott would get in on the act so that these wrestling matches would become "the wrestler versus the boxer."

On one such occasion, wrestler Cowboy Rocky Lee challenged Walcott to a fight after Jersey Joe had disqualified him a few weeks earlier in a match where Lee hit Jersey Joe in the neck. After an official challenge issued by Lee, the boxer and the "wrassler" agreed to fight ten two-minute rounds with Walcott saying that he did not want the match to go very many rounds and would "make it in one round if I can."[4] The two faced off at the Baltimore Coliseum on April 4, 1956. Lee, a 365-pound giant of a man, lumbered around the ring as Walcott, weighing in at 218 pounds, danced, jabbed and feinted. In round two, the former boxing champion landed two "well timed" right hands and Lee settled to the canvas in a delayed but well-timed fall as the crowd went wild.

In late 1955 reports came out saying that Bocchicchio had dropped Walcott as a client and the two had a falling out. Apparently, Walcott was very bitter towards Felix because he and Felix were supposed to be business partners when Felix opened up the new Bo-Bet hotel, service station and car wash. According to Dan Florio, Walcott would not confront Felix because he was afraid of his former manager. Still other reports said that Walcott and Bocchicchio had gone into business together and were quite happy. Despite what was being reported, Walcott and Felix remained friends and continued to stay in touch throughout the years.

In September 1955 Walcott received a call from Hollywood and was offered a part in an upcoming movie called *The Harder They Fall*, starring Humphrey Bogart. The film, an adaptation of the 1947 novel written by Academy Award winning sportswriter, novelist and screenwriter Budd Schulberg, was a thinly disguised life story of former heavyweight champion Primo Carnera and the scandals that surrounded his boxing career. In fact, so closely did the movie parallel Primo's life that former heavyweight champion Max Baer, Primo's nemesis in real life, was cast as the nemesis to Toro Moreno, who was Primo's counterpart in the movie.

Shortly after filming began, Primo Carnera visited the set in person. Primo, Walcott and Max spent time together reminiscing about the old days and at some point Walcott persuaded Primo and Baer to attend church. This prompted Baer to say something to the effect that it was no doubt the first and only time that three former heavyweight champions were in church at the same time.

It may have been the first time that three heavyweight champions had attended church at the same time, but it wasn't the first time that Baer and Carnera had been on a movie set together. Back in 1933, Max and Primo had starred in the movie *The Lady and the Prize Fighter* along with Myrna

Loy. Since Max was scheduled to fight Primo for the heavyweight title, Max used the opportunity to size up the giant 6'8" Primo and psych him out. Baer continuously picked at Primo, mocking his accent and playing several jokes on the huge Italian, until Primo eventually snapped and the two almost came to blows. Just a few months later Baer and Primo met in the ring for the championship. Baer gave Primo a terrible beating, knocking the giant down 11 times and stopping him for good in the eleventh round. Although Primo seemed to have a good time visiting the set, he was not happy about the film. Once he returned home, he quickly filed a lawsuit for the tune of $1,500,000, citing that the movie was an invasion of his privacy. The suit was eventually thrown out.

Jersey Joe's role in the movie was that of Toro Moreno's trainer, George. For his part, Walcott went into serious training and dumped 15 pounds, stating that he wanted to look fit for his boxing scenes. Not only did the former champion act in the movie, but while getting in shape he helped train Mike Layne, the actor playing the part of Toro Moreno. Walcott counseled the huge 6'10" 280-pound Layne in the fundamentals of boxing, so when filming began on October 31, in New York, Layne at least looked like he knew how to fight.

During filming, the former champ talked with visiting reporters. As usual, many of their questions were boxing related. When asked if he followed boxing, Walcott responded by saying that he didn't watch fights, not even on TV: "The way it is, I'm afraid if I got to watching I'd see something about one of those fighters, some weakness or something and I might get an idea that I could beat him, that maybe I could make one more fight. So, well, I just stay away."[5] When one of the reporters asked how he liked being an actor, Jersey Joe said, "I don't know yet how I feel about this acting business." Shaking his head, he added, "Anyway, I'm not an actor yet."[6]

He may not have been an actor, but Jersey Joe took to acting naturally. Having been in front of the camera many times throughout his boxing career, Walcott had no problem performing his part and received some good write-ups for his acting ability. In fact his performance was good enough to get him considered for the lead role in the *Jack Johnson Story*. All in all, filming the movie was a fun experience for Joe and he was paid well, making $8,000 for about six weeks of filming.

The Harder They Fall opened in early May 1956 with the tag line, "The movie they tried to stop!" "No punches pulled! If you thought 'On the Waterfront' hit hard ... wait till you see this one!"[7] The film, which turned out to be Bogart's last (Bogie would pass away in 1957 from cancer), enjoyed favorable reviews. Film critic of the era Bosley Crowther liked the movie, saying, "It's a brutal and disagreeable story, probably a little farfetched, and without Mr. Schulberg's warmest character — the wistful widow who bestows her favor on busted pugs. But with all the arcane of the fight game that Mr. Yorden and Mr. Robinson have put into it — along with their bruising, brutish fight scenes — it makes for a lively, stinging film."[8] Fellow critic Dennis Schwartz wrote, "The unwell Bogie's last film is not a knockout, but his hard-hitting performance is terrific."[9]

With *The Harder They Fall* a hit, Walcott was feeling quite good. Apparently, good enough to announce that he would lay claim to Marciano's recently vacated title (Marciano had retired in May 1956). It was reported that the 42-year-old Walcott was planning a comeback, but was denied a license to fight in the United States due to his age, so Bocchicchio was making plans to take Jersey Joe overseas to Europe for a possible fight. How serious Jersey Joe was about making a return to the ring is hard to say. As it turned out, nothing came of the comeback talks. Eventually, top contenders Archie Moore and Floyd Patterson fought for Rocky's vacated title, with Floyd winning the title via a fifth-round knockout of Archie.

As the 1950s drew to a close, Walcott was busy training his son Vincent, who had aspirations of following in his father's footsteps as a fighter. Walcott spent several months training and tutoring his son in the finer points of the sweet science. By late 1959, the 19-year-old Vincent, who stood 6'1" and weighed 182 pounds, was ready to start his professional career. When asked about his son's ambition to box, Walcott said it was his son's idea, not his. However, shortly before Vincent was to make his pro debut, he decided not to pursue a career in the ring. Instead, Walcott's youngest son opted to take up study for the ministry at Howard University in Washington, D.C. saying: "I feel obligated to go into the ministry. My intent is to do what God would have me do."[10] Knowing the brutality of boxing first hand and just how difficult it is to make it as a fighter, Jersey Joe was overjoyed at his son's decision to take a less painful career path.

—20—

The 1960s and the Phantom Punch

The 1960s gave rise to a young, fast talking, charismatic heavyweight by the name of Cassius Clay. After winning the gold medal in the 1960 summer Olympics, young Cassius started his professional boxing career. From 1960 to 1963 the up-and-coming fighter built a record of 19–0, with 15 knockouts, to become the number-one contender for Sonny Liston's heavyweight title.

To say that Charles "Sonny" Liston was scary is an understatement akin to calling a hungry grizzly bear dangerous. Although Liston stood just slightly over six feet, he was a freak of nature; with thick muscles and for a man of his height an incredibly long reach of 84" Sonny also had massive fists that measured over 15" around. In addition, the ex-con was a big puncher and a good boxer and possessed a scowl that could drive fear into an opponent and defeat him before a single punch was thrown.

In 1963 Sonny Liston was the reigning heavyweight champion, having crushed former champion Floyd Patterson in the first round on two separate occasions. His second defense was against the relatively inexperienced Cassius Clay, a fighter that Liston, and just about everyone else, figured would be just another knockout victim.

Perhaps underestimating his young opponent, Liston came into the fight in less than top condition and, after taking the worst beating of his career, quite shockingly, quit on his stool in the seventh round, claiming an injured shoulder. The 22-year-old Cassius Clay had shocked the world, and so began the rise of Muhammad Ali.

Most people believed that Ali's victory over the fearsome Liston was a fluke, so a rematch was arranged for November 16, 1964. From the start, the atmosphere surrounding the second fight was scary. Cassius Clay, having

20— The 1960s and the Phantom Punch

officially changed his name shortly after the first fight to Muhammad Ali, was deeply involved with the Nation of Islam and the Black Muslims, who in turn were at odds with Malcolm X and his supporters. Tension between the two groups was at the breaking point.

Then things went bad. On November 13, three days before the fight, Ali suffered a hernia and the bout had to be postponed for six months. The new date for the rescheduled match was May 25, 1965. The rescheduling caused all kinds of problems since the Massachusetts authorities who had previously sanctioned the fight now refused to endorse the rescheduled match because of fears that the promoter was involved with organized crime. As if the postponement wasn't bad enough, the situation got even worse when Malcolm X was assassinated on February 21, 1965, by members of the Nation of Islam. The next day, in what was presumed to be retaliation for Malcolm's murder, Ali's apartment was set on fire and the Nation of Islam's headquarters was bombed. Eventually, amid talks of more violence and numerous death threats, a new spot for the rescheduled fight was found in the small city of Lewiston, Maine, more than one hundred miles north of Boston.

Leading up to the fight, the identity of who would referee the bout was kept secret. There were several names that were floating around, names like Rocky Marciano, Jimmy Braddock, Jersey Joe Walcott and even Barney Felix, the referee for the first fight, but no one knew for sure. While the boxing commission was trying to make a decision as to who would get the job as referee, Walcott along with Jimmy Braddock and Joe Louis visited each fighter's camp. The trio of heavyweight greats was very much impressed with the lightning fast Ali as they watched him spar several rounds. On the other hand after visiting Liston's camp, Walcott said it appeared that Sonny was laboring during his workout, like an old fighter. With just 24 hours to go before fight time, a referee was finally decided upon. Jersey Joe Walcott got the call and the job. He immediately contacted Nat Fleischer, editor of *Ring* magazine, and the news quickly went public.

On fight night a small crowd of about 4,000 showed up to see the match. Actual numbers were said to have been around 2,000 since many people stayed home, afraid to attend because of fear of violence between the Muslims and Malcolm X's people. At about 9:00 P.M. Ali and Liston made their way into the ring, where Jersey Joe already stood at the ready. During the introductions Ali danced and shadow boxed while Liston sat brooding in his corner. After the referee gave the instructions, the fighters returned to their corners where Ali continued to bounce around on his toes until the bell sounded to start round one.

Ali came out fast to begin the round and threw a quick overhand right that caught Sonny on the side of his head. Ali followed up with a blazing fast left and right, as Liston ducked and covered up. Ali then danced around on his toes, circling to Liston's left with Sonny in hot pursuit. Liston fired a long jab and Ali smothered Liston from punching by holding for a second. Ali released Liston and danced around on his toes, bobbing and weaving. Liston shot out another long jab and again Ali held for a second, disengaged and once again retreated on his toes. Liston tried to fire a couple of jabs at the ever-moving Ali, but was far too slow to connect. Ali kept on his toes, circling Sonny as the challenger followed Ali and tried to connect with his powerful jab. Ali returned fire with a fast left right that grazed Liston's head and then got back to moving around. Liston followed the elusive Ali, shooting out occasional jabs and right hands. And then just as Liston threw out a jab, Ali came over with a lightning fast right hand that caught Sonny on the side of his jaw. So fast was the punch that most didn't even see it land; in fact, it would become known as the famous "phantom punch."

Up to this point, the fight had been fairly typical and Jersey Joe hadn't had much to do; then all hell broke loose. After Ali landed his punch, Liston went down, landing on his back and then rolled over as if to get up. Sonny only made it up about halfway and fell back down onto his back. All the while, an excited Ali was dancing around his fallen opponent, yelling "Get up, Suck'a," as Jersey Joe was telling him to go to a neutral corner, but Ali refused. Walcott then attempted to push Ali away from the fallen challenger, but had little success. As Ali danced around the ring, Liston finally got up, at which point Walcott grabbed hold of Sonny's gloves and looked over at the timekeeper. Of course, through all the excitement, Jersey Joe had not been able to start the count and had no idea how long Liston had been down. As he looked over at timekeeper Francis McDonough, he couldn't hear the count over the roar of the crowd, so he walked over to McDonough. Ali and Liston, assuming that the fight was back on, resumed fighting. Ali jumped right on Sonny with fast lefts and rights. A moment later, after being told by McDonough and Nat Fleischer that Liston had been down for 12 seconds, and had been counted out, Jersey Joe quickly separated the two fighters and signaled that the fight was over. Officially the fight was recorded as being over at the one-minute mark. In reality this wasn't even close. According to Fleischer, who was keeping

20 — The 1960s and the Phantom Punch

track of the knockdown time along with McDonough, Liston had been down for at least fifteen seconds. According to Fleischer's stop-watch, Liston went down at 1:44 and got up at 1:56 and Walcott ended the fight at 2:11.

The next day the newspapers claimed that Walcott had lost control of the fight. In fact, Liston and his team were said to be angry with Jersey Joe for not shepherding Ali to a neutral corner and giving Sonny a fair count and an opportunity to get up. This was in light of the fact that Walcott did attempt to get Ali to a neutral corner, but Ali would not go. Walcott in his defense said, "I didn't panic, I didn't blow it, I did my job. When Liston went down I tried to get Clay [Ali] to a neutral corner. He wouldn't budge. I'm sorry for my part that I wasn't able to count. But I couldn't leave Clay [Ali] alone, the way he was acting."[1] Although Walcott received a lot of negative backlash for his inability to control the fight, Ali was just as much to blame; in fact timekeeper McDonough blamed Ali for the confusion over the timekeeping. Walcott would have had every right to disqualify Ali for not going to a neutral corner. Of course, this would have added to the drama of an already drama-filled fight.

As a result of the fiasco, Walcott would never again referee a major fight, although he would go on to referee many lesser boxing and wrestling matches. As far as he and Ali were concerned, the two would become acquaintances and see each other several times over the years. Even though Walcott did not agree with Ali's religious views — even going as far as to say that if Ali was not involved with the Black Muslims the public would have an easier time accepting him as heavyweight champion — he did respect

Following his retirement from boxing, Jersey Joe became a special investigation officer on the juvenile delinquency squad of the Camden police force.

him as a fighter. In truth, Walcott thought that Ali was the greatest heavyweight champion that he had ever seen. He even went as far as to say that Ali could beat Dempsey, Louis, Ezzard, Marciano, and even a guy named Jersey Joe Walcott. In time, the excitement over the Ali-Liston fight died down and life returned to normal for Jersey Joe.

By 1968 Walcott had been a special juvenile investigator for the better part of fourteen years, and assistant community director of safety since 1964. In that time Walcott had worked hard, developed a solid reputation and was a well-respected outstanding member of the community; it was now time for Jersey Joe to take the next step. In what was, at the time, considered a bold move for an African American, Walcott announced that he would run for sheriff of Camden County, his slogan being "Win with Walcott."[2] Although he was an underdog, which was nothing new for the former champ, the race was close. In the end, more votes went to Walcott's opponent, Spencer Smith. Despite the defeat, Walcott had nothing to be sad about. Just a few months later he was promoted to head director of community affairs and made a full member of the Camden police force.

Life for Jersey Joe at this time was good. One of his greatest joys during the late 1960s was spending time with his grandchildren. One of his favorite things to do was to round up a few of them and say, "Let's go get some ice cream," at which point they would all pile into grandpop's black Lincoln Continental and drive down to the local ice cream parlor for ice cream cones.[3]

The 1960s came to a close on a sad note for Jersey Joe. On August 31, 1969, his old rival and friend Rocky Marciano was killed in a plane crash, on the eve of his 46th birthday. The news of Rocky's unexpected death was a shock to Walcott and to the boxing community.

As sad as the news of the Rock's passing was, the 1970s would hold even greater sadness for Jersey Joe. But it wasn't just sadness that awaited Walcott. The 1970s would prove to be another pinnacle decade for Walcott. He was about to make history once again.

—21—

The New Sheriff

In mid–June 1970, Walcott made a trip to Reno, Nevada, and met up with several former Golden Age champions and contenders to help celebrate Ancil Hoffman's 85th birthday on June 19. Ancil, the former manager of Max and Buddy Baer, had long since retired as a boxing manager but was still very much in touch with the boxing community. Jersey Joe arrived in town a few days before the party and spent time visiting with old friends Jimmy Braddock, Jack Sharkey, Buddy Baer, Tommy Loughran, and Two-Ton Tony Galento.

Just a few weeks after returning home from Ancil's birthday celebration, Joe's wife of 37 years, Lydia, passed away at the age of 54 at their home of a heart attack on July 4. Jersey Joe took the passing of his wife hard. A few weeks after Lydia's passing, perhaps as a way to heal, Walcott took some time off from his day job, gathered up his grandsons, and took a summer trip.

According to Vincent Cream, Jr., Walcott's oldest grandson, "During the end of the summer before the first Ali-Frazier fight, Grand Pop gathered up my brother Bill, [my] cousins Pete, Keith, and me. He told us he was gonna take us to meet Muhammad Ali. For the next two weeks, we went on an odyssey as he refereed wrestling matches all the way down [Interstate] 95 south through North Carolina to Miami, his four teenage grandsons traveling in a low-key station wagon hangin' out with their famous Grand Pop and going to meet Ali. Priceless! It was an unbelievable life experience. He told us to stay awake, look around, and see things we had never seen before. Grand Pop inspired us to dream."[1]

After several days on the road, Walcott and his grandchildren arrived at the famous Fifth Street Gym where Ali trained and together with their grandfather spent the day visiting with "The Greatest."

Shortly after returning from the summer trip, Walcott was back at work and preparing his campaign for sheriff. Never the kind of man to give up, Walcott didn't let the fact that he had lost three years earlier stop him from trying again. On April 29, 1971, Joe announced that he would be running for sheriff once again, and was nominated as the Democratic candidate. A few weeks later the race began.

Throughout his campaign for sheriff, Walcott refused to make any derogatory remarks about his Republican opponent. He hired no speechwriters, preferring instead to give all his speeches off the cuff: "I don't say anything today that I can't say tomorrow. Furthermore, whatever promises I make, I do whatever is humanly possible to live up to them and I prove that I am concerned and that I want to help, whatever the conditions are. I'm Johnny on the spot, helping and doing whatever is necessary."[2] Part of Walcott's pledge was to bring the office of sheriff closer to the people. "You must get out on the streets," he said, "you can't manage things from the sixth floor of the courthouse."[3]

For the better part of six months, Joe campaigned continuously while working his regular day job as well. Eventually, the long grueling hours took their toll, even on a man as tough as Jersey Joe Walcott. Just a few days before learning that he had won the election, Joe was admitted to Cooper Hospital and diagnosed as suffering from complete exhaustion. His doctor ordered total rest and relaxation.

On November 2, 1971, while Joe was resting in the hospital, it was officially announced that Jersey Joe Walcott had been elected sheriff of Camden County. By doing so, Walcott made history as the first African American to be elected as a sheriff, not just in Camden, but in the entire state of New Jersey. In addition to that, Jersey Joe Walcott had won the election by the widest margin ever, 46,061 votes to 38,040.

Although he was supposed to be resting, Walcott received permission from his doctor to leave the hospital briefly to attend his swearing-in ceremony held at the Camden police station on November 9. With his oldest son Arnold, Jr., who was a lieutenant on the Camden police force, standing at his side, Jersey Joe stood proudly, raised his right hand, and took the oath of office. It was one of the proudest moments of Walcott's life as well as a significant event in New Jersey's history. Just to show that there were no hard feelings, Joe took his defeated opponent out to lunch a couple of days later.

A week later, feeling rested and happy with his victory, the new sheriff was interviewed at his office, where he said: "A man's got to have more than the cheers of the crowd. To me, if I can walk down the street in any

21— The New Stuff

Jersey Joe (center) takes the oath of office as sheriff of Camden County, New Jersey, on November 9, 1971. At left is his son, Arnold Cream, Jr., and at right is Judge Louis Goldman.

given town and the people remember things I've done with my life besides fighting, that's a lot more important. When I was a fighter it was understood that the fellow that could knock the most people down is the fellow who will reach the top the fastest." As sheriff, Jersey Joe's philosophy was: "The fellow that can pick up the guy who is a fallen human being and help him to find his way, I think that is as great a challenge as boxing and believe you me this is what will be done."[4]

As sheriff, Walcott kept all of the promises that he made during his campaign, especially the one about bringing the sheriff closer to the people. At times Joe could be found walking the streets of Camden and surrounding neighborhoods, seeking out both youngsters and older people with problems and trying to help them and to bring them hope. Due to his efforts, he gained the title "the champion of the underdog" from the people that he helped.

It was around this time that Joe met and married Riletta Twyne, an elementary school principal and prominent member of the Camden community. The two would stay married until Walcott's death and share in several adventures that included trips to Europe. As a result of Riletta's accomplishments in her life, she became a New Jersey state freeholder (legislator) and was honored by having a school named after her.

Walcott's time as sheriff only lasted one term. After nearly four years on the job, Joe announced that he would not run again. Instead he wanted to get back on the streets, back to helping young people and helping keep people out of jail. There was some talk of his running for mayor. There is little doubt that the people would have elected him but Joe said that politics wasn't for him.

In late March 1974, Walcott officially submitted his resignation as sheriff to New Jersey governor Brendan T. Byrne. He wasn't without a job for long. Almost immediately he went back to his old job with the New

Walcott playfully raises the hand of boxer Yaqui Lopez (left) as if he were the referee declaring Lopez to be champion.

Jersey Department of Community Affairs. This time though, his job would be a little different. His new position would include setting up special athletic programs and working directly with mentally retarded and physically handicapped kids. Joe's other duties included helping run employment programs for poor youngsters and their families.

As it turned out, Walcott greatly enjoyed working with handicapped children, and took pleasure tutoring the kids in running, swimming, and jumping. As Joe said, "In my entire career the best thing that ever happened to me is when Governor Byrne gave me this job. It's been the most rewarding thing in my life. Furthermore, it makes guys like me who have been blessed with a good physical body and some ability feel how small I am."[5] Walcott said the hardest part of his job was the bad handicaps that tear at your heart. As much as Walcott enjoyed working with the kids, the kids also loved having the burly former champ around.

On May 28, 1975, Walcott received some sad news. His greatest rival, Ezzard Charles, the man he had fought four battles with and had won the heavyweight title from, passed away at the age of 53 from complications brought on by Lou Gehrig's disease. The bad news didn't end there. Just a few weeks later on June 17, 1975, Walcott received the news that his longtime friend and manager, the fiery Felix Bocchicchio, had died at his home at the age of 68.

As the 1970s wound down, Walcott was credited with yet another outstanding milestone. In June 1977, Governor Byrne appointed Walcott to the position of boxing commissioner for the New Jersey State Athletic Commission, once again being the first African American to hold the position.

— 22 —

The Passing of a Legend

In 1981, another of Walcott's greatest rivals passed away. Joe Louis, the great Brown Bomber, died on April 12. "It's too bad we all can't be in heaven," said Walcott. "That's where the Brown Bomber is now and I would give almost anything to speak to him just one more time. I hate to admit it now, but back when I was trying to get the title from Joe, I wanted to hate the man. I wanted to go into that ring mean and beat him bad. When I look back now, after all these years, I have to admit I'm still sorry that I couldn't beat him. But I can't say how happy I am that I never could bring myself to hate Joe. Nobody could."[1]

In January 1984, Jersey Joe stepped down as New Jersey's boxing commissioner at the mandatory retirement age of 70. After what probably amounted to two lifetimes of work, it was the right time for Walcott to stop, especially since his health was beginning to decline. About a year before, Joe had been diagnosed with diabetes and was experiencing heart problems as well.

By the 1990s, Jersey Joe Walcott was a living legend and an icon. He was also a part of a fading group of boxers from a bygone era commonly referred to as the Golden Age of Boxing. In June 1990, Jersey Joe Walcott, along with several of the Golden Age fighters that were still alive, as well as many that had passed away, was inducted into the newly opened International Boxing Hall of Fame in Canastota, New York. Walcott, along with his son Arnold, Jr., attended the first induction ceremony and was overjoyed at being inducted. With his induction, Jersey Joe Walcott achieved boxing immortality. It was something that he truly deserved, since he was one of the original masters and all-time greats of the boxing ring. In the Boxing Hall of Fame, Jersey Joe would share a place next to the several of greatest pugilists that had ever lived, fighters such as Jack Dempsey, Joe Louis, Sugar Ray Robinson and Muhammad Ali.

22 – The Passing of a Legend

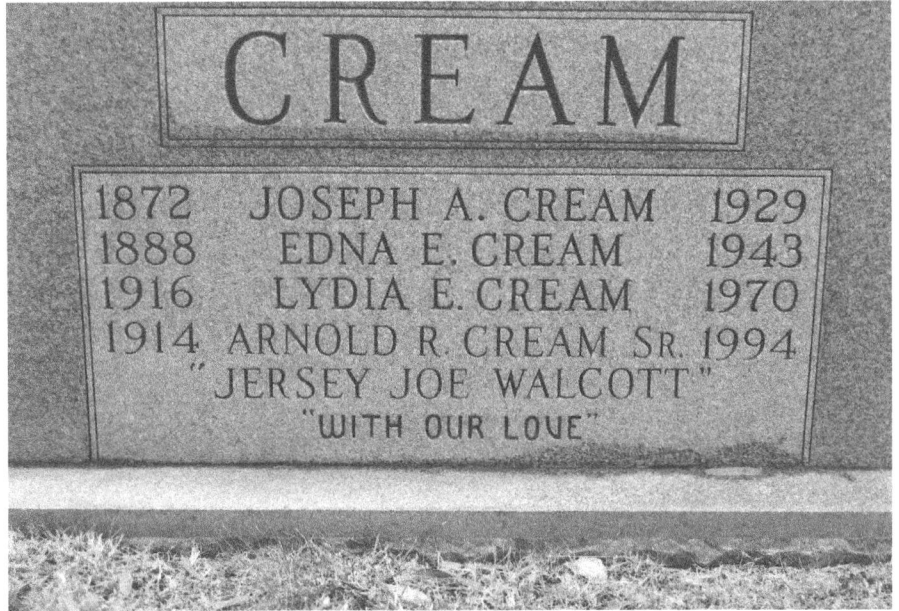

Jersey Joe Walcott's family grave site in Camden, New Jersey.

By 1994, Jersey Joe's health had suffered greatly and he was making frequent trips to the hospital for dialysis due to his diabetes. At the time, Jersey Joe was living with his daughter Ruth, since she was closest to the hospital. On February 24, Arnold's two sons, Vincent Sr. and Arnold Jr., took their ailing father to the hospital. The very next day, February 25, 1994, Jersey Joe Walcott passed away at Our Lady of Lourdes Medical Center in Camden, New Jersey, at about 11:30 P.M. He was 80 years old.

On the day of Walcott's funeral, the flags in Camden and at the Boxing Hall of Fame were flown at half staff. Despite a severe snowstorm that was covering Camden in ice, about a thousand people braved the treacherous weather to pay their respects. The service was a two-hour eulogy at Haddonfield United Methodist Church that was tinged with reflections, humor and tributes to the boxing legend.

Camden Mayor Arnold Webster was one of several prominent people to speak. He said that, "the world has lost a hero and friend."[2] Walcott was also remembered by other speakers as a role model, especially for youngsters in the segregated Merchantville area. The Rev. Edward Dorn said, "Every one of us tried to imitate our hero Jersey Joe Walcott. He taught us a lesson; we can overcome our circumstances."[3] State assembly-

The Jersey Joe Walcott memorial in Camden, New Jersey.

man John Watson said, "He held the title with grace and dignity. He made Camden proud."[4]

It wasn't that people just came to say good-bye to one of the truly greatest fighters of all time; they came to say good-bye to a truly great man, a man who was a kind and caring soul, and a friend to many. The legacy that Walcott left behind went beyond his accomplishments in the boxing ring. His work with children and people in need showed the kind of man he really was. Quite simply, he was a good man, and a man who was repeatedly described to this author as a soft-spoken gentleman, who always had a smile on his face.

His rise from poverty further showed the kind of man he was. Through the force of his indomitable will, Jersey Joe Walcott lifted himself up from a life that had given him a one-two punch from the beginning. It's a testament to the man's character that even though he began with so little, he accomplished so much. He proved that through hard work, dedication, and honesty, a person can overcome incredible odds and achieve their dreams. If there was one word that could sum up Arnold Raymond Cream's amazing life, that word would be "triumphant."

Appendix: Jersey Joe Walcott's Fight Record

52-18-2 (32 by knockout)

Date	Opponent	Place	Result
Sept. 9, 1930	Cowboy Wallace	Vineland, NJ	KO 1
Oct. 10, 1930	Jimmy O'Toole	Camden Conv. Hall, NJ	KO 4
Oct. 24, 1930	Frank Mitchell	Camden Conv. Hall, NJ	KO 4
Apr. 20, 1931	Carl Mays	Waltz Dream Arena, NJ	KO 2
No Known Fights in 1932			
May 5, 1933	Bob Norris	Camden Conv. Hall, NJ	KO 1
July 28, 1933	Henry Taylor	Pennsauken Arena, NJ	TKO 1
Nov. 16, 1933	Henry Taylor	New Broadway AC, PA	LD 6
No fights in 1934			
May 1935	Al Lang	Camden Conv. Hall, NJ	KO 1
Aug. 27, 1935	Lew Alva	Pennsauken Arena, NJ	KO 1
Oct. 1, 1935	Pat Roland	Camden Conv. Hall, NJ	KO 4
Oct. 29, 1935	Al King	Camden Conv. Hall, NJ	KO 1
Nov. 26, 1935	Roxy Allen	Camden Conv. Hall, NJ	KO 7
Jan. 21, 1936	Al Ettore	Camden Conv. Hall, NJ	LTKO 8
Mar. 16, 1936	Willie Reddish	Philadelphia Arena, PA	WD8
April 28, 1936	Joe Colucci	Camden Conv. Hall, NJ	KO 4
June 4, 1936	Billy Ketchell	Camden Conv. Hall, NJ	D 10
June 16, 1936	Louis LePage	Coney Isl Velodrome, Brooklyn, NY	KO 3
June 22, 1936	Phil Johnson	Phillies Ballpark, Philadelphia, PA	KO 3
July 14, 1936	Billy Ketchell	Pennsauken Arena, NJ	D 10
Aug. 1, 1936	Carmen Passarella	Camden Conv. Hall, NJ	WD 8
Sept. 1, 1936	Billy Ketchell	Pennsauken Arena, NJ	LD 10
May 22, 1937	Tiger Jack Fox	Rocklin Palace, NY	LKO 8
Sept. 3, 1937	Joe Lipps	Garden Pier, Atlantic City, NJ	KO 2
Sept. 25, 1937	Elmer Ray	Rocklin Palace, NY	KO 3
Oct. 9, 1937	George Brothers	Rocklin Palace, NY	LD 8
Jan. 10, 1938	Freddie Fiducia	Philadelphia Arena, PA	WD 8
Jan. 20, 1938	Jim Whitest	Olympia A.C., PA	WD 8

Appendix

Date	Opponent	Place	Result
Mar. 25, 1938	Art Sykes	Cambria A.C., PA	KO 4
April 12, 1938	Lorenzo Pack	Camden Conv. Hall, NJ	KO 4
May 10, 1938	Tiger Jack Fox	Camden Conv. Hall, NJ	LD 10
June 14, 1938	Roy Lazer	Fairview Arena. Camden, NJ	LD 8
Dec. 23, 1938	Bob Tow	114th Infantry Armory, Camden, NJ	WD8
Aug. 14, 1938	Al Boros	Meadowbrook Bowl, Newark, NJ	WD 8
Nov. 18, 1938	Curtis Sheppard	Rocklin Palace, NY	WD 8
Jan. 19, 1940	Tiger Red Lewis	Cambria A.C., PA	TKO 6
Feb. 12, 1940	Abe Simon	Laurel Gardens, Newark, NJ	LTKO 6
June 27, 1941	Columbus Grant	Memphis, TN	KO 3
Inactive 1942–1943			
June 7, 1944	Felix DePaoli	Batesville A.C., NJ	WD 8
June 28, 1944	Ellis Singleton	Batesville A.C., NJ	KO 3
Jan. 11, 1945	Jackie Saunders	Camden Conv. Hall, NJ	TKO 2
Jan. 25, 1945	Johnny Allen	Camden Conv. Hall, NJ	LD 8
Feb. 22, 1945	Austin Johnson	Camden Conv. Hall, NJ	WD 6
Mar. 15, 1945	Johnny Allen	Camden Conv. Hall, NJ	WD 8
Aug. 2, 1945	Joe Baksi	Camden Conv. Hall, NJ	WD 10
Sept. 20, 1945	Johnny Denson	Camden Conv. Hall, NJ	KO 2
Oct. 23, 1945	Steve Dudas	Patterson, NJ	TKO 5
Nov. 12, 1945	Lee Q. Murray	Baltimore Coliseum, MD	WDQ 10
Dec. 10, 1945	Curtis Sheppard	Baltimore Coliseum, MD	KO 10
Jan. 30, 1946	Johnny Allen	Camden Conv. Hall, NJ	KO 3
Feb. 25, 1946	Jimmy Bivins	Cleveland Arena, OH	WD 10
Mar. 20, 1946	Al Blake	Camden Conv. Hall, NJ	TKO 4
May 24, 1946	Lee Oma	Madison Square Garden, NY	WD 10
Aug. 16, 1946	Tommy Gomez	Madison Square Garden, NY	TKO 3
Aug. 28, 1946	Joey Maxin	Public Service Ballpark, NJ	LD10
Nov. 15, 1946	Elmer Ray	Madison Square Garden, NY	LD 10
Jan. 6, 1947	Joey Maxin	Philadelphia Convention Hall, PA	WD 10
Mar. 4, 1947	Elmer Ray	Orange Bowl, Miami, FL	WD 10
June 23, 1947	Joey Maxin	Gilmore Field, Los Angeles, CA	WD 10
Dec. 5, 1947	Joe Louis*	Madison Square Garden, NY	LD 15
June 25, 1948	Joe Louis*	Yankee Stadium, NY	LKO 11
June 22, 1949	Ezzard Charles*	Comiskey Park, Chicago, IL	LD 15
Aug. 14, 1949	Olle Tandberg	Raasunda Football Stadium, Sweden	TKO 5
Feb. 8, 1950	Harold Johnson	Philadelphia Arena, PA	KO 3
Mar. 3, 1950	Omelio Agramonte	Madison Square Garden, NY	TKO 7
Mar. 13, 1950	Johnny Shkor	Philadelphia Arena, PA	KO 1
May 28, 1950	Hein Ten Hoff	VFR Stadium, Mannheim, Germany	WD 10
Nov. 24, 1950	Rex Layne	Madison Square Garden, NY	LD 10
Mar. 7, 1951	Ezzard Charles*	Olympia Stadium, Detroit, MI	LD 15
July 18, 1951	Ezzard Charles*	Forbes Field, Pittsburgh, PA	KO 7
June 5, 1952	Ezzard Charles*	Municipal Stadium, Philadelphia, PA	WD 15
Sept. 23, 1952	Rocky Marciano*	Municipal Stadium, Philadelphia, PA	LKO13
May 15, 1953	Rocky Marciano*	Chicago Stadium, Chicago, IL	LKO 1

Result Key: KO, Win by knockout; TKO, Win by technical knockout; WD, Win by decision; LD, Lost by decision; LKO, Lost by knockout; LTKO, Lost by technical knockout; D, Draw; *For the heavyweight championship

Notes Concerning Fight Record

Not all of Jersey Joe Walcott's fights have been located. In fact, several may have never been reported at all. As far as can be estimated, about a dozen fights are missing from his record. Walcott himself said that he had several that never made it into the record books.

In an article from the *Chicago Times*, dated September 22, 1952, Walcott said that he fought "Wild" Bill Kent. This fight has yet to be found and probably happened sometime during the early 1930s.

Phil Sacks claimed to have fought and beat Walcott in 1929 by four-round KO. This fight has yet to be verified and would pre-date Walcott's first confirmed professional fight with Cowboy Wallace. Frank "Big Boy Baker" Giannelli also claimed to have fought Jersey Joe sometime in the early 1940s. This fight is not confirmed.

Other fights that have been reported on www.cyberboxingzone.com, but not verified:
(1) Ted Movan, 1929–1930, the fight was reported as a loss for Walcott.
(2) Joey Bazonne, 1932, listed as a 6 round decision win for Walcott.
(3) Leo "Deacon" Kelly, 1932, listed as a 5 round knockout loss for Walcott.
(4) Teddy Graham, 1933, listed as a 4 round knockout loss for Walcott.

Exact date of the Al Lang fight in May 1935 is unknown

Hall of Fame Inductions

Ring Boxing Hall of Fame in 1969
New Jersey Boxing Hall of Fame in 1972
World Boxing Hall of Fame in 1983
International Boxing Hall of Fame in 1990

Walcott's Measurements

Height: 6' 0"
Weight: 195 lbs.
Reach: 74 inches.
Neck: 17 inches
Chest, normal: 40 inches
Chest, expanded: 43 inches
Waist: 35 inches
Forearms: 13 inches
Biceps: 16 inches
Wrist: 7 ½ inches
Fist: 12 inches
Thigh: 21 inches
Calf: 14 inches
Ankle: 9¾ inches

Chapter Notes

Chapter 1

1. Arnold maintained throughout his career that January 31, 1914, was his birth date. A date of May 1913 was reported on the 1915 census and lists Arnold's age as two years old at the time the census was conducted, which was on June 1. According to Arnold's age on the 1930 census, 16 years old, and his age at the time he was married on April 15, 1933, 19 years old, this birth date is possible; although on the 1920 census Arnold's age is listed as five when the census was conducted on January 1. According to this date and age Arnold could not have been born in 1913. It should be noted that the 1915 census lists Arnold's mother's birth date as 1887 which does not match the 1888 date that is reported by all other sources. The same census report also incorrectly lists Arnold's father's place of birth as Delaware and his birth date as 1877 which would make him much younger than all other reported birth dates. Eventually an official birth certificate was filed on March 27, 1936, which showed Arnold's birth date to be January 31, 1914. Arnold's mother was present as a witness and signed the certificate.

2. Joseph's age and birth dates vary widely on the federal census reports, as does his arrival date to the U.S. This birth date is the one listed on his death certificate.

3. Most newspaper articles researched say that Joseph came to America in 1880 at the age of eleven as a stowaway. The data collected from census reports does not support these claims. The 1900 census report lists his arrival as 1887. The 1905 census has his arrival date at about 1891. The 1910 census has a date of 1889. The 1920 lists his arrival as 1889 as well.

4. The 1915 census lists Edna's birth date as June 1887. All other census reports list her date of birth as May 1888.

5. Arnold's age at the time of his father's death was verified by Vincent Cream.

6. Most sources state that Arnold quit school after his father passed away. The 1930 census states that Arnold had not attended school even before his father passed away. Arnold's grandson Vincent believed Arnold actually quit school in the eighth grade at the age of thirteen, so he could work.

7. Jersey Joe Walcott, with Lewis Burton, "I'll Lick Joe Louis Again," *Saturday Evening Post*, June 1948, 136.

8. Ibid., 117.

9. Ibid., 20.

10. Richard Bak, *Joe Louis: The Great Black Hope* (Dallas: Taylor, 1996), 239.

11. Kathleen J. Crane, *Images of Pennsauken* (Charleston, SC: Arcadia, 1997), 95.

12. Walcott, "I'll Lick Joe Louis Again," 21.

13. Ibid.

14. Ibid.

15. Walcott told his grandsons that he used the same moves and tricks he learned as a kid when he fought as a professional.

16. Walcott, "I'll Lick Joe Louis Again," 21.

17. This story was told by Jersey Joe to his grandsons, who in turn told it to the author.

18. As told to the author by Vincent Cream.

19. As told to the author by Walter Sikorski.

20. Walcott, "I'll Lick Joe Louis Again," 21.

Author's Note on Arnold's age: During my research into the history of the Cream family I searched the census records for 1905, 1910, 1915, 1920 and 1930. I found Arnold's father, Joseph, his mother, Edna, his older brother Joe and his sister Ruth listed on the 1910 census. Arnold was not listed as he was not yet born. A search for the 1920 and 1930 U.S. census turned up nothing for Joseph Cream, Edna Cream or Arnold Cream. It was only by searching through several hundred names that I chanced upon an Arnold Creem for the 1920 census. I clicked on the name and before my tired eyes appeared the Creem family, Joseph, Edna, Ruth, Joseph Jr. and Arnold. The last name had been misspelled, instead of the correct last name of Cream (with an "a") the last name came up on the census as Creem (with an "e").

Arnold's age at the time of the census, January 1, 1920, is listed as five. If Arnold's birth date of January 31 is correct it would mean that he would turn six on January 31, 1920. On the 1930 census his age at the time of April 1, 1930, is listed at 16 which would support his claim that he was born in 1914. It wasn't until a later search of the 1915 census report that a birth date of May 1913 was found. It should be noted, as stated in footnote number one above, that the information on the 1915 census appears incorrect. This birth date is very possible as the ages listed on the 1930 census and on his marriage certificate support this date as well as the 1914 birth date. The only age that does not support the 1913 birth date is the age listed on the 1920 census, which is five years old. The 1920 census was conducted on January 1 and Arnold's age is listed as five, which would prove he could not have been born in 1913, if the listed age of five is correct. Regardless whether he was born in May 1913 or eight months later on January 31, 1914, there is no way (according to the census reports) that he could have been age 35 when he fought Louis and no way he could have been age 41 to 45 when he fought Marciano.

Chapter 2

1. Walcott, "I'll Lick Joe Louis Again," 21.
2. Ibid., 136.
3. Ibid.
4. "Policeman Killing Suspects Taken For Ride," *Brownsville Herald*, November 1, 1933, 1; "Police Hunt Executioners," *Hagerstown Daily Mail,* November 2, 1933, 1.
5. Franklin Anderson, "The Life Story of Jersey Joe Walcott," *Oakland Tribune*, December 26, 1947, 23.
6. Walcott, "I'll Lick Joe Louis Again," 136.
7. *Camden Morning Post*, October 11, 1930, 26.
8. <www.cyberboxingzone.com>.
9. Walcott, "I'll Lick Joe Louis Again," 138.
10. Ibid.
11. Ibid.

Chapter 3

1. Walcott, "I'll Lick Joe Louis Again," 138.
2. Ibid.

3. Ibid.
4. Lancing McCurley, "Reddish-Walcott Brawl Looks Better Than Windup," *Philadelphia Daily News*, March 15, 1936.
5. Walcott, "I'll Lick Joe Louis Again," 141.
6. Ibid.

Chapter 4

1. Matt Ring, "Ettore Shatters Haynes' Winning Streak," *Philadelphia Daily News*, June 23, 1936.
2. From a 1974 interview conducted by IBRO member John A. Bardelli.
3. Walcott, "I'll Lick Joe Louis Again," 141.
4. Ibid.
5. Ibid.
6. Ibid., 118.
7. Irving Rudd, *The Sporting Life* (New York: St. Martin's, 1990), 41–43.

Chapter 5

1. Walcott, "I'll Lick Joe Louis Again," 118.
2. Ibid.
3. Ibid.
4. A cast of Abe's massive fists can be seen at the International Boxing Hall of Fame in Canastota, New York.
5. Walcott, "I'll Lick Joe Louis Again," 119.
6. Bill Kelly, "Jersey Joe Walcott the Improbable Champion," <www.fightbeat.com>, 1.

Chapter 6

1. Kelly, "The Improbable Champion," 2.
2. Walcott, "I'll Lick Joe Louis Again," 120.
3. Ibid.
4. Ibid.
5. Ibid.
6. Ibid.
7. Ibid.
8. As told to the author by Vincent Cream.
9. Walcott, "I'll Lick Joe Louis Again," 120.
10. Ibid.
11. Ibid.
12. Ibid.
13. Ibid.
14. As told to the author by Vincent Cream.
15. Walcott, "I'll Lick Joe Louis Again," 120.
16. Ibid.
17. Ibid.

Chapter 7

1. Fourteen knockouts is incorrect. As far as can be verified, Walcott had nine wins during that time period, five by knockout, and suffered one loss.
2. Walcott, "I'll Lick Joe Louis Again," 120.
3. Ibid.

Chapter 8

1. Walcott, "I'll Lick Joe Louis Again," 120.
2. Ibid., 122.
3. Ibid.

Chapter 9

1. "Walcott-Louis Go Stirs Controversy," *Dixon Evening Telegraph*, August 1, 1947, 7.
2. Ibid.
3. Ibid.
4. Kelly, "The Improbable Champion," 1.
5. Ibid.
6. Maxwell Stiles, "Jump, Jump, Jump, Jim Crow," *Long Beach Press Telegram*, August 2, 1947, p.6
7. Joe Louis, *Joe Louis: My Life* (New York: Harcourt Brace Jovanovich), 201.
8. "Walcott in Seclusion," *Winnipeg Free Press*, November 26, 1947, 18.
9. Quote from film of the Jersey Joe Walcott vs. Joe Louis fight.
10. Walcott, "I'll Lick Joe Louis Again," 122.
11. Quote from film of the Jersey Joe Walcott vs. Joe Louis fight.
12. Bak, *Joe Louis: The Great Black Hope*, 240.
13. "Walcott Barely Misses Capturing Joe Louis' Title," *Titusville Herald*, December 6, 1947, 10.
14. Ibid.
15. Ibid.
16. Ibid.
17. Ibid.
18. Ibid.
19. Ibid.
20. Joe Louis Barrow, *Joe Louis: 50 Years an American Hero* (New York: McGraw-Hill, 1988), 162.

Chapter 10

1. "Big Welcome for Walcott" *San Antonio Light*, December 8, 1947, 23.
2. Walcott, "I'll Lick Joe Louis Again," 122.
3. "Joe Louis Says Next and Last Fight Will Be with Walcott," *Walla, Walla Union Bulletin*, January 1, 1948, 12.
4. Ibid.
5. Murray Rose, "Louis Issues Ultimatum to Walcott," *Mattoon Daily Journal Gazette*, February 19, 1948, 8.
6. " Walcott Agrees to Louis Terms for a June Bout," *Yuma Daily Sun*, February 27, 1948, 6.
7. Jack Saunders, "Shep Says Jersey Is Too Speedy for Louis," *Pittsburgh Courier*, June 5, 1948, 13.
8. "Walcott Style Is Question in June Bout," *Utah Standard Examiner*, May 21, 1948, 25.
9. Ibid.
10. Ibid.
11. Bak, *Joe Louis: The Great Black Hope*, 241.
12. "Walcott Pleased with Condition," *Hagerstown Morning Herald*, June 3, 1948, 11.
13. Ibid.
14. Quote from film of the Jersey Joe Walcott vs. Joe Louis fight.

15. "I Was Fighting the Referee Instead of Louis, Says Walcott," *Oakland Tribune,* June 26, 1948, 6.
16. Ibid.
17. Ibid.
18. Ibid.
19. Bak, *Joe Louis: The Great Black Hope,* 242.

Chapter 11

1. "Jersey Joe Walcott and Pilot Part Ways," *Bluefield Daily Telegraph,* August 8, 1948, 7.
2. Ibid.
3. "Pugs Happy, Pilots Scrap," *Oakland Tribune,* June 5, 1949, 27.
4. Ibid.
5. "Mintz Invades Walcott's Lair," *Racine Journal,* June 8, 1949, 22.
6. Bak, *Joe Louis: The Black Hope,* 247.
7. "Joe Walcott's Manager Won' Let Louis Box," *Davenport Democrat and Leader,* June 12, 1949, 84.
8. "Galento Picks Walcott," *Mattoon Daily Journal Gazette,* June 13, 1948, 5.
9. "Old Jersey Joe Does 300 Road Miles," *Mt. Vernon Register News,* June 18, 1949, 8.
10. "Both Expect to Win, If That's Surprising," *Charleston Daily Mail* June 22, 1949, 14.
11. "Charles Wants Action," *Racine Journal Times,* June 23, 1949, 23.
12. "Calls Ezzy Sneaky Hitter," *Logansport Press,* June 23, 1949, 8.
13. Ibid.
14. Ibid.
15. Charles Chamberlain, "Leather Flinging Fails So Walcott Flings Mud," *Wisconsin Rapids Daily Tribune,* June 23, 1949, 13.
16. Jack Cuddy, "Walcott Complains," *Davenport Democrat and Leader,* June 23, 1949, 27.
17. "Charles Wants Action."
18. Ibid.
19. Chamberlain, "Leather Flinging Fails."
20. "Calls Ezzy Sneaky Hitter."

Chapter 12

1. "Walcott Fight Tandberg Soon," *Pacific Stars and Stripes,* July 25, 1949, 3.
2. Ibid.
3. "Jersey Joe, Olle Tandberg Fight Sunday," *LaCross Tribune,* August 12, 1949, 7.
4. "Abe Green Blasts Snub of Title Bout," *Long Beach Press Telegram,* July 31, 1949, 29.
5. "Charles, Louis Bout Sought," *Salt Lake Tribune,* August 13, 1949, 26.
6. Ibid.
7. Ibid.
8. "Jersey Joe Honored," *Long Beach Independent,* September 18, 1949, 46.
9. "Sudden Collapse of Walcott Foe Stirs Ring Probe," *Middletown Journal,* February 9, 1950, 21.
10. Ibid.
11. "Angry Omelio Agramonte Vows to Retire Jersey Joe Walcott," *Altoona Mirror,* March 2, 1950, 27.
12. Ibid.
13. Ibid.

14. Ibid.
15. Ibid.
16. Murray Rose, "Walcott Wants to Meet Charles or Louis," *Lowell Sun,* March 4, 1950, 7.

Chapter 13

1. "Charles' Injury Brings Forth Title Claim From Jersey Joe," *Billings Gazette,* March 29, 1950, 11.
2. Ibid.
3. "Trainer Gives Ten Hoff 50–50 Chance to Win," *Pacific Stars and Stripes,* May 17, 1950, 10.
4. "Jersey Joe Wins Decision Over Ten Hoff, German Heavy Champion," *Bradford Era,* May 29, 1950, 11.
5. Ibid.
6. "Jersey Joe Walcott Out Points German Heavyweight," *San Antonio Express,* May 29, 1950, 14.
7. "Walcott Decisions Germany's Ten Hoff," *Winona Republican-Herald,* May 29, 1950, 12.
8. Dick Habein, "Walcott Wants 50G's for Rex Bout," *Pacific Stars And Stripes,* July 21, 1950, 11.
9. Ibid.
10. Ibid.
11. "Walcott Open Battle in Court for Gate Share," *Galveston News,* July 22, 1950, 15.
12. Ibid.
13. Ibid.
14. "Walcott is 4–1 Favorite in Bout With Layne Tonight," *Hamilton Journal,* November 24, 1950, 21.
15. "Relentless Rex Layne Surprises Walcott," *Charleston Daily Mail,* November 25, 1950, 5.
16. Ibid.
17. "Layne Trounces Jersey Joe Walcott in Upset," *Daily Review,* November 25, 1950, 9.

Chapter 14

1. Murray Rose, "Charles Retains His Crown With TKO Win Over Oma in Tenth," *Capital Times,* January 13, 1951, 7.
2. "Fireman Take Joe Home," *Pacific Stars and Stripes,* February 11, 1951, 9.
3. "Charles Wants Final Showdown With Louis," *Altoona Mirror,* February 27, 1951, 16.
4. "Walcott Changes Style for Charles," *Sandusky Register News,* February 28, 1951, 14.
5. Ibid.
6. "Charles-Walcott Pronounced Fit for March 7 Title Battle," *Long Beach Independent,* March 1, 1951, 30.
7. " Charles and Walcott Close Training Camp, *Terre Haute Star,* March 6, 1951, 8.
8. Jack Cuddy, "Charles is Favorite in Detroit Match," *Mansfield News Journal,* March 3, 1951.
9. Ibid.
10. "Ezzard Wary of Jersey Joe," *Charleroi Mail,* March 6, 1951, 6.
11. "Charles Brick Ticket Sales," *Racine Journal,* March 6, 1951, 12.
12. "Jeering Boos Ring in Champion's Ears," *Long Beach Independent,* March 8, 1951, 25.

13. Ibid.
14. Ibid.
15. Ibid.
16. Ibid.
17. Ibid.
18. Murray Rose, "Champ's Ear Injured, Louis Match Postponed," *Pacific Stars and Stripes,* March 10, 1951, 9.
19. "Walcott Signs to Fight Ezz," *Lethbridge Herald,* June 8, 1951, 13.
20. Ibid.
21. Joe Bradis, "Jersey Joe Unworried About Fight," *Titusville Herald,* July 10, 1951, 8.
22. Ibid.
23. Ibid.
24. "Jersey Joe Looking Sharp," *The Evening Standard,* July 3, 1951, 8.
25. Ibid.
26. Bradis, "Jersey Joe Unworried About Fight."
27. Ibid.
28. Ibid.
29. "Charles Miffed Over Remarks by Jersey Joe Walcott," *Mason City Globe Gazette,* July 12, 1951, 16.
30. Ibid.
31. "Walcott Plans to Be Fighting Champion," *Ft. Wayne Journal Gazette,* July 20, 1951.
32. Remembrance of words spoken by Jersey Joe Walcott's father, Joseph Cream.
33. Words of Jersey Joe Walcott, as told to his grandsons and recounted to the author.
34. "Underdog Walcott Wins," *Sheboygan Press,* July 19, 1951, 31.
35. Ibid.
36. "Jersey Joe to Be Fighting Champion," *Lowell Sun,* July 19, 1951, 42.
37. Ibid.
38. Ibid.
39. "Underdog Walcott Wins."
40. "Jersey Joe to Be Fighting Champion."
41. Ibid.
42. "Jersey Joe Knocks Out Charles in Seventh Round" *Ft. Wayne Journal Gazette,* July 19, 1951.

Chapter 15

1. Russell Sullivan, *Rocky Marciano: The Rock of His Times* (Urbana: University of Illinois Press, 2002), 197.
2. Wilfred Smith, "Walcott Slips into Role of Champ Easily," *Chicago Tribune,* July 19, 1951.
3. Gene Ward, "Walcott Keeps Promise Made to Young Hero-Worshiper," *Chicago Tribune,* July 19, 1951.
4. "Champ Cheered by 100,000 Throng," *Ft. Wayne Journal Gazette,* July 21, 1951, 21.
5. "Fighters Row Over Return Match Dates," *Santa Fe New Mexican,* August 1, 1951, 7.
6. Ibid.
7. "Charles Lets Walcott of Hook," *Charleroi Mail,* August 2, 1951, 5.
8. Ibid.
9. "Boxing Board Demands Walcott Defend Crown Soon," *Syracuse Herald Journal,* January 19, 1952, 9.

10. "Walcott IBC Reach No Decision on Next Title Bout Opponent," *Cumberland Evening News*, February 7, 1952, 18.
11. Ibid.
12. "Charles Ready Anytime, Age Creeping on Joe?" *Portsmouth Herald*, May 23, 1952, 6.
13. Ibid.
14. Al Warden, "Ross Picks Charles Over Walcott," *Ogden Standard Examiner* May 4, 1952, 12.
15. "Proves I'm the Real Champ, Walcott," *Charleston Daily Mail*, June 6, 1952, 9.
16. Ibid.
17. Ibid.
18. Ibid.
19. Ibid.

Chapter 16

1. Gayle Talbot, "I Can Lick Anybody, Rocky," *Winnipeg Free Press*, July 28, 1952, 16.
2. Jack Hand, "Marciano KO's Kid Matthews in Two Rounds," *Reno Evening Gazette*, July 29, 1952, 11.
3. "Tunney Foresees Rocky as Champ," *Charleston Daily Mail*, August 6, 1952, 7.
4. "Tendler Picks Walcott by KO Inside of Six," *Chester Times*, September 4, 1952, 28.
5. "Louis Says Walcott to KO Marciano Within 6 Rounds," *Long Beach Press Telegram*, September 16, 1952, 12.
6. "Jersey Joe to Meet Marciano in September 23 Bout in Philadelphia," *Albuquerque Journal*, August 18, 1952, 9.
7. "Marciano Overrated," *Chester Timse*, August 20, 1952, 18.
8. "Rocky, Jersey Joe Exchange Boasts," *Twins Falls Time News*, August 28, 1952, 11.
9. "Walcott to Spar at Night," *Lowell Sun*, August 31, 1952, 49.
10. "Tennis Keeping Jersey Joe Alert," *Cedar Rapids Gazette*, September 7, 1952, 43.

Chapter 17

1. Quote from film of the Jersey Joe Walcott vs. Rocky Marciano fight.
2. Ibid.
3. Ibid.
4. Russell Sullivan, *Rocky Marciano: The Rock of His Times* (Urbana: University of Illinois Press, 2002), 124.
5. Ibid.
6. Quote from film of the Jersey Joe Walcott vs. Rocky Marciano fight.
7. A.J. Liebling, *The Sweet Science* (New York: Viking, 1956), 96.
8. Ibid.
9. Sullivan, *Rocky Marciano*, 126.
10. Liebling, *The Sweet Science*, 97.
11. Ibid.
12. As told by Walcott's grandsons to the author.
13. Sullivan, *Rocky Marciano*, 128.
14. Liebling, *The Sweet Science*, 99.
15. Sullivan, *Rocky Marciano*, 128.
16. Quote from film of the Jersey Joe Walcott vs. Rocky Marciano fight. 17. Interview in film of the Jersey Joe Walcott vs. Rocky Marciano fight.
18. Sullivan, *Rocky Marciano*, 129.

19. "Marciano KO's Walcott in Thirteenth to Take Title," *Janesville Daily Press,* September 24, 1952, 14.
20. Ibid.
21. Sullivan, *Rocky Marciano,* 129.
22. "Marciano KO's Walcott," 14.
23. Ibid.
24. Ibid.
25. Sullivan, *Rocky Marciano,* 129.

Chapter 18

1. "Walcott Wants Pilot Around," *Tucson Daily Citizen,* January 17, 1953, 9.
2. "Marciano, Walcott Sign for Rematch," *Newport News,* February 26, 1953, 23.
3. Ibid.
4. Jack Cuddy, "Here's How Jersey Joe Was Rocked to Canvas by Marciano," *Charleston Daily Mail,* May 16, 1953, 6.
5. Ibid.
6. Ibid.
7. Ibid.
8. Ibid.
9. Ibid.
10. Ibid.
11. Ibid.
12. Jack Cuddy, "Walcott Counted Out At 2:25 of First Round," *Logansport Pharos Tribune,* May 16, 1953, 6.
13. Ibid.
14. "Marciano Put Walcott Out in First Round," *Chicago Telegram,* May 16, 1953.
15. Cuddy, "Walcott Counted Out," 10.
16. "Walcott to Seek Another Title Bout," *Waterloo Daily Courier,* June 7, 1953, 41.
17. Ibid.
18. Sullivan, *Rocky Marciano,* 134.

Chapter 19

1. "Walcott's Son Gives Up Boxing for Ministry," *Corpus Christi Times,* January 14, 1960, 23.
2. William F. Sperry, "Walcott Says Prayer, Help of Parents Only Delinquency Solution," *Connellsville Courier,* August 22, 1955, 1.
3. Ibid.
4. "Walcott Cools Off Wrestler," *Charleston Daily Mail,* April 4, 1956, 11.
5. Bob Myers, "Joe Still Punching," *Portsmouth Herald,* November 1, 1955, 5.
6. "Jersey Joe Making Picture Debut," *Pacific Stars and Stripes,* November 11, 1955, 15.
7. "Martini's 'Harder They Fall' Is Brutal Tale of Fight Racket," *Galveston News,* May 6, 1956, 57.
8. "The Harder They Fall," *New York Times,* May 10, 1956.
9. "The Harder They Fall," *Ozus' World Movie Reviews,* December 17, 2004.
10. "Walcott's Son."

Chapter 20

1. "Didn't Panic Walcott Insists," *Winnipeg Free Press,* May 27, 1965.
2. "Jersey Joe Walcott to Enter Politics," *Joplin Globe,* June 2, 1968.
3. As told to the author by Jersey Joe's grandson.

Chapter 21

1. As told to the author by Vincent Cream.
2. "Jersey Joe Picking Up People Now," *Charleston Daily Mail,* November 9, 1971.
3. *Bennington Banner,* February 13, 1973.
4. "Jersey Joe Begins New Career," *Danville Bee,* November 9, 1971.
5. "Walcott Teaches Handicapped, Retarded Kids," *Cumberland Times,* March 27, 1977.

Chapter 22

1. "Louis Was Loved by All," *Winnipeg Free Press,* April 13, 1981.
2. "Mourners Pay Tribute to Walcott," *Indiana Gazette,* March 4, 1994.
3. Ibid.
4. Ibid.

Bibliography

Anderson, Franklin. "The Life Story of Jersey Joe Walcott." *Oakland Tribune*, December 24–29, 1947.
Bak, Richard. *Joe Louis: The Great Black Hope*. Dallas: Taylor, 1996.
Barrow, Joe Louis. *Joe Louis: 50 Years an American Hero*. New York: McGraw-Hill, 1988.
Callis, Tracy, Chuck Hasson, and Mike DeLisa. *Philadelphia Boxing Heritage 1876–1976*. Charleston, SC: Arcadia, 2002.
Crane, Kathleen. *Images of Pennsauken*. Charleston, SC: Arcadia, 1997.
Liebling, A.J. *The Sweet Science*. New York: Penguin, 1956.
Louis, Joe. *Joe Louis: My Life*. New York: Harcourt Brace Jovanovich, 1978.
McLoone, Maureen. *Merchantville*. Charleston, SC: Arcadia, 2001.
Mead, Chris. *Champion—Joe Louis, Black Hero in White America*. New York: Penguin, 1985.
Rudd, Irving. *The Sporting Life*. New York: St. Martin's, 1990.
Sullivan, Russell. *Rocky Marciano: The Rock of His Times*. Urbana: University of Illinois Press, 2005.
Walcott, Jersey Joe, with Lewis Burton. "I'll Lick Joe Louis Again." *Saturday Evening Post*, June 1948.
Ward, Gene. "A Punch and a Prayer." *Chicago Tribune*, July 20–25, 1951.

Periodicals

Albuquerque Journal
Altoona Mirror
Billings Gazette
Blue Field Daily Telegram
Bradford Era
Camden Evening Edition
Camden Morning Post
Capital Times
Cedar Rapids Gazette
Charleroi Mail
Charleston Daily Mail

Chester Times
Chicago Telegram
Chicago Tribune
Connellsville Courier
Corpus Christi Times
Cumberland Evening News
Cumberland Times
Daily Review
Danville Bee
Dixon Evening Telegraph
Evening Standard, Pennsylvania
Fort Wayne Journal Gazette
Galveston News
Hagerstown Morning Herald
Hamilton Journal
Indiana Gazette
Long Beach Independent
Janesville Daily Press
Joplin Globe
La Cross Tribune
Lethbridge Herald
Logansport Press
Long Beach Press Telegram
Lowell Sun
Mansfield News Journal
Mason City Globe Gazette
Mattoon Daily Journal Gazette
Middletown Journal
Mount Vernon Register News
Newport News
Oakland Tribune
Pacific Stars and Stripes
Philadelphia Daily News
Pittsburgh Courier
Portsmouth Herald
Racine Journal
Reno Evening Gazette
Ring Magazine
Salt Lake Tribune
San Antonio Express
San Antonio Light
Sandusky Register
Santa Fe New Mexican
Sheboygan Press
Syracuse Herald Journal
Terre Haute Star
Titusville Herald
Twin Falls Times News
Utah Standard

Walla, Walla Union Bulletin
Waterloo Daily Courier
Winnipeg Free Press
Winona Republic Herald
Wisconsin Rapids Daily Tribune
Yuma Daily Sun

Interviews

Riletta Cream
Ruth Cream
Vincent Cream
Maureen McLoone
Walter Sikorski, Jr.

Archival Sources

Camden Historical Society
New Jersey State Historical Society
Sacramento Library

Video

Jersey Joe Walcott vs. Ezzard Charles
Jersey Joe Walcott vs. Joe Louis
Jersey Joe Walcott vs. Rocky Marciano

Web Sites

www.ancestry.com
www.boxrec.com
www.cyberboxingzone.com
www.dvrbs.com/people/camdenpeople.com
www.fightbeat.com
www.thesweetscience.com

Index

Aaron, George 189
AAU Amateur National Championship 63
Abramson, Jess 178
Adams, Baba 98
Adams, Frank ("Spike") 106
Adolf, Hitler 30
Agramonte, Omelio 114, 115, 116, 117
Albertani, Francis 71
Alexander, Ella Eliza 8
Alexander, Gus 39
Alexander, Joseph 8, 9, 12
Alexander, Mary 8
Alexander, Thelma 8
Ali, Muhammad *see* Clay, Cassius
Ali Shuffle 49
Allen, Joe 14, 64, 74, 95
Allen, Johnny 49, 50, 53, 54
Allen, Roxie 15, 15, 24, 38, 46
Alva, Lew 23
Amos, Bertha 8
Amos, Howard 8
Amos, Ida 8
Amos, Louisa 8
Amos, Marion 8
Amos, May 8
Amos, Walter 8
Amos, William 8
Amos, Willie ("The Joplin Ghost") 11, 34
Amos 'n' Andy 11
Ancil, Hoffman 199
Angelo, Joey 90
Anthony, Quinn 40
Arcadia Boxing Gym 18, 19, 20, 21, 22, 23, 27
Arcel, Ray 52, 141
Armstrong, Louis 11

Aspery, Jack 138
Atkins, Larry 54, 98
Atlantic City, New Jersey 18, 155, 160, 162
Auletto, Rocco 15

Bad Durkheim 122
Baderfield, Atlantic City 160
Baer, Buddy 199
Baer, Max 40, 59, 92, 134, 191, 192, 199
Baksi, Joe 50, 51, 58, 67, 70, 97, 100, 110, 112
Balogh, Harry 76, 83
Baltimore Coliseum 52, 191
Barney, Felix 195
Barone, Nick 49
Baroudi, Sam 101
Barton, George 156
Baseball 11
Bass, Benny 165
Battalino, Battling 49
Battling Mack's Boxing Gym 13, 14, 15, 16
Baum, Benny 115
Bear Lake, Michigan 91, 92
Bellmawr, New Jersey 16
Belofl, Joey 113
Benton, George 165
Berlin, Germany 126
Beshore, Freddie 116, 119, 127
Bettina, Melino 33, 54, 97
Bible 10
Bill, Kent ("Wild") 162
Bivins, Jimmy ("The Cleveland Spiderman") 52, 54, 55, 56, 57, 58, 75, 98, 100, 101
Black, Julian 28, 69
Black Murderers Row 100

225

Index

Black Muslims 197
Blackburn, Jack 11, 19, 20, 21, 22, 27, 34, 49, 69
Blake, Al 58, 162
Bo-Bet Hotel and Car Wash 46, 191
Bocchicchio, Andrew 44
Bocchicchio, Claudine 44
Bocchicchio, Felix 44–52, 54, 58, 60, 62, 64, 65, 68, 74, 83, 86, 98, 101–103, 106–109, 111, 112, 113, 115, 118–121, 123, 127, 133, 134, 135, 138, 140, 141, 144, 147–149, 151, 154–156, 159, 160, 163, 178, 180–183, 186–188, 191, 203
Bocchicchio, Mrs. 108
Bocchicchio, Nicky ("Anthony") 44, 46
Bocchicchio, Ronald 44
Bogart, Humphrey 191, 192
Boris, Al 38
Boston Garden 90
Bournemouth, Dorset, United Kingdom 111
Boxing Commission 59
Boyd, Edna 33
Braddock, Jimmy ("Cinderella Man") 25, 31, 34, 55, 69, 134, 165, 195
Brando, Marlon 40
Bridge, Benjamin Franklin 18
Brighton, New Jersey 17
Brockton, Massachusetts 165
Brook, Bill 37
Brooklyn Dodgers 101
Brothers, George 35, 36
Brown, Freddie 172
Brunner, George E. 86, 89, 149, 150
Bruno, Angelo 46
Bruns, George K. 119, 120
Buckley, Johnny 117
Bulge, Battle of 60, 61
Bureau of Vital Statistics, Camden 71
Burk, Jackie 152
Burly, Charley 54, 100, 101
Byrne, Brendan T. 202, 203

Cahalan, Dr. Joseph 134
Calabrese, Phil 165
California Football Team 84
Calloway, Cab 11
Camaguey, Cuba 114
Camden, New Jersey 8, 14–17, 24, 25, 31, 37, 42, 46, 71, 76, 86, 107, 108, 122, 128, 142, 148, 149, 150, 165, 184, 190, 201

Camden Armory 38, 44, 98
Camden Athletic Club 44, 46, 47, 86, 128
Camden Ball Park 63
Camden Convention Hall 17, 23, 29, 37, 38, 44, 49, 50, 51, 58, 65, 89
Camden Police Force 190, 198, 200
Campbell, Louis 46
Campbell Soup Factory 9
Cannon, Jimmy 86
Canzoneri, Tony 49
Carnera, Primo 26, 116, 134, 191, 192
Carpentier, George 123
Casella, Peter 46
Castle, Gandalfo 111
Castle, Heidelberg 123
Cavalier, Paul 51, 63
Center Air Port, New Jersey 86
Century Athletic Club 53
Cerdan, Marcel 98
Charles, Amos 8
Charles, Ezzard ("Cincinnati Cobra") 7, 12, 42, 54, 56, 63, 97–112, 116, 117, 118, 120, 127, 128, 129, 130, 131, 132, 135–148, 151, 152, 154–159, 189, 198, 203
Charleston, South Carolina 90
Charron, Robert 121, 122
Chicago Cubs 161
Chicago Golden Gloves 92
Chicago Stadium 140, 182, 184
Christenberry, Bob 154, 155
Christoforidis, Anton 54, 100
Cincinnati Cobra 7
Clario, Tommy 152
Clark, Dr. Ray 139
Clark, S., Jr. 161
Clay, Cassius ("Muhammad Ali") 49, 194–199, 204
Clayton, Zach 156, 157
Cleveland Arena 54, 56
Cliffside, New Jersey 98
Cohen, Harry 27
Cole, George 11
Comiskey Park 99, 103
Conn, Billy 54, 55, 56, 70, 73, 82, 88, 134
Connellsville, Pennsylvania 190
Corum, Bill 178
Cream, Arnold, Jr. ("Buddy") 20, 38, 120, 127, 128, 200, 201, 204, 205
Cream, Barbara 8

Cream, Bertha 8
Cream, Bill 199
Cream, Carol 43, 44
Cream, Doris 34
Cream, Edna 7, 9, 10, 17
Cream, Elva 24, 38
Cream, George 8
Cream, Joseph 7, 71, 72
Cream, Lester 8
Cream, Lydia 18, 21, 24, 32, 42, 43, 142, 148, 151, 188, 199
Cream, Naomi 8
Cream, Norma 8
Cream, Robert 8
Cream, Ruth (Arnold's daughter) 38, 145, 205
Cream, Ruth (Arnold's sister) 8
Cream, Vincent, Sr. 42, 140, 193, 205
Cream, Vincent, II 199
Crime, Joseph Alexander 8
Crocker, Richard 18
Cromwell, Lew 135
Crosby, Bing 11
Crowther, Bosley 193

Daggert, Charley 65, 165, 168, 169, 172, 173, 175, 178
Dagrosa, John ("Ox") 114, 172
Daniels, Abe 190
De La Cruz, Francisco 68
Delaware River 11
Dempsey, Jack 29, 63, 69, 72, 92, 116, 159, 160, 161, 198, 204
Denson, Johnny 51
Detroit, Michigan 76
DiMaggio, Joe 84
Donofrio, Frank 37
Dorazio, Gus 31, 37, 50
Dorn, Edward Rev. 205
Douglas, Al 34, 35
Dowling, Jim, 31
Dry Branch Georgia 54
Duaphin, Johnny 16
Dudas, Steve 51
Duncan, Leo 31
Dyes, Cliff 91

Ebbert's Field, New York 63
Eckert, Ray 152
Egan, Eddie 59, 70, 71, 84, 87, 88, 99
Ella, Edna 8
Ettore, Al 24–26, 31, 37, 72

Europe 113
European Command (EUCOM) 121

Fairview Arena 38
Farr, Tommy 134
Feducia, Freddie, 37
Feitz, William 46
Fever, Typhoid 21, 22, 24
Fifth Street Gym 199
Firpo, Lou 159
Fleischer, Nat 112, 153, 195, 196, 197
Florio, Dan 48, 49, 64, 74, 81–84, 89, 91, 95, 101, 109, 132, 144, 147, 155, 178, 184, 186, 188, 191
Florio, Nick 48, 49
Forbes, Frank 83, 87, 130
Forbes Field 140, 142
Ford, Bernal 190
Foster, Maud 100
Fox, Linwood Jack ("Tiger Jack Fox") 29, 33, 34, 37, 38
Frankfurt, Germany 120
Freeman, Harrison 111
Friedman, James 120
Fullman, Frank 61, 93

Galento, Tony ("Two Ton") 37, 102, 103, 165, 199
Gans, Joe 19
George Cole Boxing Gym 11
German Allied Bank commission 127, 128
German Financial Ministry 127
Giardello, Joey 165
Gilmore, Reggie 68
Gilmore Field 67
Gleason's Gym 50
Goettert, Joachim 126
Golden Gloves 63, 69
Goldman, Charley 161, 186
Goldman, Herb 100
Goldman, Louis 201
Goldstein, Ruby 63, 76, 83, 87, 130
Gomez, Tommy 60, 61, 62
Graziano, Rocky 116
Greb, Harry 18
Great Depression 189
Green Abe 67, 70, 109
Greenwood Lake, New Jersey 64
Grenloch Amusement Park, New Jersey 74, 90, 101, 133

Index

Grossingers 160
Guarino, Bert 44

Haddonfield United Methodist Church 205
Hagen, Richard 92
Hall, John 48
Hamas, Steve 32
The Harder They Fall 191, 192, 193
Harlem Globetrotters 156
Haynes, Leroy 26, 31, 37, 74
Hays, Grover 25
Heidelberg 121
Heidelberg Hawks 122
Hindenburg 33
Hoff, Max ("Boo Boo") 18
Hoff, Paul 32
Hoffman, Harry 163
Holliday, Billy 11
Hollywood, California 67, 191
Hollywood Stars (baseball team) 67
Homestead High School 9
Homesteadville 7
Hospital, Coopers, New Jersey 9, 21, 24, 32, 200
Houston, J.M. 103, 106
Howard, Amos 8
Howard University, Washington D.C. 193
Hoxter, Helen M 18
Hunt, Harry 155

Illinois State Athletic Commission 103, 106, 186
Ingber, Lou 115
International Boxing Club (IBC) 99, 127, 132, 135, 139, 151, 155, 159, 160, 162, 181, 182, 184
International Boxing Hall of Fame 114, 204, 205
International Boxing Research Organization (IBRO) 100

The Jack Johnson Story 192
Jacobs, Mike ("Uncle Mike") 58, 59, 60, 64, 65, 67, 69, 70, 97
Jeanette, Joe 11, 29
Jefferies, James J. 99
Johnson, Austin 49, 50, 74, 90
Johnson, Harold 31, 100, 112, 114
Johnson, Jack 13, 14, 29, 42, 166
Johnson, Jim ("Battling") 30

Johnson, Marv 130, 131
Johnson, Melody 100
Johnson, Phil 31, 112
Jordantown, New Jersey 8
Jordantown Cemetery 9

Keach, Mickie 37
Kearns, Jack ("Doc") 63, 65, 66, 68, 71
Kelly, Bill 44
Ketchell, Billy ("The Millville Plowboy") 29, 32
King, Al 23, 38
Kinkaid, Charles 145, 148
Klucka, Basil 29
Koch, Arthur 123
Koenig, Leo 120, 121
Koerner, Gustav 190
Korea 151
Krug, E.C. 142
Kulpmont, Pennsylvania, 50

The Lady and the Prize Fighter 191
Lafayette, Alabama 69
Lambert, Jay 129
Lamps, Kerosene 10
Landes, Sydney 20
Langford, Sam 11, 19, 30
Lansing, McCurley 26
Lastarza, Roland 49, 188
Laurel Garden, New Jersey 40
Lawrenceville, Georgia 100
Layne, Mike 192
Layne, Rex 127, 129, 130, 131, 132, 134, 136, 140, 154
Lazer, Roy 38
Lee, Rock ("Cowboy") 191
Legion of Merit (award) 69
Lenahan, Joe 138
LePage, Louis 29
Lesnevich, Gus 54, 89, 92, 97, 98, 100, 109, 111, 132
Levy, Dr. Joseph 114
Liebling, A.J. 170, 171, 173, 174, 177, 180
Lipps, Joe 34
Liston, Charles 194, 195, 196, 197, 198
Logson, Bill ("Wild") 152
Lone Ranger 11
Lopez, Yaqui 202
Lorber, Philip 120
Lou Gehrig's Disease 203
Loughran, Tommy 25, 156, 187, 199
Louis, Joe ("Brown Bomber") 7, 12, 21,

22, 27–31, 34, 40, 51, 52, 55–58, 62, 64, 65, 67–88, 90–96, 99, 100, 107, 109, 112, 116, 117, 120, 127, 128, 129, 130, 132, 134, 135, 136, 139, 148, 151, 152, 154, 156, 159, 160, 165, 186, 198, 204
Louis, Marva 28
Loy, Myrna 191, 192
Lucas, Johnny 14
Luciano, Charles ("Lucky") 46
Lydia, Cream 10, 12, 20

Mack, Battling 13, 14
Madison Square Garden 58, 59, 60, 61, 64, 70, 71, 76, 77, 83, 84, 90, 98, 108, 114, 116, 129, 130, 154
Magnolia Avenue, 6201, 10
Main, Lewiston 195
Malcolm X 195
Manda, Angelo 182
Mandel, Sammy 1
Manheim, Germany 121, 125
Manheim Boxing Association 123
Manheim Stadium 122
Mann, Nathan 20
Mannheim, Germany 113, 122
March of Dimes 90
Marciano, Rocky ("The Brockton Blockbuster") 12, 53, 100, 116, 132, 140, 152, 154, 159, 160, 161, 162, 165, 166, 167, 168, 170, 172, 173, 174, 175, 176, 177, 178, 179, 181, 182, 184, 185, 186, 187, 188, 193, 195, 198
Markowitz, Harold 106
Marsello, Tommy 16
Marsello, Vic 44, 46, 48
Marshall, Lloyd 100, 101
Marshall, Miles 139
Massi, Pasquale 46
Matchtown 7, 47
Matthews, Frankie 18
Matthews, Harry ("Kid") 100, 155
Mauriello, Tami 50, 54, 58, 62, 64, 70, 97
Maxim, Joey 52, 54, 62, 63, 65, 66, 67, 97, 100, 108, 113, 116, 132, 134, 140, 165
Maxwell, Marilyn 67
Mays, Carl 18
McDonough, Francis 196, 197
McKeesport, Pennsylvania 141, 148, 157
McQuinn, George 84

McTiernan, Buck 143, 144, 157
McVey, Sam 30
Meadowbrook Bowl 38
Merchantville, New Jersey 7, 8, 12, 13, 16, 18, 28, 42
Merchantville High School 88
Merit, Dan 38
Miller, Davey 106
Miller, Ray 63
Mills, Freddie 97, 111
Mintz, Jake 102, 103, 106, 109, 110, 134, 139, 141, 146, 151, 156
Mitchell, Frankie 18
Mitchell, Terry 31
Momence Country Club 101
Monroe, Martin 83, 87
Montgomery, Bob 90
Moore, Archie ("The Old Mongoose") 53, 54, 100, 101, 112, 165, 193
Moran, Pete 26, 27, 37
Moreno, Toro 191
Morgan, Dan ("Dumb Dan") 92
Morrison, Herbert 33
Mt. Ephraim, New Jersey 188
Mueck, Frank 123
Municipal Stadium 156, 164
Murray, Jimmy 181
Murray, Lee Q. 52, 53, 54, 56

Nation of Islam 195
National Boxing Association (NBA) 67, 70, 98, 99, 106, 109
Neil J. Award 112, 154
Nelson, Carl 28
Nelson, Pete 163
New Broadway Athletic Club 20
New Jersey 7, 9, 10, 61, 67, 76, 96, 108, 127, 148, 164, 200
New Jersey Department of Community Affairs 203
New Jersey State Freeholder 202
New York 18, 92, 93, 102, 109, 111, 112, 114, 133, 152, 160, 162, 182, 186, 192
New York Boxing Writers Association 112
New York Ship Yards 42
New York State Athletic Commission 70, 86, 87, 88, 90, 99, 109, 154, 155, 160, 203, 204
New York Yankees 84
Newhall, Freddie 162, 163
Norris, Billy 91

Norris, James D. ("Jim") 99, 139, 151, 154, 155, 160, 164, 181, 182
Norristown, Pennsylvania 152
Nova, Lou 40, 50

O'Loughlin, Tommy, 62
Olympic Athletic Club 37
Olympic Stadium 135, 136
Oma, Lee ("Loose-Leaf") 59, 60, 100, 131, 132, 139
On the Waterfront 40
Orange Bowl, Florida 66
O'Toole, Jimmy 17, 18
Our Lady of Lourdes Medical Center 205
Overlin, Ken 100, 121, 122

Pack, Lorenzo 37, 38
Panter, Dale 129
Paoli, Del 43
Parker, E.E 8
Parker, P.S. 8
Passarella, Carmen 32
Pastor, Bob 54
Patterson, Floyd 49, 193, 194
Peaceful Valley Country Club 101
Pearl Harbor 42, 54
Pennsauken, New Jersey 7, 8, 12, 16
Pennsauken Arena 20, 23, 32
Pennsauken Police Force, 189
Pennsylvania Athletic Commission 172
Pep, Willy 116
Phantom Punch 196
Philadelphia Arena 37, 112, 117, 149
Philadelphia General Hospital 152
Philadelphia Municipal Stadium 155, 160, 165
Pinto, Charles 111
Pirrone, Paul 31
Pleasantville, New Jersey 140, 141, 155, 160
Police Gazette (magazine) 89
Pollino, Dominick 46
Pollock, Ed 177
Pompton Lakes, New Jersey, 57, 73
Pope Pius the XII 111
Poverty 10
Powers, Tyrone 67
Prince, Eddie 14, 15
Ptomkin, Mr. 44

Raasunda Football Stadium 110
Radio 11

Raft, George 67
Rainbow Gardens, Pennsylvania 141, 148
Ray, Elmer ("Violent"; "Bear Cat"; "Kid Violent Ray") 34, 35, 62–66, 67, 97, 100, 101
Red, Lewis ("Tiger") 39
Reddish, Willie 25, 26, 31, 52
Requiem for a Heavyweight 40
Rhine-Main Airport, Hamburg, Germany 120
Rhode Island 162
Rickets 8
Riedel, Paul 121
Ring (magazine) 100, 112, 153, 195
Ring, Matt 31, 178, 188
Robinson, "Sugar" Ray 59, 63, 165, 204
Rocklin Palace 33, 34, 35, 36, 38, 53
Rohr River 60
Roland, Pat 23, 163
Rome, Italy 111, 127
Rosen, Charles 138
Rosen, Clarence 136
Rose's Tavern 135
Ross, Barney 156, 165
Roxborough, John 69
Royals, Battle 35
Rudd, Erving 36
Russell, Belle 100
Ruxx, Conny 126

S-3 (drive-in movie theater) 164
Saddler, Sandy 165
San Francisco Kezar Stadium 181
Satterfield, Bob 140, 165
Saturday Evening Post 80
Saunders, Jackie 49
Savold, Lee 50, 54, 63, 97, 111, 116, 126, 140
Saxton, Johnny 152
Scalzo, Petey 49
Schmelling, Max 27, 29, 30, 31, 57, 69, 84, 124, 134
Schneider, Heinz 120
Schulberg, Bud 191
Schwetzinger 121
Schwetzinger Castle 121
Scrapple 9
Seaman, Manny 88, 92
Seven Angels (promotion company) 97, 98
Sharkey, Jack 92, 117, 199
Sheppard, Curtis ("Hatchet Man") 39, 52, 53, 54, 64, 91, 162

Sheridan, Al 101
Shkor, Johnny 117, 118, 119
Sikora, Frank 184, 185, 187
Sikorski, Walter 13
Sikorski, Walter, Jr. 13
Sikorski's Boxing Gym 13
Simon, Abe 39, 40, 41, 42, 69, 72
Sinatra, Frank ("Old Blue Eyes") 67, 68
Singleton, Elis 43
Skelly, Lena 42
Slater, Jimmy 141, 148, 149, 157
Smith, Billy ("Oakland") 162
Smith, Red 147
Smyth, Andrew 110
Solomon, Jack 97, 116
Steinman, Harry 112
Stevens, Floyd 134
Stillman, Lou 115
Stillman's Gym 11, 116
Stockburger, Charles 16
Strauss, Sol 70, 71
Streeter, Keith 199
Streeter, Pete 199
Stuttgart, Germany 120
Sunset Hills Golf and Country Club 101
Superman 11
Sweden, Stockholm 108, 122
The Sweet Science 171
Swiden, Art 141
Sykes, Art 37

Talton, Lydia Eleanor 18
Tandberg, Olle 68, 70, 108, 109, 110
Tannas, Tom 139, 151, 154
Taylor, Bud 19
Taylor, Henry 20, 52
Taylor, Herman 164 160, 164
Taylor, Roy ("Tiger") 92
Teiger, Milton J. 128
Television 11
Tendler, Lou 160, 165
Ten Hoff, Hein 113, 114, 119, 120, 122, 123, 124, 125, 126, 127, 128
Thomas, John 58
Thorp, Wilson J. 132
310th Infantry 60
Toledo State Juvenile Home 152
Trainer, Joseph 106
Tunney, Gene 88, 116, 159, 160, 165
Turner, Florence 98
Turner, Gil 154
Turner, Lana 67

20th Century Sporting Club 58, 70, 90, 97, 98, 116
28th Transportation Battalion 122
Twine, Riletta 202

United Methodist Church 18
U.S. Army 101
United States Senate Committee 190

Valentino, Pat 112
Valley Forge General Hospital 152
Vasa Street 109
Vella, Joe 75
Velodrome, Coney Island 29
Victor, Indian 17
Vineland, New Jersey 16

Walcott, Joe ("The Barbados Demon") 19, 24
Walcott Shuffle 49, 113, 166
Waldorf Astoria hotel 154
Walkaway 49, 67, 74, 78, 79, 91, 92, 106, 113, 126, 136, 167
Walker, Mickey 65
Wallace, Edward ("Cowboy") 16, 17
Waltz Dream Arena 18
Watson, Jack 117, 118
Watson, John 205
Webster, Arnold 205
Webster, Joe 48, 49, 51, 54, 59, 65, 67, 86, 88, 98, 128
Weil, Al 116, 129, 162, 172, 173, 181
Weinberg, Bill 59
Weinhelm, Town of 122
West Indies, Netherlands 98
White, Larry 39
Whitest, Jim 37
Willard, Jess 166
William Penn Hotel 147
Wills, Harry 11
Wilson, Eddie 74
Woodcock, Bruce 97, 111, 116
World War I 17, 115
World War II 42, 54, 101
Wurzburg Warriors 122

Yale 39
Yankee Stadium 90, 182
YMCA 90

Zale, Tony 98

www.ingramcontent.com/pod-product-compliance
Ingram Content Group UK Ltd.
Pitfield, Milton Keynes, MK11 3LW, UK
UKHW041945140426
5217IPUK00014B/663